AF560791

Strategic
INDUSTRIAL RELATIONS AND LABOUR LAWS

BOOKS BY THE SAME AUTHOR

- Business Ethics and Managerial Values
- Management of Change & OD
- New Compensation Management
- Business Ethics and Corporate Governance
- Training and Development
- International HRM
- Managing Cultural Diversity
- Constructive Industrial Relations and Labour Laws
- International Practices in Industrial Relations
- HRM: Competitive Advantage
- Performance Management
- Team Leadership
- Strategic Industrial Relations and Labour Laws
- Non-Profit Organisations
- Strategic HRM

Forthcoming

- New Horizons in Management
- Managing Organisational Behaviour
- Winning Teams
- Total Quality Management (TQM)
- Organisation Theory and Design
- Emerging Trends in Human Resource Development
- Strategic Management
- Emerging HRM
- Business Ethics and Global Values
- Managing Relations
- Industrial Psychology

Strategic INDUSTRIAL RELATIONS AND LABOUR LAWS

S.K. BHATIA
Director
Human Resource Management Foundation, New Delhi
and
Senior Faculty,
Business Management Institutes

Formerly: • Director (Personnel), Oil India Ltd.
• Director (Pers. and PR),
Mekaster Group Co's.
• Add. General Manager (Pers. and Admn.)
Bharat Heavy Electricals India Ltd.

Foreword by

DR. S. CHANDRA
Chairman
PAN Asian Management Foundation and
Corporate Director, New Delhi
Former Senior Faculty
Administrative Staff College of India,
Hyderabad

DEEP & DEEP PUBLICATIONS PVT. LTD.
F-159, Rajouri Garden, New Delhi-110027

Strategic
INDUSTRIAL RELATIONS AND LABOUR LAWS

ISBN 978-81-8450-061-5

Typeset by S.S. COMPOSERS,
3190, Mohindra Park, Shakur Basti, Delhi 110034 India.

Printed in India at SARAS GRAPHICS PVT. LTD.
8, Rai Industrial Area, Sonepat (Haryana)

Published by DEEP & DEEP PUBLICATIONS PVT. LTD.
F-159, Rajouri Garden, New Delhi 110027 India.
Phones: 25435369, 25440916
E-mail: ddpbooks@yahoo.co.in • ddpubs@gmail.com
Sales Showroom:
2/13, Ansari Road, Daryaganj, New Delhi 110002 India. • Telefax: 23245122

Dedicated to my wife

KUSUM

for her infinite patience,

understanding and inspiration

and

- **NEERAJ, PULKIT**
- **ARUNIKA, ARJUN**

Contents

Part Three

FUTURISTIC ISSUES IN INDUSTRIAL RELATIONS

PART FOUR

RECOMMENDATIONS AND GUIDELINES

ANNEXURES

Foreword

Industrial Relations Policy in India has evolved over a period of five decades through a process of tripartite consultations and in the light of then prevailing socio-economic and political conditions and circumstances. Since many of the substantive and procedural laws were enacted piecemeal they not only lacked the much desired synergy but suffered from severe systemic and operational weaknesses. Aggressive pursuit of sectional interests, "We-They" syndrome, combative postures in collective bargaining, strong disagreements on basic issues like optimization of productivity, technological upgradation, deployment of manpower, strengthening trade unions, collective bargaining, cost conservation, profit sharing, etc. queered the pitch for bipartite cooperation. Industrial enterprises consequently lost million of mandays due to strikes, lockouts and other forms of industrial actions every year. Financial viability of enterprises and creation of national wealth were thus dealt a severe blow. Repeated attempts made by the Government to evolve tripartite consensus on long-term vision of labour policies and strategies, rationalizing and reforming multitude of labour laws, fine-tuning the labour policy with the liberalized economic policy and allowing a level playing field to industrial and trading organizations to compete with multinational enterprises have thus far not been successful at all. India, in my view, is a classic example of what ails industrial relations in a developing country and what should not be done to reform labour laws.

Human resource is a very critical factor in economic development and a major source of competitive advantage. Our Industrial Relations Policy, should therefore, capitalize this advantage to create national wealth and be friendly to both—labour and business. It should optimize human dignity, quality of life, optimize utilization of labour and other resources through structural adjustments, multi-skilling, technological upgradation, empowerment of employees, fair and competitive compensation, etc. Labour laws should facilitate strong, unified and depoliticized trade unions, to ensure bipartite trust, cooperation and industrial harmony at enterprise and industry level. The very trying conditions through which India is passing through currently and the challenges it would have to confront in the very near future, it will have to create a work culture that is driven more by responsibility rather than rights. Innovations in labour policy are the need of the hour to build confidence of national and international investors as well as among employees and their chosen leaders.

This very learned treatise on "Strategic Industrial Relations and Labour Laws" by Mr. S.K. Bhatia is a timely and valuable addition to the existing literature on the subject for it very comprehensively deals with multi-dimensional aspects of a fascinating discipline of study. Mr. Bhatia, whom I have known as a professional colleague for more than two decades is a very eminent professional colleague and dedicated scholar. He has backed the entire text with reflective analysis as well as deep and practical insights gained by him during his long and distinguished career as a practicing executive and faculty member in numerous institutions of Business Management. Without undermining the erudite and comprehensive coverage of Parts I and II covering forty chapters, serious students of industrial relations, researchers and Human Resource Executives will find the Sections III and IV on futuristic issues, recommendations and guidelines especially very stimulating and rewarding learning experience. While complementing Mr. Bhatia for his dedication I strongly recommended this book to all those who, for long, have been looking for a one-stop reference manual.

DR. S. CHANDRA
Chairman,
Pan Asian Management Foundation &
Corporate Director
Former Senior Faculty,
Administrative Staff College of India,
Hyderabad

Preface

Just as every birthday in the life of a person provides the much-needed opportunities for reflection and introspection, every book gives the author a chance to think of what more could be done to make his work more readable and useful for the readers. It gives an occasion for embellishing the work and updating facts and figures.

It is encouraging for the author to know that there is demand for and this book has been found useful by the students of the subject.

In order to help the students to test themselves of concepts, to understand the problems, and to learn out of situations, the following new features are included:

(a) Objective type questions on different laws,
(b) Practical problems on laws, and
(c) Case studies

Thus, this book seeks to acquaint the readers not only with the concepts and principles but also the practices. I look forward to hearing from my discerning readers on the utility of these features so that some more can be introduced in the subsequent edition.

A unique feature is to include few chapters which lay focus on strategic aspects of industrial relations. Objective of these chapters is of optimising the interests of the employer and those of employees and creating a congenial atmosphere in the 'work place', thus, increasing the welfare of the nation.

Learning is a never ending process. It takes time and lot of effort. So does writing a book. That has been my reasoning to my wife, Kusum. My sincere appreciation to her patience.

Last, but by no means the least is the contribution of my publishers M/s Deep & Deep Publications Pvt. Ltd. to give a unique look to this book a new look. A special word of thanks is least I can offer to this dynamic team.

New Delhi

S.K. BHATIA

Acknowledgements

Text books for educational purpose are a team project. While my name is on the cover of this book, literally, it is combined contribution of the writings of so many scholars and authors from whose distinguished works, ideas and valuable contributions have enabled me in completion of this book. As far as possible, I have tried to include their names and publication in each chapter and list of references. Every effort has been made to gratefully acknowledge them, but if any have been inadvertently overlooked, I crave their indulgence. I shall make necessary arrangement to acknowledge at the first opportunity.

Some articles were collected from various sources—newspapers, seminars, magazines and text books, during long years of service and used as teaching material. Unfortunately, these sources were not noted and it is impractical to offer acknowledgements. I express my thanks to those who contributed anonymously to this book.

I am immensely grateful to my son, Neeraj and daughter-in-law Pulkit, in USA, who not only arranged my study visits to USA, but also helped in arranging the literature on the subject, from various sources such as Libraries, Bookstores and Internet, etc. Company of little Arunika and playful Arjun made my study tours more lively and interesting. I thank my wife for her unfailing support and encouragement throughout this project.

Finally and most important my daughter's family Namita, her husband Atul, loving children Malvika and Geetka in UK for learning, inspiration and joy.

I thank Deep & Deep Publications Pvt. Ltd. for managing the book into its final form.

New Delhi

S.K. BHATIA

Part One

INDUSTRIAL RELATIONS

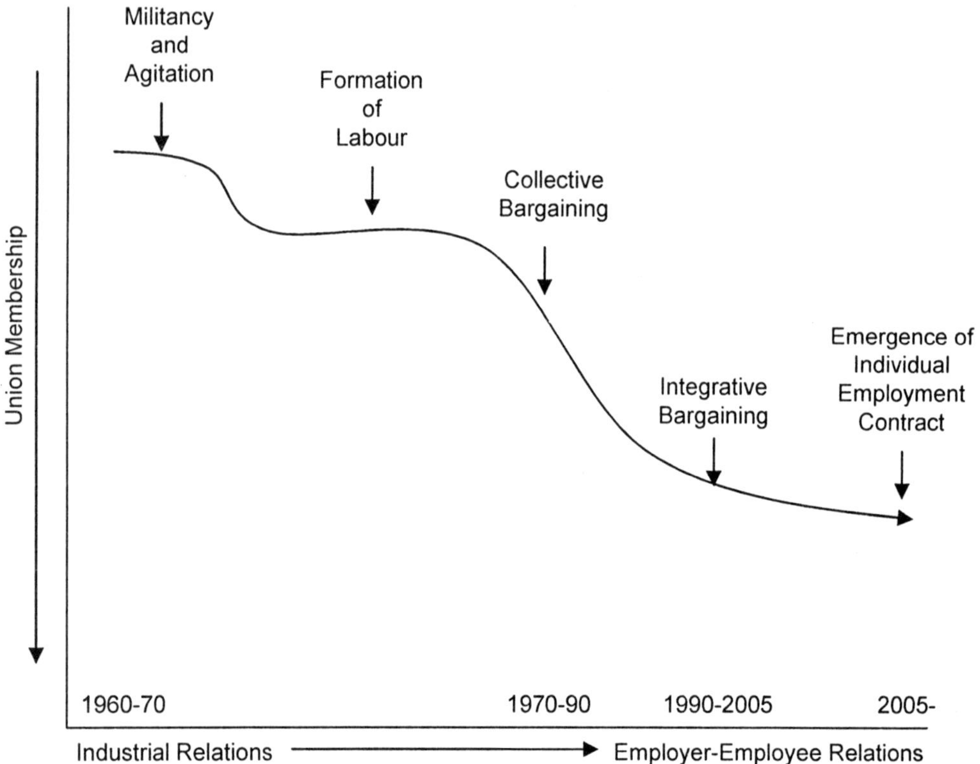
Union Membership
Militancy and Agitation
Formation of Labour
Collective Bargaining
Integrative Bargaining
Emergence of Individual Employment Contract
1960-70
1970-90
1990-2005
2005-
Industrial Relations
Employer-Employee Relations

Industrial Relations

Concept, Objectives and Factors for Good Industrial Relations

In this opening chapter, we would like to understand some basic aspects of industrial relations. We shall share the importance of study of industrial relations, its meaning, objectives, parties involved and significance of good employer-employee relationship in the organisations.

Over the years, the relationship between employer and employee has changed from master and servant to one of contract of employment between management (as employer) and a worker (as employee). This contract covers rights and obligations of both sides in respect of nature of working conditions, discipline, wages and benefits, security of employment, nature of work to be performed, productivity and social security, etc. The industrial relations are often viewed as constraints which limit the ability of the management. But neglect of industrial relations function by employer can lead to problems like, indiscipline, lack of mutual trust, frustration and alienation of workers, coercive practices by trade unions.

MEANING OF INDUSTRIAL RELATIONS

According to Dale Yoder, industrial relations is collective relationship between employees' (trade) union and employer which grows out of employment. The concept also means the relationship between employees and management in the day-to-day working of industry. The subject of industrial relations includes the distinct areas:

- Individual relations and joint consultation between employers and workers at work place,
- Collective relations between employers and their organisations and the trade unions, and
- The part played by the state (government) in regulating these relationships.

FEATURES OF INDUSTRIAL RELATIONS

(i) Industrial relations are outcome of employment relationship in an industrial enterprise.

(ii) As a regulated relationships the focus of it is on rule-making by participants so that there may be un-interrupted production.

(iii) The work situation may provide methods of adjustment and cooperation with each other.

(iv) The government agencies involve to shape the industrial relation through laws, rules and awards.

(v) The important actors (parties) of industrial relations are employees or their trade unions, employers and their associations and government. The actors in industrial relations are explained in model below:

MODEL

Actors in Industrial Relations

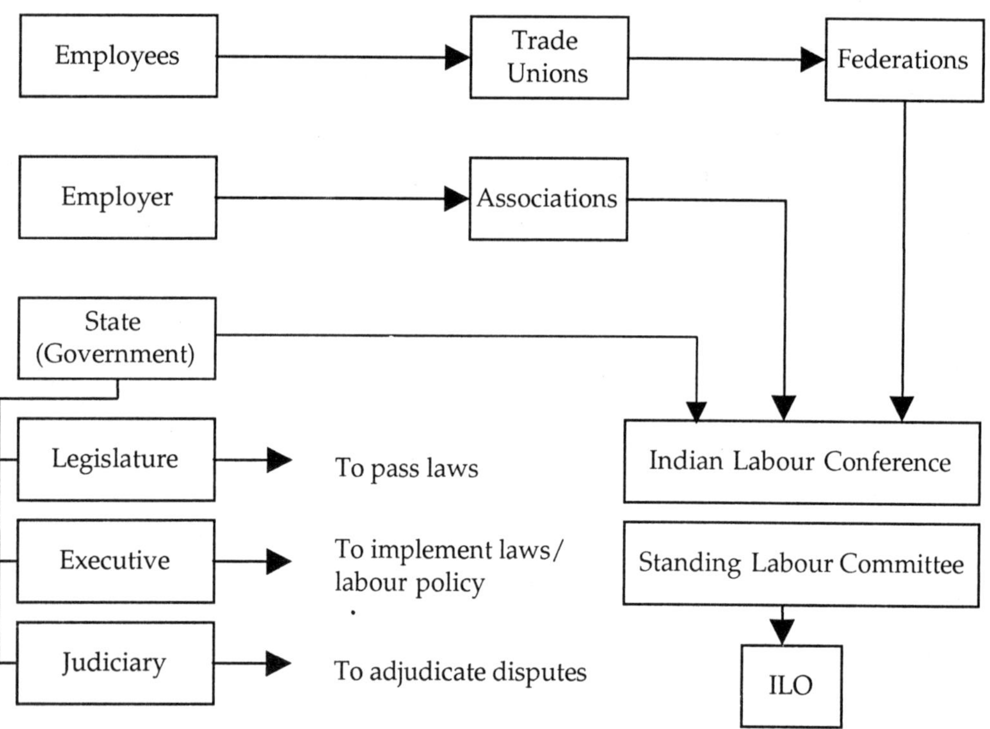

It has become necessary to secure cooperation and involvement of three actors, i.e. workers, management and state.

OBJECTIVES OF INDUSTRIAL RELATIONS

The objectives of Industrial Relations are:

(i) Development and promotion of harmonious labour-management relations.
(ii) Maintenance of industrial peace, goodwill and avoidance of industrial strife—the conflicts. To safeguard interests of labour, management, industry and national economy as a whole.
(iii) Establish industrial democracy based on labour partnership in management.
(iv) To raise productivity level.
(v) To boost the discipline and morale of workers.
(vi) Industrial prosperity is largely dependent on good industrial relations.
(vii) To improve worker's lot with a view to solve their problems through mutual negotiations and consultation with the management.

Significance of good industrial relations or industrial peace can lead to numerous benefits such as, harmonious relation between the trade unions and the management, higher productivity, high morale, fair benefits to workers, entering of long-term agreements through collective bargaining, establishment of industrial democracy, higher morale and facilitate changes in technology, innovative systems.

FACTORS/CONDITIONS FOR GOOD INDUSTRIAL RELATIONS

Good industrial relations refer to harmonious relations between the trade unions and employees. These depend on variety of factors and even we can improve them. Some of these are:

1. History of Industrial Relations in an Enterprise

A good history is marked by harmonious relationship between management and workers in an enterprise. Once militancy is established as a mode of operations, there is tendency to continue. It takes time to change.

2. Economic Satisfaction of Workers

Reasonable wage and benefits are important for workers which should be comparable in other similar organisations.

3. Social and Psychological Satisfaction

Establishing worker participation in management, machinery for redressal of grievances, suggestion schemes, job enrichment, effective two-way communication, regular union-management negotiations, etc. are important aspects.

4. Off-the-Job Conditions

Living conditions of workers are equally important. We employ the "whole person". His home life is not totally separable from his work life.

5. Enlightened and Responsible Trade Unions

Trade unions may promote the status of labour without jeopardising the interests of enterprise. Trade unions to explain about workers' responsibilities towards the organisation to employees. Trade unions can maintain good relations with management and avoid militancy and strikes. Trade union can develop and encourage right kind of leadership. Infact politicalisation and multiplicity of unions leads to rivalry and indiscipline amongst trade union workers.

6. Choice of Strategy of Cooperation or Conflict in Relations

Choice of a strategy as maintaining harmonious/cooperative relations or conflict/confrontation by both the parties, i.e. Management and Unions. They have to work together to make industrial cooperation/harmony as success.

7. Negotiating Skills and Attitudes of Management and Workers to be Developed

- Both parties should have approach to arrive at agreement and not only raise conflicts.
- Parties must have confidence on each other. Empathy and open mind are important. Reliance on collective bargaining is vital.
- Mutual trust and respect in negotiations.
- Both parties should develop constructive approach and believe in honouring agreements.

8. Public Policy and Legislations

Government to intervene in enforcing labour laws so as to prevent conflicts/fires rather than to try stopping them after these start.

9. Education of Workers

Better education to workers so that they adopt sense of responsibility and problem-solving approach. Workers should not be misled by trade union leaders who have their own axe to grind, i.e. self-interest in certain situations.

10. Standing Orders Containing Employment Terms

Industrial employment standing orders determining terms and conditions of service should be finalised by the management and every employee should know these.

TO SUM UP

The establishment of good industrial relations depends on the constructive attitude on the part of both management and the unions.

(i) The essential factors for healthy and congenial industrial relations are the existence of strong, independent, responsible trade unions. Trade unions now have to play an important role by *cooperating* with the management as survival of the organisation under competitive environment is under stake.

(ii) The promotion of collective bargaining in good faith with the majority union. However, under liberalised economy organisations are seeking to promote labour-management *cooperation through consultations* rather than collective bargaining.

(iii) A fair and independent machinery for the peaceful settlement of industrial disputes by the state.

(iv) The existence of good human relations, i.e. mutual respect, understanding, good will and recognition of dignity.

(v) Provision for the bipartite committees to evolve personnel polices, code of conduct and code of discipline.

(vi) Management has to take initiative to persue harmony as goal and institutionalise schemes such as—two-way communication with employees, transparency in actions, promotion of information about the organisation, participative management quality of competence of industrial relations professionals, etc.

(vii) Industrial relations theme of parties has to shift from *conflict* towards *cooperation, collaboration, participation* and *partnership* for success in global competitive environment.

2

Strategies for Developing Employment Relationship

The employment relationship between managements and employees is a factor that can make a significant impact on the degree to which organizational effectiveness is achieved. Although relationships between employers and employees are subject to continuous day-to-day development, negotiation and change, it is necessary to take a strategic view on how a lasting and positive relationship can be established. Motivation of employees is related to the beliefs they have about how they and others are expected to behave employment relationship.

In this chapter following aspects of the employment relationship are described:

1. Meaning of employment relationship
2. Basis of employment relationship
3. Concept of psychological contract
4. Developing employment relationship strategies
   - 4.1 Develop a positive psychological contract
   - 4.2 Increase commitment
   - 4.3 Create a climate of trust

1. MEANING OF THE EMPLOYMENT RELATIONSHIP

The term 'employment relationship' describes the relationships that exist between employers and employees in the workplace. These may be formal, e.g. contracts of employment, procedural agreements, or they may be informal, in the shape what managers and employees have to offer and are willing to deliver.

2. BASIS OF THE EMPLOYMENT RELATIONSHIP

(i) Written Contract

The starting point of the employment relationship is an *undertaking by an employee* to provide skill and effort to the employer in return for which the *employer provides* the employee with a salary or a wage. Initially the relationship is founded on a legal contract. This may be written contract but the absence of such a contract does not mean that no contractual relationship exits.

(ii) Implied legal rights and obligations

Employers and employees still have certain implied legal rights and obligations. The employer's obligations include the duty to pay salary or wages, provide a safe workplace, to act in good faith towards the employee and not to act in such a way as to undermine the trust and confidence of the employment relationship. The employee has corresponding obligations, which include obedience, competence, honesty and loyalty.

(iii) Employer has power to dictate

An important factor to remember about the employment relationship is that generally it is the *employer who has the power to dictate the contractual terms* unless they have been fixed by collective bargaining. Individuals, except when they are much in demand, have little scope to vary the terms of the contract imposed upon them by employers.

3. THE PSYCHOLOGICAL CONTRACT

The employment relationship is governed to a considerable extent by the psychological contract.

This expresses the combination of beliefs held by an individual and his employer about what they expect of one another. It can be described as the set of reciprocal but unwritten expectations that exist between individual employees and their employers. It creates attitudes and emotions that form and govern behaviour. A psychological contract is implicit. It is also dynamic—it develops over time as experience accumulates, employment conditions change and employees re-evaluate their expectations. The notion of a psychological contract implies that *there is an unwritten set of expectations operating at all times between every member of an organization and the various managers* and others in that organization.

(a) Employee Expectations

The aspects of the employment relationship covered by the psychological contact will include, from the *employee's point of view*:

- *Trust in the management* of the organization to keep their promises—to 'deliver the deal';
- Rewarded equitably in accordance with their contributions;
- How they are *treated* in terms of fairness, equity and consistency;
- Provided work which uses their abilities;
- *Security* of employment.
- Scope to demonstrate *competence;*

- Career expectations and the opportunity to develop skills;
- How they are doing i.e. feedback; and
- *Involvement* and influences.

(b) Employer Expectations

From the *employer's point of view,* the psychological contact covers such aspects of the employment relationship as—

- Commitment to the organization,
- To be competent,
- To put effort; and work hard,
- To be compliant.
- Loyalty to organization,
- To enhance the image of the organization with its customers, clients and suppliers.

(c) A Balanced Psychological Contract

A balanced psychological contract is necessary for a continuing, harmonious relationship between the employee and the organization. However, the violation of the psychological contract can signal to the participants that the parties no longer shared (or never shared) a common set of values or goals.

(d) Unarticulated Assumptions

The concept highlights the fact that employee/employer expectations take the form of *unarticulated assumptions.* Disappointments on the part of management as well as employees may therefore be inevitable. These disappointments can, however, be alleviated if *managements appreciate that one of their key roles is to manage expectations,* which means clarifying what they believe employees should achieve, the competencies they should possess and the values they should uphold. And this is a matter not just of articulating and stipulating these requirements but of discussing and agreeing them with individuals and terms. The psychological contract governs the *continuing development of the employment* relationship, which is constantly evolving over-time.

However, sometimes these unexpressed expectations are not fulfilled and parties do not feel right and even cheated.

4. DEVELOPING EMPLOYMENT RELATIONSHIP STRATEGIES

Aim of strategies for developing the employment relationship is to

4.1 Develop a positive psychological contract

4.2 Increase commitment

4.4 Create a climate of trust

None of these aims can be achieved overnight if the situation is one of a negative psychological contract, poor commitment and an absence of trust. That is why a strategic approach is necessary, which sets out longer-term aims and the programmes to accomplish them but recognizes that the programmes will have to be flexible in the sense of being able to respond rapidly to new circumstances.

4.1 Strategies for developing a positive psychological contract

A positive psychological contract is worth taking seriously because it is strongly linked to higher commitment to the organization, higher employee satisfaction and better employment relations. Again this reinforces the benefits of pursuing a set of progressive HRM practices.

They also emphasize the importance of a *high-involvement climate* and suggest *HRM strategies for developing the contract*, such as the provision of opportunities for learning, training and development; focus on job security, promotion and careers; minimizing status differentials; fair reward system; and comprehensive communication and involvement processes.

The particular practices that can be incorporated in the strategy include:

(a) During recruitment interviews—presenting the unfavourable as well as the favourable aspects of a job in a 'realistic job preview';
(b) In *induction programmes*—communicating to new starters the organization's personnel policies and procedures and its core values, indicating to them the standards of performance expected in such areas as quality and customer service, and spelling out requirements for flexibility;
(c) By issuing and *updating employee handbooks* that reinforce the message delivered in induction programmes;
(d) By encouraging the development of *performance management processes* that ensure that performance expectations are agreed and reviewed regularly;
(e) By encouraging the use of personal development plans that spell out how continuous improvement of performance can be achieved, mainly by self-managed learning;
(f) By using *training and management development* programmes to underpin core values and define performance expectations;
(g) By ensuring through manager and team leader training that managers and team leaders understand their role in managing the employment relationship through such processes as performance management and *team leadership;*
(h) By encouraging the *maximum amount of contract*—between managers and team leaders and their team members to achieve mutual understanding of expectations and to provide a means of two-way communication;
(i) By adopting a general policy of transparency-ensuring that on all matters which affect them, employees know what is happening, why it is happening and they are implemented fairly and consistently;
(j) By *developing HR procedures* covering grievance handling, discipline, equal opportunities, promotion and redundancy and ensuring that they are implemented fairly and consistently;
(k) By *developing and communicating HR policies* covering the major areas of employment, development, reward and employee relations;
(l) By ensuring that the *reward system is developed and managed* to achieve equity, fairness and consistency in all aspects of pay and benefits; and
(m) Generally, by *advising on employee relations procedures*, processes and issues that further good collective relationships.

These strategies for managing the employment relationship by *developing a positive psychological* contract cover all aspects of people management. It is important to remember, however, that this is a continuous process. The effective management of the relationship means ensuring that values are upheld and that a transparent, consistent and fair approach is adopted in dealing with all aspects of employment.

4.2 Commitment Strategy

The concept of commitment refers to feelings of attachment and loyalty and as such plays an important part in HRM philosophy. Commitment is to the relative strength of the individual's identification with, and involvement in, a particular organization. It consists of three factors:

- A strong belief in, and acceptance of, the values and goals of the organization.
- A strong desire to remain a member of the organization.
- A readiness to exert considerable effort on behalf of the organization.

A commitment strategy will be concerned with the development of *communication, education and training* programmes, initiatives to increase involvement, particiption and 'ownership', and the introduction of performance and reward management processes.

4.3 Create climate of trust

(a) The meaning of trust

Trust, as defined by the Oxford English Dictionary, is a firm belief that a person may be relied on. An alternative definition has been provided by Shaw (1997) to the effect that trust is the 'belief that those on whom we depend will meet our expectations of them'. These expectations are dependent on 'our assessment of another's responsibility to meet our needs'.

(b) A climate of trust

A high-trust organization has been described by Fox (1993) as follows:

Organizational participants share certain ends or values; bear towards each other a diffuse sense of long-term obligations; offer each other spontaneous support without narrowly calculating the cost or anticipating any short-term reciprocation; communicate honestly and freely; are ready to repose their fortunes in each other's hands; and give each other the benefit of any doubt that may arise with respect to goodwill or motivation.

(c) Developing a high-trust organization

Trust is a *cultural norm* which can rarely be created intentionally because attempts to create trust in a calculative manner would destroy the effective basis of trust. Trust is an *outcome of good management*. It is created and maintained by *managerial behaviour* and by the development of better mutual understanding of expectations—employers and employees. Issues of trust are not in the end to do with managing people or processes, but are more *about relationships and mutual support* through change.

More specifically, trust will be developed if *management acts equitably and consistently, if a policy of transparency is implemented,* if intentions and the reasons for proposals or decisions are communicated both to employees generally and to individuals, if there is *full involvement* in developing reward processes, and if *mutual expectations* are agreed through performance management.

Failure to meet these criteria, wholly or in part, is perhaps the main reason why so many performance-related pay schemes have not lived up to expectations. If trust is lost, admission by top management that it has paid insufficient attention in the past to employees' diverse needs and take action.

References

Michael Armstrong, 'Managing People', Crest Publishing House, New Delhi.

Guest, D., 'The State of the Psychological contract in Employment', Institute of Personnel and Development, London.

Hiltrop, S.M., 'The changing psychological contract', *European Management Journal*, September, pp. 286-92.

S.K. Bhatia, Strategic Human Resource Management, Deep & Deep Publications Pvt. Ltd., New Delhi.

3

Causes of Industrial Disputes and Machinery for Prevention and Settlement of Industrial Disputes

In this chapter, we give details of machinery set-up in India for prevention and settlement of industrial disputes. We also give various causes of industrial disputes.

CAUSES OF INDUSTRIAL DISPUTES

The causes of industrial disputes or unrest may be grouped in four broad categories:

(a) Industrial Factors

Grievances relating to employment, i.e. work, wages, bonus, hours of work, privileges, conditions of employment and obligations of employees and other factors are:

- Attitude of workers.
- Increasing prices and demand for increases in dearness allowance.
- Indiscipline and violence among the workers.
- Worker's resistance to rationalisation, introduction of new machinery and change of place of factory.

(b) Management's Attitude towards the Workers

- Disinterest of the management to discuss with the workers.
- Management's unwillingness to recognise a particular trade union.
- Not involving the workers in decision-making.
- Inadequate communication.

(c) Role of Government Machinery

- Not successful in implementing labour laws.
- Inability of conciliation machinery of the Labour department to do its job and employees and management's loss of confidence in that.
- Irrelevance of certain provisions of labour laws in the context of challenges of present industrial climate and imperatives of development due to competitive environment.

(d) Other Causes

- Affiliation of trade unions with political parties, political leadership thereby bringing pressures for accepting their demands.
- Political instability and poor centre-state relations contribute to industrial conflicts.
- Another factor is character crisis, in values of trade union leaders, trade union rivalry.
- Need for change in outlook and attitudes of parties including management.

So there is increasing tendency among industrial workers to resort to strike and militancy. They forget that strike is the last resort in their armoury.

Some important sources of Union-Management conflict can be summarised as under:

(i) Profit

Both agree organisations to make profit but trade unions feel they are not getting enough pay and benefits. Unions contest the distribution of profits.

(ii) Security of Jobs

Earlier organisation goal was to provide jobs. It is now replaced by organisation to provide security of job due to competitive environment.

(iii) Right to Manage

Management would like to retain decision-making authority and ward-off encroachment. However, trade unions seek to increase bargaining issues.

(iv) Seniority

Unions plead for seniority principle for promotion, and giving of other benefits, etc. and disregard competence and ability as subjective criteria. However, managements resist seniority system in favour of productivity and merit.

(v) Productivity

Productivity is a result of labour, capital, technology and other factors. The problem is in determining how much productivity is due to labour and how much other factors. Workers want more compensation for more productivity.

(vi) Inflation

Linking wages to cost of living index while managements would like allowances to be linked with productivity and performance.

Industrial Relations Scene at Present

Industrial relations are complicated by factors such as—growing indiscipline, frequent break-down of law and order and political pressure.

Industrial relations are in impasse. Organisations are busy in fire-fighting based on strategy of conflict. Industrial relations managers are busy in settling disputes and dealing with unions at the cost of constructive work. Most of the problems are connected with weaknesses of trade unions.

Besides state role needs re-orientation due to various factors:

(a) Legislation is protective of labour and welfare-oriented.
(b) Executive machinery has failed in implementation of labour laws.
  - Executives develop political bias and considerations.
  - Government intervention is control-oriented of settling disputes, rather than positive building of industrial relations.
  - Executive machinery has more reliance on compulsory adjudication rather than encouraging voluntary settlement and collective bargaining.

(c) Judiciary gives pro-labour interpretations.

So challenge lies in seeking stable-protective industrial relations environment instead of fire-fighting. Managements should learn to live with the unions. Some changes required are:

(i) Reform of labour laws which is overdue and requires to be expedited.
(ii) Government to make preventive and settlement of disputes machinery more effective.
(iii) Collective bargaining is the only hope and parties to prefer integrative bargaining rather than distributive bargaining. Orientation towards bipartite system is the need of the hour.
(iv) Managements have to build healthy industrial relations through continuing dialogue and build cooperative relationship with unions. Employers and employees have to understand the necessity of working together.
(v) Produce more and distribute more is to be the slogan.

MACHINERY FOR PREVENTION AND SETTLEMENT OF INDUSTRIAL DISPUTES

Machinery for prevention and settlement of industrial disputes comprises of:

(A) Statutory Machinery, and
(B) Voluntary Machinery.

(A) STATUTORY MACHINERY

The Industrial Disputes Act, 1947 provides the mechanics of dispute—resolution and set-up the necessary structure so as to create cogenical climate.

What is an 'Industrial Dispute'?

An 'industrial dispute' means any dispute or difference between employers and employers, or between employers and workmen, or between workmen and workmen, which is connected with the terms and conditions of employment of any person.

Who can Raise a Dispute?

A dispute is said to have arisen when some demand is made by workmen and it is rejected by the management or *vice versa* and the demand is relating to the employment. A workman can raise a dispute. However, it is pertinent to note that a dispute between an employer and single workman does not fall within the definition of industrial dispute, but if the workman as a body or a considerable section of them make a common cause with the individual workman then such a dispute would be an industrial dispute.

However, certain individual disputes relating to dismissal, discharge, retrenchment or termination of services of a workman, are also covered. The Act implies even to industrial establishments employing a single workman. But dispute in relation to a person who is not a 'workman' within the meaning of the Act is not an industrial dispute under Section 2(k).

The Industrial Disputes Act, 1947 provide for creation of different authorities to preserve industrial harmony, prevention and settlement of industrial disputes. These are:

1. Work Committee

In establishments where hundred or more workers are employed,

(a) The appropriate government may require the employer to set-up works committee.
(b) It is composed of equal number of representatives of workmen and management who are chosen with consultation of the trade union.
(c) Its functions are to preserve amity and establish cordial relations and to resolve differences of opinion on matters of common interest.

The works committee is purely consultative body and thus have not made much progress and are ineffective forum, baring few exceptions in some organisations.

2. Conciliation Officer

The conciliation officer may be appointed by the government for specified area or specified industries.

Duty of conciliation officer is to mediate in and promote the settlement of industrial disputes.

Where industrial dispute exists or is apprehended and relates to public utility, conciliation officer shall hold conciliation proceedings and it is mandatory. In such cases conciliation officer will investigate the dispute and induce the parties to come to amicable settlement. However, he cannot take the decision.

He has to send report of settlement to his government. If no settlement is reached then also he has to report to the government giving reasons on account of which settlement could not be reached. Conciliation officer to normally submit report within 14 days of commencement of conciliation proceedings. Duty of the conciliation officer is administrative and not judicial in nature.

If an agreement is reached by the parties, it is binding on both the parties.

3. Board of Conciliation

The government may notify constitution of board of conciliation for promoting settlement of an industrial dispute. Its role is also consultative like conciliation office.

4. Court of Enquiry

The government may constitute a court of enquiry to inquire into any matter connected with an industrial dispute. In the case of board of conciliation the object is to promote settlement of an industrial dispute. But in the case of a court of enquiry object is to inquire into and reveal the causes of an industrial dispute.

5. Voluntary Arbitration

It is voluntary method of resolving individual disputes if dispute is not settled by negotiating parties. Here both parties are willing to go to an arbitrator of their choice and submit to his decision. Arbitrators are named by the parties in the written agreement. The number of arbitrators can be one or even more than one. Legal sanctity to this mode of settlement of industrial disputes was given in 1956 when Section 10A was introduced in Industrial Dispute Act.

6. Adjudication

The Industrial Disputes Act provides for three-tier system of adjudication of industrial disputes. The cases either may be referred by government to court after the receipt of failure report from conciliation officer or directly by any party. Labour courts and industrial tribunal may be constituted by the state government while national tribunal is constituted by the central government.

(i) Labour Courts

Functions of labour courts are relating to matters as under:

(i) Legality of an order passed by an employer under the standing orders,
(ii) Application and interpretation of standing orders,
(iii) Discharge or dismissal of workman,
(iv) Withdrawal of any customary concession or privilege,
(v) Illegality or otherwise of a strike or lock-out, and
(vi) All matters (not specified for industrial court).

(ii) Industrial Tribunals

The functions:

(i) All matters within jurisdiction of labour courts,

(ii) Wages,
(iii) Compensatory and other allowances,
(iv) Hours of work and rest intervals,
(v) Leave with wages and holidays,
(vi) Bonus, Provident Fund and Gratuity,
(vii) Shift working,
(viii) Classification of grades,
(ix) Rule of Discipline, and
(x) Retrenchment and closure of establishment.

(iii) National Tribunal

The national tribunal shall be constituted by the Central Government (only) when undertakings in more than one state is affected by such industrial dispute and is of 'national importance' and matters relate to functioning of labour and industrial courts.

7. Grievance Settlement Authority

It is to be set-up by enterprises where 50 or more workers are employed. This is for settling of individual grievances of employees. Individual disputes are to be referred to the courts when not settled at grievances authority level.

8. Welfare Officer

Another preventive measure is under the Factories Act, 1948, i.e. the appointment of welfare officer in the organisation if workers are 500 or more.

9. Standing Orders

Another preventive measure is certification of standing orders by enterprises under the Industrial Employment Standing Orders Act, 1946. These standing orders require enterprises to lay down uniform terms and conditions of employment of workers.

10. Central and State Industrial Relations Machinery

Central Industrial Relations Machinery consists of the Chief Labour Commissioner and Regional Labour Commissioner together with Labour Enforcement Officers. The machinery has Regional Offices. Their main functions are:

(i) prevention, investigation and settlement of industrial disputes in industries, or enforcement of labour laws and awards,
(ii) verification of union membership,
(iii) fixation of minimum wages, etc., and
(iv) central implementation and evaluation machinery ensures implementation of code of discipline, labour laws, awards and settlements, takes preventive action by settling disputes, evaluates major strikes and lock-outs, evaluates labour laws and policy decisions and suggests measures to improve them.

11. Other Preventive Measures

Some other provisions laid down in Industrial Disputes Act, 1947 which discourage disputes are as under:

(a) According to Sec. 9A of Industrial Disputes Act, an employer cannot make any change in conditions of service without giving to the workers a 21-days' notice and follow the prescribed procedure for changing them.

(b) Defining of unfair labour practices on part of employees/unions and employers which have deterrent affect as penalties are provided under [Section 2(ra)] of Industrial Disputes Act, 1947.

(c) Provisions of laws relating to lay-off, retrenchment and closure and also regarding lock-out and strikes which imposes restrictions on the employers and employees.

In nutshell statutory preventive and settlement machinery can be summarised as under:

1. Works Committee 2. Conciliation Officer 3. Board of Conciliation	(for consultation)
4. Court of Enquiry 5. Voluntary Arbitration	(for enquiry)
6. (a) Labour Courts (b) Industrial Tribunals (c) National Tribunal	(for adjudication)

7. Grievance Settlement Authority
8. Welfare Officers
9. Standing Orders
10. Centre and State Industrial Relations Machinery
11. Other Preventive Measures

(B) VOLUNTARY MACHINERY

Box I

Interpret I.D. Act to Avoid Industrial Unrest and to Secure Industrial Peace

The Industrial Disputes Act provides machinery for regulating the rights of the employers as well as employees to lock-outs and strikes and to settle any dispute in peaceful and harmonious manner by providing for negotiations, mediations, voluntary arbitration or compulsory adjudication by the authorities created under the statute. While interpreting different provisions of the Act, an attempt has to be made to avoid industrial unrest, and to secure industrial peace. The appropriate machinery has actually been provided to achieve that end. Conciliation is most important and desirable way to achieve it. While dealing with indsutrial disputes, the courts have always emphasised on doctrine of social justice, which is founded on basic ideal of socio-economic equality as enshrined in the preamble of our Constitution.

luntary machinery for settlement of industrial disputes is based on Code of Discipline announced in 1958. The code was approved by all central organisations of workers and employers in 16th Indian Labour Conference at the initiative of then Labour Minister Shri G.L. Nanda.

1. Code of Discipline, 1958

It contains matters where:

(i) Labour and managements agree,
(ii) Managements agree,
(iii) Unions agree,
(vi) Arbitration procedure under code of discipline,
(v) Model grievance procedure laid, and
(vi) Criteria for recognition of unions and rights of recognised union.

2. Tripartite Bodies

1. Indian Labour Conference,
2. Standing Labour Committee,
3. Industrial Committees, and
4. Tripartite Committee on International Labour Organisation Conventions, 1954.

3. Formation of Permanent Negotiating Machinery

For Railways and Post and Telegraphs (PNM) in 1951. The machinery is three-tiers—at division level, zonal railway level and *ad hoc* tribunal with equal number of representatives of labour and management with a neutral as chairman.

4. Formation of Joint Consultative Machinery for Central Government Employees (JCM), this is also three-tier

5. Collective Bargaining to be Encouraged

6. Workers' Participation in Management Scheme to be Introduced through Formation of Shop Councils and Plant Council

7. Functioning and Review of Code of Discipline

(i) The Code reflects the policy of the government to build-up an industrial democracy on voluntary basis and is the sheetanchor of Mahatma Gandhi's philosophy of industrial relations. It aims at preserving industrial peace with the help of employers and employees. It represents a voluntary moral commitment and is not a legal document. The Code, which aims at providing an alternative to conflict for the resolution of disputes, worked very well for some time after its adoption.

The machinery (Central Implementation and Evaluation Machinery) set-up at the central and state levels for the implementation of the Code receives reports of breaches, investigates and then reports the findings to the employers' or workers' national level organisations for taking suitable steps. It assists in the implementation of the Code of Discipline, labour enactments, awards and agreements and takes preventive action in order to avert strikes and lock-outs, settles long-pending disputes, brings about out-of-court settlement of cases pending in the High Court and the Supreme Court, and ensures that the proposed labour appeals are screened by the screening committees set-up by the central organisations of employers and workers before they are taken to the courts. The implementation machinery also persuades employers and unions to evolve grievance procedures for the reduction of day-to-day grievances of individual workers. It undertakes evaluation studies on the working of labour laws, awards, policies, programmes, major disputes, etc. It also exercises a restraining influence on employers and workers when they seem to be heading towards unilateral or direct action.

(ii) In the early years, the Code focussed the attention of the parties on their obligations under the various labour laws, and enjoined upon them a stricter observance of these and other obligations associated with work in an industrial environment. The fact that the parties got together and openly accepted the need for stricter adherence to certain basic propositions was itself an achievement when breaches were enquired into and openly discussed in tripartite committees. The very process of discussion procedure was a restraining and sobering effect on the parties and instances of gross violations of law and repudiation of responsibilities declined. The National Commission on Labour thought that the Code had only a limited success and a limited use.

(iii) It is to be noted that some provisions of code of discipline such as: (a) penalties for unfair labour practices, (b) provision of voluntary arbitration, and (c) setting of governance authority in an enterprise and prohibition of strike/lock-out without notice, have been included in the Industrial Disputes Act, 1947. Matters relating to recognition of union as bargaining agent has been included in the Maharashtra Recognition of Unions and Prevention of Unfair Labour Practices Act, 1971.

(iv) Industrial Truce Resolution, 1962. With the Chinese attack in October 1962, an emergency was declared in the country, and it was realised that production should not be jeopardised in any way. Employers' and workers' representatives, in a joint meeting of their organisations held on November 3, 1962 at New Delhi, passed a resolution, saying that:

> "No effort shall be spared to achieve maximum production, and management and workers will strive to collaborate in all possible ways to promote the defence efforts of the country."

As a result of the acceptance of this Resolution, there was a sharp decline in the number of disputes and in the number of mandays lost. Workers not only worked for extra hours but also contributed to the National Defence Fund. Emergency Production Committees were set-up, both at the Centre and in the S tates to improve production and productivity. But the Resolution lost its importance when prices rose sharply and disputes erupted once again.

Trade Unions and their Functions

Definition

"Trade union is a continuous association of wage-earners for the purpose of protecting and advancing the conditions of their working lives."

—Sydney and B. Webb

WHY EMPLOYEES JOIN UNIONS?

Objectives

Employees join unions due to following reasons:

(1) Trade unions will protect employee's economic and vocational interest. As such serve as instrument of defence and security of employment.
(2) Trade unions look after employee's welfare.
(3) Trade unions safeguard and improve conditions of work and service, i.e. wages, etc.
(4) Trade unions will communicate their views of the management.
(5) Trade unions will restrain managerial authoritarianship. Trade unions will oppose management discretions.
(6) Trade unions will strengthen their bargaining power. They are seen as an instrument regulating the relationship between employers and employees.
(7) Trade unions highlight class distinction to reduce workers' dissatisfaction. They join to overthrow capitalism.
(8) To exercise leadership role as office-bearer of trade union. This satisfies their ambition to get ahead which they aspire.
(9) Trade unions help in developing rational personnel policies which are fair in treatment.

ARE UNIONS NECESSARY?

Union is a body of workers/employees working in an organisation, who fights for their rights and other benefits with the organisation. Unions play an important role in preventing exploitation of employees by their employers. Over the years, the relationship between employer and employees has changed from *master and servant* to *contract* between employer and employee. Earlier it was a one-sided relationship with employer wielding absolute power to hire and fire employees. Intervention of trade union prevent one-sided exploitation by the employer and to wield countervailing power over them.

Workers look to unions to provide the following:

(a) Job security to the workers/employees,
(b) Safeguard workers' interest,
(c) Improve the working conditions in the organisation,
(d) Helping employees in developing skills according to the job entrusted to them,
(e) Enable the workers' participation in management,
(f) Protect rights of the workers, i.e. wages and salary, etc.,
(g) Helps in maintaining good industrial relations, and
(h) Negotiating with management on industrial conflicts.

In some organisations where strength of employees is large, it is very difficult for the management to deal with all the employees. In such a situation, the management deal with the Trade Unions and in turn unions deal with the employees.

TRADE UNION STRUCTURE

There are four types of trade unions:

(i) *A Craft union* is formed by workers belonging to same occupation or specialisation irrespective of industry, e.g. Indian pilots' guild, electricians join to secure more favourable terms.
(ii) *Industrial union* is formed on the basis of industry, e.g. cotton textile factories—Rashtriya Mill Mazdoor Sangh, Mumbai, for worker's solidarity and avoids separate bargaining by employee's unions.
(iii) *General union* embraces all workers whatever industry or craft in a place, e.g. Jamshedpur Labour Union.
(iv) Another aspect of the structure of unions relates to *pattern of relationship* between:
    (a) National level federations,
    (b) Regional level federations, and
    (c) Plant level unions.

FORMATION OF TRADE UNIONS

Due to scenario of exploitation of workers led to birth of unions and era of government regulation and control. Trade unions are now part of industrial organisations to pursue the interests of employees collectively to influence management decisions. Even be in competition with the management for employee's loyalty.

FUNCTIONS OF TRADE UNIONS

These are given under four groups:

(a) Functions Relating to Trade Union Members

(1) Safeguard workers' interest against exploitation by employer or leaders.
(2) Protect workers from unfair labour practices by employer.
(3) Provision of healthy, safe and conducive working conditions by employer.
(4) To ask for rewards to be associated with work performance.
(5) Get benefits from organisation for health, housing, education, recreation, etc.
(6) To help in grievance redressal of employees.
(7) To foster labour-management participation and cooperation.
(8) To make workers conscious of their rights and duties.

(b) Functions Relating to Industrial Organisation

(1) To increase production and productivity.
(2) To help maintenance of discipline.
(3) To promote cordial relations between the management and workers.
(4) To create favourable opinion of the management among workers.
(5) To facilitate communication with the management.

(c) Functions Relating to Union Organisation

(1) To improve financial position of trade union by increasing subscription.
(2) To train members in leadership.
(3) To augment communication between union and members.
(4) To curb inter-union rivalry.
(5) To avoid unfair labour practices.
(6) To review relevance of union objectives in the context of social change.
(7) To maintain records of union.

(d) Functions Relating to Society

(1) To help national development—family planning, national integration, afforestation.
(2) To launch campaigns against social evils, i.e. corruption, communalism, casteism, price rise, hoarding, smuggling, dowry, illiteracy, etc.
(3) To help the government and mobilise people participation.

HISTORICAL DEVELOPMENT OF TRADE UNION IN INDIA

- First Trade Union was formed in 1890—Bombay Mill Hands Association by Mr. Lokhande to demand amendment of Factories Act, 1881. Then several unions followed to fulfil specific demands and of temporary nature. Also to lend support to national independence movement.
- In 1918—Ahmedabad Textile Labour Association was born when dispute was settled by the intervention of Gandhiji in Ahmedabad Textiles.
- In Madras, B.P. Wadia formed Madras Labour Union.
- International Labour Organisation was established in 1919—This influenced formation of All India Federation of Trade Unions.
- After World War I, 1919—Large number of strong Trade Unions got formed by—Annie Besant in Madras and M. Gandhi in Ahmedabad. After 1924 all major All India Left-Wing Trade Unions got formed for class struggle.

The Trade Union Act, 1926

Some of the provisions of the Trade Union Act, 1926 are as under:

(a) Any 7 members or more can apply for registration to the Registrar of Trade Unions.
(b) Trade unions to regulate relations between:
  (i) workmen,
  (ii) between employers and workmen, and
  (iii) between employees.
(c) Procedure for cancellation of registration is prescribed in the Act.
(d) Rights and liabilities of registered trade unions are:
  - Can make payment of salaries to office-bearers?,
  - Can spend for defending legal action against trade unions?,
  - Can spend for publication of periodicals?,
  - Can create political fund for trade union members for fighting elections to local municipalities, and
  - Provides immunity from civil action to office-bearers in furtherance of trade union activity. Registered trade union is a legal entity.

ADVENT OF INDEPENDENCE

Advent of independence quickened the pace and growth of trade unions due to government's changed outlook towards labour and awakening in the country. Further reasons for growth were economic distress due to World War II. Involvement of political parties in trade unions, inter-union rivalry, etc. So some major central organisations of workers are as follows:

(i) The Indian National Trade Union Congress (INTUC) formed by the Congress party.
(ii) The All India Trade Union Congress (AITUC) formed by Communist Party of India.
(iii) The Hind Mazdoor Sabha (HMS) formed by Socialists.
(iv) Centre of Indian Trade Unions (CITU) formed by Marxists-Communists.
(v) Bhartiya Mazdoor Sangh (BMS). Affiliated to BJP party.

WEAKNESSES OF TRADE UNION MOVEMENT IN INDIA

Some of these weaknesses of trade unions are:

(i) Multiplicity of trade unions as seven persons can form a union.
(ii) Inter-union rivalry.
(iii) Intra-union factions.
(iv) Absence of criteria for recognition of bargaining agent.
(v) Politicalisation of trade union and association of outsiders with enterprise unions.
(vi) Philosophy and approaches of unions which advocate:
- Adversial relationship (war-fare) conflict with management.
- Class struggle-oppression and exploitation by employers.
- Adoption of pressure tactics, militancy, indiscipline, intimidation, black-mailing towards management.
- No role of unions as social change agents and welfare of workers but self-centred.

(vii) Low membership due to lack of interest by union leaders.
(viii) Absence of paid office-bearers.
(ix) Weak financial position due to low membership, non-collection of dues.
(x) Lack of public customers and community interest.

MEASURES TO STRENGTHEN TRADE UNIONS

(i) One union one industry so as to avoid multiplicity of trade union.
(ii) Linking of trade unions to political parties to be curbed.
(iii) Development of internal leadership.
(iv) Financial stability by raising monthly subscription from members and introduction of check-off system under which each worker can individually authorise the employer to deduct membership fee from his wage.
(v) Expansion of union activities for its members, social, education and cultural areas—Trade unions to participate in the development programmes of the country.
(vi) Laying of criteria for recognition of unions to strengthen as bargaining agent.

5

Profile of New Industrial Labour Force in India and Emerging Employer-Employee Relations in New Economy

I. PROFILES OF LABOUR FORCE

1.1 The profile of industrial labour force has undergone changes from the time factories were set-up in early 1940's in India. The labour force was purely with agricultural background. It was mostly rural, illiterate, and migratory in character. They were hardly committed to factory working and returned to villages at will. This was *first generation* of industrial workers.

1.2 After 1960's with the setting up industrial training institutes and vocational training centres, the profile of industrial labour force underwent marked change with industrialisation. Some characteristics of *second generation* labour force are given as under:

Profile of Industrial Worker (Second Generation)

The industrial workers are:

- Knowledgeable, qualified and skilled and wants *direct information* from his supervisor.
- Not satisfied with *managerial functioning* and wants *fast decisions*.
- *More secure* in employment once he enters and shows *defiance* of his superiors comes from middle urban class.
- Demands *better work environment* and facilities but willing to adjust to work environment.
- Wants to *participate* and be consulted in his work activity and decision-making.
- Educated employees pressurise supervisors to change the job, if it is not challenging, to suit their creative ambitions. *Selective about the work* they would like to do.

- Fatalism leading to *cynicism* that things cannot be improved in factories.
- Have high *emotional needs* when in crisis, e.g. sickness or bereavement in family.
- Hesitant to move from one region to the other for job.

1.3 Around 1990's the profile of new labour force has further changed in view changed environments of global competition, high-tech, internet-era, knowledge revolution and social awareness in improving standards of living. Now primary factor of production is knowledge for wealth creation. The change is towards service sector and knowledge-based economy. The *third generation* workforce is well educated and IT-oriented. They have competitive efficiency and contribute to higher productivity. They have better living standards. Brief file is as under:

Profile of new labour force (Third Generation)

Following aspects of new generation employees are covered as under:

(1) Characteristics of new generation employees.
(2) Retention strategies.

(1) Characteristics of new generation employees

A breed of employees, that are between 18-24 years of age are smart, practical, *fiercely ambitious* and restless. They have inquiring minds and zealous spirit. They have *obsession to acquire* higher and more saleable skills. This is, their only guarantee to a better job and the *recipe to speedy success* in a fast changing world.

They are used to office interiors which are inviting, comfortable, yet *formal work spaces*. Lounging areas, jukeboxes, food courts, gymnasium, etc. They have got all. They are more comfortable with informal, flexible roles rather than a fixed set of responsibilities. They thrive on *multi-tasking*. This also makes them more vulnerable to changing jobs, or switching careers.

A *less hierarchical* workplaces suit them best and they would prefer to converse on first name basis. Their workplace need to be fun, relaxed and unconventional. They do not need stuffy cabins for them, as they have to spend 12 hours a day there, five days a week. They work hard and harder.

(2) Retention strategies

It is quite a task to keep Generation 'Y' hooked to one job and one employer for long. Because they do not identify with old-fashioned jargon like 'loyalty'. Their primary commitment is "We, Me and My Career Success . . . the faster I get there, the better." *So how to retain them. Best bet would be to appreciate their unique areas of strengths and build on those.* Ambition is second nature to today's young workforce. They are used to aiming for the stars and believe they can go places, much faster than their predecessors. Says a youngman, my father built a home when he retired, I can do it by the time I am 30 years. They have *over-confidence* and are optimistic. They want to be at the top from day one. What makes them think they can get to the top fast? Here is a tip. Be generous with some *direct and objective feedback*, while ensuring that it does not wash away that bubbly spirit. The trick is to help them start with smaller, attainable goals and be more practical about taking on higher levels of responsibility. Tap the potential of that limitless energy by assigning multiple projects.

Generation 'Y' employees are perfect *team players*. In fact, they would rather work in a team, rather than be singled out for an individual function. The opportunity to interface with intelligent and innovative colleagues can act a huge motivator for these people.

Another hint is *to build trust* with sincere, open and honest communication, share information and encourage two-way flow of ideas. Help them get a taste of loyalty, by offering *involvement in participative forums.* Office functions and events like annual days are great platforms for freshers to show their abilities.

Time-bound assignments where they can prove their mettle to handle complexities are perfect. Facilitate them in assessing and identifying their hidden potential, and challenge them to make effective use of their special skills and talents. Generation 'Y' have a tendency go get *bored easily,* so make sure you keep them on their toes, with pressure and excitement.

Coaching and mentoring can be useful tools when it comes to moulding them. Their raw energy and unending enthusiasm, when tempered with appropriate guidance and encouragement from seasoned and respected professionals, can provide these youngsters, an ideal foundation that will ultimately transform them into smart managers of tomorrow.

They can flourish, if they are provided with state-of-the-art resources. The lack of high tech environment will not be welcome for them. Provide state-of-art *training to retain them.* Allow ample breathing space . . . *autonomy* and *independence* to experiment in their area, and learn from their mistakes. *Listen* to them as they recount their experience of last weekend.

Their *dreams* may be different from yours, and their work styles too, but they may score as high as yours, in much lesser time, because they mean business.

2. EMERGING EMPLOYER-EMPLOYEE RELATIONS IN NEW ECONOMY

1. Employer-employee relations in new economy.
2. H.R. practices and staffing strategy which will be in continual flux.
3. Role of managers in knowledge millennium.

2.1 Employer-employee relations in new economy

Employer-employee relations now require a whole new approach to management and management practices in different aspects.

(a) Talented men are becoming free agents

Slow-moving, rigid, long-term employment in one company, corporate loyalty, climb-the-ladder model is moving to new fast-moving, free-markets. The employees with most marketable skills are in greatest demand. They can increasingly see themselves fending for themselves as sole proprietors of their skills and abilities. They seem to move from one new opportunity to next.

Employees are adaptable, independent, techno-literate, information savvy and entrepreneurial. They are short in supply, as most organizations need them.

In the new economy, the individual, not the employer is in the driver's seat. When he leaves the employer, his skills, ability and experience which adds value goes with him. Employees are in commanding position.

(b) Work place is becoming more flexible

Now rule is you get the work done wherever you can. Business organizations have become more flexible to compete in today's high-tech, fast paced knowledge driven, global economy.

(c) Employer-employee relationship—A balance of power

(i) The old feudal employment relationship of internal hierarchy and insulated from market forces is dead. In *free market environment* everyone gets what he can negotiate. Talented people who cannot negotiate best deals for themselves are going to be left behind. Like-wise employers who cannot negotiate with best talent will not be able to retain people to get work done.

(ii) Organisation may *avoid investment in training for long-term basis* as employees are going to leave. The trend is to train people on an as-needed basis. *Just-in-time training* allows learners to select precise information they require to till skills and knowledge gaps as they occur. In fact, in new economy, acquiring new knowledge and competencies is individual's responsibility. To keep one self-marketable and competitive is one's role.

2.2 HR Practices and staffing strategy in new economy will be in continual flux

(i) In new economy the employers shall do three things

First, *shrink their core group*. Second, grow a *fluid talent pool* that employer can draw on as needs be. Third, employer will *maintain an internal group* of contributors who are not permanently assigned to any particular responsibilities and who can be deployed to fill in staffing gaps any where. Employer has to do selective hiring.

(ii) Retention

Employer will *retain the best people* on the basis of an ongoing negotiation with each individual on their own unique terms. They will be employers new life long-term employees.

(iii) Performance management

To bring out the very best in best people, managers will create clarity on ongoing basis in their roles and responsibilities.

(iv) Rewards and incentives

In the just-in-time workplace, (long-term rewards are out of place) rewards are to be given with speed and creativity. Managers to understand that different people are motivated by different incentives and thus to customize the same.

(v) Encourage flexible work arrangements

As flexible work arrangements give higher productivity, and stronger employee commitment, these will be enouraged by employers.

2.3 Role of Managers in knowledge millennium

(a) The role of managers is undergoing change. Managers are becoming as *performance management coaches* who give fast feedback effectively which is specific, timely and accurate.

(b) For meeting *cultural differences* manager has to observe 3 R's, i.e. *recognize, respect* and *reconcile* differences between employees. Wealth in new economy is *created in alliances.* In mergers and acquisitions managers have to recognize that there are cultural differences and thus respect each culture and reconcile the opposing views by discovering special aspects of excellence within different cultures. Organizations that can reconcile cultural differences better are at much advantage at creating wealth.

(c) Managers to integrate 3 Qs, i.e. Mental, Emotional and Spiritual quotients. Spiritual quotient allows us to understand situations deeply and enable us to question what we are doing and where it will lead to. Meaning of situation gives us a sense of higher purpose and values, a long-term commitment to the future.

(d) There are various things for a leader *to be progressive* in an organisation are as under:

First, leader has to *involve everyone* to improve the organisation, i.e. he has to be highly participative.

Second, leader should be willing to *trust people* i.e. *team*. He has to be sensitive, supportive and understanding of their feelings and emotions.

Third, critical *trait for leadership* that he has to be committed to think about where the organisation is headed and how it needs to change. Leader has to become the agent of change. Manager has to develop a long-term focus and resist short-term temptations and pressures.

Fourth, "new ideas" are redefining what managers should be doing and how they should be doing it.

Fifth, *development of vision, values and vitality* are essential for leadership role.

Sixth, knowledge leader has to pay more attention to the *health of knowledge worker* where he can renew himself and his mind. It is caring for knowledge potential. He has to maintain worklife balance for his men.

Seventh, to become *a manager of choice* with focus on relation building with employees by helping them to develop their know-how, trust building by his characteristic of credibility, fairness and respect, and organizational brand building by enhancing organisation's image through achievement of strategic goals.

6

Trade Union Strategies in the wake of Declining Trends in Unionism

According to D.K. Srivastava, trade unions, world-wide, are experiencing difficulties on many counts in general and retention of quality membership in particular. There has been substantial erosion both in membership as well as bargaining power of unions. In order to remain relevant and effective too, unions in many competitive economies of the world are becoming "part of solution" rather "part of the problem". In such an environment, trade unions in India have also shown marked change in their approach and activities towards betterment of work culture *vis-a-vis* productivity. Changes in the strategies of unions towards changes taking place in the wake of globalization are discussed under following heads:

1. Reasons for declining trends in unionism.
2. Strategies adopted by unions to cope with eroding-base and changed business environment.
   - 2.1 Reorient thinking and attitudes.
   - 2.2 Profit-centre mindset and performance culture.
   - 2.3 Focusing on decent work and work-life balance.
   - 2.4 Adopting familial approach in order to get good deals.
   - 2.5 One union in one company.
   - 2.6 Group of strategies in changed environment.
3. Labour responses and initiatives with MNCs.
4. To conclude.

I. REASONS FOR DECLINING TRENDS IN UNIONISM

The important reasons for the declining influence of trade unions could be identified as follows:

(i) The volatile market, increasing competition and emerging business compulsions have diluted the needs of unions. Direct dialogue between employees and management has further weakened the position of unions.

(ii) *Relocation of manufacturing* operations to non-unionised sites and outsourcing of non-core activities has marginalized unions to a great extent. Unions seem helpless to evolve suitable counter strategies to ward-off side effects of restructuring.

(iii) The profile *vis-a-vis aspirations of new generation of workforce* have changed drastically and there exists a mismatch between agenda of unions and expectations of new workers.

(iv) Non-adherence to the democratic values within a union, resulting in growing alienation of the rank and file.

(v) The existing *union leadership* seems neither interested in the future of workers nor development of quality inside leadership.

(vi) *Changing attitude of government* in granting permission to closure and/or retrenchment has adversely impacted on union development.

In addition, there are weaknesses in trade union movement in India as under: (Figure 1)

FIGURE I

Weaknesses of Trade Union Movement in India

Some of these weaknesses of trade unions are:

(i) Multiplicity of trade unions as seven persons can form a union and get it registered.
(ii) Inter-union rivalry.
(iii) Intra-union factions.
(iv) Absence of criteria for recognition of bargaining agent.
(v) Politicalisation of trade union and association of outsiders with enterprise unions.
(vi) Philosophy and approaches of unions which advocate:
- adversial relationship (warfare) conflict with management.
- Class struggle-oppression and exploitation by employers.
- Adoption of pressure tactics, militancy, indiscipline, intimidation, black-mailing of management.
- No role of unions as social change agents and welfare of workers but self-centred.

(vii) Low membership due to lack of interest by union leader. (see Box 1)
(viii) Absence of paid office-bearers.
(ix) Weak financial position due to low membership and non-collection of dues.
(x) Lack of public, customers, consumers and community interest.

In the backdrop of all the odds for unions when even survival is at stake, it is very difficult to regain the position back to normalcy. However, unions still are hopeful to make their presence worthy to the companies in general and workers in particular. It is hoped, with a planned strategy and an understanding behaviour, unions will bounce back in near future. The increasing number of matured internal leaders and better relationships with management is a good sign for unionism; the only problem with internal leadership is lack of professionalism and skills. If these two things can be improved, this will benefit both unions as well as management. What are the important strategies being adopted by unions to strengthen their positions?

Box I

(i) Density of trade unions out of 92 countries:
- Only 14 had a rate of more than 50 percent,
- In 48 the rate less than 20 percent.

(ii) Loss of trade union membership:

Country	*Less percent*	*During*
• France	25	1975-85
• England	3 million	in five years
• USA	Drop in union membership from 35% in 1953 to less than 17% in 1983 (30 years)	
• Japan	Membership dropped from 55% in 1949 to 29% in 1985	
• India	Membership declined from 92.95 lakhs in 1989 to the lowest 31.34 lakhs in 1993	

Result: Equation between labour and management has altered trade union movement in India was built during first quarter of 20th century and movement had grown economically and politically powerful. But during last decade of 20th century, trade unions lost their membership and prominence due to their activities like protests, strikes, etc. and weakened their movement as a whole.

Source: ILO, 1997 and Labour Bureau, 1998 from D.K. Srivastava's article.

2. STRATEGIES ADOPTED BY UNIONS TO COPE WITH ERODING-BASE AND CHANGED BUSINESS ENVIRONMENT

2.1 Re-orient thinking and attitudes

In the context of eroding-base, the unions will have to re-orient their thinking and attitudes because the demands upon business organisation are more exacting than those in a protected market environment. Unions will have to develop a long-term perspective of relationships, and not one of solving specific service-related issues alone.

2.2 Profit-centre mind-set and performance-based culture

Unions have now started understanding and accepting the importance of business realities like profitability and productivity to be seen as a part of package deal with the management. Unions, accordingly, have started supporting performance-based rewards.

2.3 Focusing on decent work and work life balance

In the era of multi-tasking *vis-a-vis* increasing workload, unions have started projecting aspects like flexible work schedule and work-life balance. The quality of work-life and decent treatment to employees are being reworked at workplaces.

2.4 Adopting familial approach in order to get good deals

The changing posture of union and management has also helped in evolving a familial or collaborative approach both by management and workers. The good results of such arrangements are being reflected in the behaviour as well as work of employees.

2.5 One union in one company

Unions, after weakening their power due to multiplicity, are now developing an arrangement that supports not only "one union in one company" formula but also independence from any outside leadership. Unions are now actively working to develop and support inside leadership.

2.6 Group of strategies in changed environment

The strategies of trade unions in the wake of change could be identified as good governance, offering new services, expanding union base, opening up new areas of negotiation, collective action for institutional benefits and building new alliances. These are explained as under:

(i) Internal good governance

The unions will have to consider development of internal management system within their own organisations. The union leaders will need training because the job of trade unions will require assessment of long-term plans for growth of the enterprise so that the jobs can be secured, besides problem-solving on day-to-day basis. They need to identify softer areas of management such as people and system development and see how balance is achieved to benefit both the organisation and the people dependent upon it.

- One way to promote *union democracy* is to introduce an element of professionalism within unions in matters such as the selection or of union leaders, their succession planning, development of leadership potential among rank and file membership, etc.
- The unions will need *both professionals and research* inputs to help them decide on their policy and strategy. They will have to improve their financial position to sustain a viable organisation.
- The strength of a union lies in its being able *to get support of the general public,* and for this purpose the unions have to consider themselves as an instrument of the society, and constantly bear in mind that their actions should give strength to the society as a whole for the effectiveness of the trade unions. Unions have to avoid traffic blockages due to processions and strikes in consumer industries to devoid consumers of daily items.

(ii) Offering new services

Trade unions in India may benefit from the experiences of their counterparts across the globe. Some attractive services could be offered by trade unions as in different countries.

Compared to the western counterparts, unions in India also face difficulties due to (a) small size and membership, (b) lack of unity in central trade unions, (c) low subscription rate, and (d) improper use of union funds.

(iii) Expanding union-base

(a) There is nothing secret about declining number of factories and employment in organised sector in the last ten years or so. Considering the fact that there is no better alternative to downsizing and outsourcing, unions should work to *organise the unorganised sector.* This strategy, although fragile, will serve two purposes: first, better social security for unorganised workers will reduce huge cost differences between organised and unorganised sector workers which has been a source of attraction for employers; second, unions will get a readymade strength of workforce to join them. It is not correct to project that contract workers are happy with their exploitation on many counts, rather they have started forming groups to pressurise principal employers to provide facilities like canteen, medical and transport, etc. at par with unionised category. The international unions are likely to put pressure on developing countries for providing better monetary and other benefits in order to discourage their employers from outsourcing manufacturing operations to labour-intensive countries.

(b) The *absence of women from the trade union* movement has reflected in limiting the union base. With more number of women workers entering into jobs, unions will have to present them "special packages" in a more meaningful and effective manner. The broader concerns of women workers related to work flexibility, child care benefits, tax concessions, leadership opportunities in union and more paid holidays, etc. will have to be incorporated in the subsequent agendas for negotiations.

(c) In view of large number of *middle-aged employees* opting out from jobs through VRS, unions should evolve a policy to get in touch with such employees who are likely to join alternate jobs in small firms. Unions should emphasize on extending certain facilities like medical care to employees and their families even after retirement. Union should also help in settling of these employees in the post-VRS situation.

(iv) Opening up new areas of negotiation

In the wake of globalisation the pattern of bargaining is changing worldwide with scope for greater autonomy at the enterprise level. While management is continuously putting pressure on the unions to accept higher productivity, eliminating certain practices that they consider wasteful, and strict disciplinary standards through counter proposals, unions have no option but to accept them. Unions should work seriously to understand the implications of increasing work load on the health of workers and raise voice against *exploitative practices*. They should also demand more *voice in decision-making*, about composition of contract workers, outsourcing and VRS. The Mumbai-based unions have also opened up new areas of negotiation like contracting out non-core activities (Cadbury), enhanced *ex-gratia* payments in case of death of worker (Colgate Palmolive), replacing retrenchment with VRS (Asian Paints), deferring massive retrenchment (Voltas), separate settlements for contract workers (Cadbury), redeployment of surplus labour (Cadbury), one time settlement of court cases (Voltas) and effective consultations with union on production matters (Crompton Greaves). Decentralised bargaining has given lot of freedom to the management but the competition between settlements of different units of the same company is still very tough and challenging.

(v) Collective action for institutional benefits

- In this strategy the main focus should be to ensure that workers' rights and interests are incorporated into legislation or other regulatory instruments of the labour market. Trade unions should aim at successfully lobbying with the public authorities so as to *influence national economic and social policies*. Neither the Government nor the unions have created a forum to examine in depth the implications of the market economy for the unions.

- Labour laws in India are scattered and confusing; there is an urgent need to *judiciously consolidate them* in an effective manner. If unions decide to work together for evolving bare minimum *social security benefits for unorgaised sector*, this will be a real contribution on the same lines as what they did for industrial workers at its initial stage.
- India, being a founder member of ILO, has ratified only three out of eight core labour standards. We need to address the specific issues that have blocked us to ratify core labour standards. It will be suicidal if we see our strength at the cost of long-run development of citizens.

(vi) Building new alliances

- The unions would have to examine seriously the possibility of *mergers of different unions*. They need to build their strength internally and also combine their resources to influence the thinking of policy-makers. They would also have to establish closer links with trade unions in other countries to benefit from the experiences of their counterparts elsewhere. It is inevitable that unions have to build an independent constituency. They will have to strengthen their organisation management considerably and professionalise.
- In Mumbai unions showed positive results of unity in Voltas and Cadbury. These unions follow a unified command while negotiating with respective managements at different locations in India.
- A *solidarity committee of trade unions*, comprising of veteran trade union leaders, has been formed to provide a forum to the voice of unions in Mumbai. Such efforts should be appreciated, as there is dearth of genuine union leaders who can understand the problems of workers and respond promptly. There is also a move to unite all unaffiliated unions in Mumbai and if this gets some success the union movement will get a new twist.

3. LABOUR RESPONSES AND INITIATIVES WITH MNC's

Cooperation between labour groups in different countries in their conflicts with MNC's is minimal. However, trade union strategies include:

(i) *Information exchanges* among union of different countries which helps them persue claims with the company as well as cite precedents from other countries during bargaining. The labour unions have formed international trade secretaries (ITSs). There are 15 ITSs which function to provide world-wide links of national unions in a particular trade or industry (e.g. metals, chemicals, transport) world-wide. It mainly facilitate the exchange of information. The primary goal of each ITS is to achieve bargaining with each of the MNC in its industry.

(ii) Most common *union tactic* is to strike for temporary suspension of functions so as to exert pressure. The very existence of the firm may be threatened by a prolonged strike. However, unions have to exercise caution before resorting to strike as some MNCs enjoy formidable financial strength. The bargaining power of a union may be weakened by MNCs adopting some practice such as sourcing its products or

Box 2

New Role of Trade Unions: Unions commonly known as protest organisations who never take up any development activities. To quote Dr. N.R. Sheth, *IJIR*, Oct. 2001, are at crossroads. They are on divergent path. One wonders they would like to map the new path early. They have to redefine their social responsibilities in relation to unemployed, contract workers. They may like to explore ways for development of new leadership for new trade unionism appropriate for the global society in the years ahead."

Unions can play a developmental role:

(i) By building human resource management philosophy, values and practices in trade unions so that they are responsible for human resource development. Union leaders can to develop employees.
(ii) Provide workers with right information regarding role of trade unions in an organisation by explaining mission and plans of the organisation.
(iii) Redefine trade union role as one of developmental rather than a protest institution in the organisation.
(iv) By building linkages between union and different groups through human resource development.
(v) Counselling or guidance of workers on their social problems, i.e. drinking, indebtedness, absenteeism, etc.
(vi) Role in family and vocational guidance, i.e. children's education, career growth, investment of money, etc.
(vii) Move from traditional role to developmental role:

Traditional Role	*Developmental Role*
• Agitator	• Trainer
• Blackmailer	• Educator
• Crisis dealer	• Counsellor
• Grievance Handler	• Motivator
• Coercive Bargainer	• Facilitator
• Productivity bargainer	• Communicator

components across different countries, or threaten to move production facilities to other location. Ford, for example, treated British Unions to move manufacturing unit to Europe unless British workers abandoned their demands. Such threats have risks of plant closure or rationalisation, on the ability of a union to organise strike.

(iii) Next tactic sought by labour unions is lobbying for restrictive national legislations. To prevent export of jobs via MNCs/investment policies (outsourcing in USA).
(iv) Assistance to foreign bargaining unit by providing support in other countries in several ways. These includes refusing to work overtime when that output would supply the market normally served by striking workers' production, or sending financial aid to workers in other countries, and presenting demands simultaneously to their management.

(v) National legislation in some countries provides for worker representation on boards of directors, supervisory boards, restricts entry of foreign worker and/or foreign investment outflows. It is problem that most future regulations will be at the national rather than international level.

(vi) Finally, labour unions seek intervention from the international labour organisation (ILO), UNCTAD, European Union (EU) and Organisation for Economic Cooperation and Development (OECD). ILO has identified a number of workplace-related principles that should be adhered by all nations. In 1997, the ILO adopted a code of conduct for MNCs. The voluntary guidelines cover disclosure of information, competition, taxation, employment, financial and industrial relations, science and technology.

In sum, labour strategies are information exchanges, simultaneous negotiations or strikes, and refusal to work overtime, etc. Further, in reality, developments in industrial relations indicate a shift in focus of industrial relations system at the enterprise level.

4. TO CONCLUDE

To conclude, industrial relations systems may not take much deviation, but actors in the industrial relations may be required to play a more coordinated role:

- Government to play the role of facilitator,
- Trade union to play a balanced role of keeping the interest of management too, and
- The management fulfils its role towards individual.

Thus, emphasis may shift from industrial relations to human relations in diverse workforce.

References

This an abstract of D.K. Srivastava, 'Trade Union Response to Declining Membership Base', *Indian Journal of Industrial Relations,* April 2006, New Delhi. Gratefully acknowledged.

Venkata Ratnam, C.S. (1994), Labour and Unions in a Phase of Transition, Friedrich Ebert Stiftung.

Venkata Ratnam, C.S. (2000), "India and International Labour Standards", *Indian Journal of Industrial Relations,* Vol. 35, No. 4, April, pp. 461-85.

Dayal, Ishwar (1997), "Are Unions Losing Influence", *Indian Journal of Industrial Relations,* Vol. 33, No. 2, October, pp. 245-53.

Dayal, Ishwar (1999), "Union-Management Relations in the Changing Business Environment", *Indian Journal of Industrial Relations,* Vol. 35, No. 2, October, pp. 211-23.

Hoerr, John (1991), "What Should Unions Do?", *Harvard Business Review,* May-June, pp. 30-45.

Report of National Commission on Labour (Second), 2002, Government of India.

Ramaswamy, E.A., "Changing Economic Structure and Future of Trade Unions", *Indian Journal of Labour Economics,* Vol. 42, No. 4, Oct.-December 1999, pp. 785-92.

S.K. Bhatia, "Human Resource Management: A Competitive Advantage" (2006), Deep & Deep Publications Pvt. Ltd., New Delhi.

S.K. Bhatia, "International Human Resource Management" (2006), Deep & Deep Publications Pvt. Ltd., New Delhi.

S.K. Bhatia, Strategic Human Resource Management, Deep & Deep Publications Pvt. Ltd., New Delhi.

7

Strategies in Industrial Relations in India

The following aspects are covered:

1. Industrial relations approaches.
2. Factors influencing IR strategy.
3. Strategy for establishing good industrial relations.
4. Emerging trends in trade union-management relations.
5. Feasibility of HRD approach to unionised employee.
6. Shift in IR—based on dependency syndrome (disputes resolution under government agencies) to collaborative dialogue.
7. Importance of role of three actors in IR system.

I. INDUSTRIAL RELATIONS APPROACHES

IR is associated with regulating of activity of employment. Two terms *industrial relations* and *employee relations* are inter-changeably used. While IR is traditional term reflects unionised manual workers within manufacturing sector. The other term employee relations is used for less unionised white collar employment in service and commercial sectors.

Three different approaches in IR are:

(1) *Unitary approach* legitimises the interests of management and employees as being same and emphasises management's role of governing in the best interests of the organisation, as a whole.

(2) *Pluralistic perspective* refers to separation of ownership and workers and acceptance of conflict in both spheres. According to it, role of trade unions is legitimate and resolution of conflict is through compromise and agreement.

(3) *Radical markist perspective highlights class conflict* without which society will stagnate. It is between those who own capital and those who supply labour. There is imbalance and inequities in economy. Conflicts can be resolved by changing society, so trade unions should develop political awareness and activity.

2. FACTORS INFLUENCING INDUSTRIAL RELATIONS STRATEGY

Two sets of factors, internal as well as external, influence employee relations strategy:

(a) The internal factors are:

- The attitudes of managements to employees and unions.
- The attitudes of employees to management.
- The attitudes of employees to unions.
- The inevitability of the differences of opinion between management and unions.
- The extent to which management can or wants to exercise absolute authority to enforce decisions affecting the interests of employees.
- The present and likely future strength of the unions.
- The extent to which there is one dominating union or the existence of multiple unions leading to inter-union rivalry.
- The extent to which effective and agreed procedures for discussing and resolving grievances or handling disputes exist within the company.
- The effectiveness of managers and supervisors in dealing with industrial relations' problems and disputes.
- The prosperity of the company, the degree to which it is expanding, stagnating or running down and the extent to which technological changes are likely to affect employment conditions and opportunities.

(b) The external factors are:

- The militancy of the unions—nationally or locally.
- The effectiveness of the union and its officials and the extent to which the officials can and do control the activities of supervisors within the company.
- The authority and effectiveness of the employers' association.
- The extent to which bargaining is carried out at national, local or plant level.
- The effectiveness of any national or local procedure agreements that may exist.
- The employment and pay situation—nationally and locally.
- The legal framework within which industrial relations exist.

Employee relations is an extremely broad concept. The important segments of industrial relations include collective bargaining, grievance handling, discipline enforcement, and disputes settlement.

3. STRATEGY FOR ESTABLISHING GOOD INDUSTRIAL RELATIONS

IR activities are to contribute to overall industrial goals such as productivity, labour peace and industrial democracy. Some areas of focus are:

(i) *Constructive attitude* on the part of both management and unions.

(ii) *Optimising the interests* of the employer and those of employees fields such as:
- Wage and salary administration, retirement and medical benefits, worker's compensation issues,
- Career prospects training and development, and
- Discipline and redress of grievances, counselling.

(iii) *Labour-management relations* to be based on union recognition; collective agreements and settling industrial disputes and to be regulated through legal structure. Managing of IR by collaborative *problem-solving approach.*

(iv) In global business to maintain high productivity for survival of organisation. Some *areas to focus are*: upgrading technology and production methods, re-training and re-deployment of surplus labour.

(v) Having *industrial democracy*, i.e. workers' involvement in decision-making process.

(vi) New collective bargaining (CB) approach to reach a *win-win solutions.* Both parties to collaborate to find a solution acceptable to each of them. The goal is to change negotiation from a zero-sum-game to a positive-sum-game.

(vi) Management has to take initiative to pursue *harmony as goal* and institutionalise schemes such as—two-way communication with employees, transparency in actions, sharing of information about the organisation business, participative management, competence of industrial relations professionals, etc.

(vii) Industrial relations theme of parties to *shift from conflict towards cooperation,* collaboration, participation and partnership for success in global competitive environment.

4. EMERGING TRENDS IN TRADE UNION-MANAGEMENT RELATIONS

Some trends are as under:

(i) The institution of *trade union is getting weak.* Employers are going in for non-unionism, such as IT companies and some service sectors.

(ii) Collective bargaining is being decentralised and replaced by *collaborative bargaining and individual bargaining.*

(iii) *Voluntary Retirement Scheme* (VRS) and disinvestment/privatisation are almost accepted facts of IR.

(iv) Changing pattern of compensation management from fixed time rate are replaced by *variable/performance-based wages.*

(v) Low-productive jobs in organised sector are replaced by sub-contracting these.

(vi) *Government is aligning its labour policies* with business imperatives such as—Second National Labour Commission has recommended: (a) Employment of contract labour on all activities of organisation including core activities, (b) Retrenchment of workmen without obtaining government permission if workmen strength in company less than 300 employees, and (c) Establishment of special economic zones. All these show government attitude.

(vii) The *attitude of judiciary* is also changing from pro-labour. The recent judgements of the Supreme Court about Contract Labour in Steel Authority case (2001) and Tamil Nadu Government case on strike (2003) sent clear messages to the trade unions that court's mean business.

(viii) There are proposals for labour law simplification/codification.
(ix) There has been ease in labour inspection of establishments to overcome harassment and corruption.
(x) There has been use of Sec. 10(3) of Industrial Disputes Act declaring strikes illegal.
(xi) Use of police for diluting labour struggle.
(xii) Re-engineering and rationalisation of work—job mobility, re-deployment, shedding surplus manpower, etc.
(xiii) Multi-skilling is an accepted requirement.
(xiv) Encouragement to employee involvement, participation and communication.
(xv) Enterprise-based unionism.
(xvi) Diluting of political ideology by the trade unions.
(xvii) Keeping in view emerging economic scenario, government policies to make shift from regulating and control to *facilitate disputes resolution and economic development*. There is gradual decline in role of state of intervention and focus on consensus development at all levels. Government have to shift from pro-labour to a balanced approach keeping the interests of both employees and employers.

This trend is going to be accelerated in future.

5. FEASIBILITY OF HRD APPROACH TO UNIONISED EMPLOYEES

1. HRD approach

While the term "Personnel function" is associated with prescriptive, critical evaluative punitive approaches and the term "Human Resources Development" (HRD) function is associate with positive, dynamic development orientation.

The *HRD approach* holds the view that human resources through their willing efforts to achieve the organisations objective are assets and decide the destiny of the organisation. The employees are no longer cogs in the wheel of the organisation, but are active agents shaping their own future and future of the organisation. The HRD approach is proactive rather than a reactive. It has visionary stance rather than a fire fighting. It believes in developmental actions rather than procedural bound approach.

The study of HRD philosophy and practices clearly demonstrate that this approach is quite opposite to the reality of industrial relations approach. The IR approach believes in enforcement of rules, regulations, grievances, discipline, enquiries, sanctions, unions, disputes, negotiations, litigation, slogans, strikes, go slow, gheraos, mandays lost, wage loss, production loss, damages, insolevence, terror despair, despondency.

On the other hand, the HRD philosophy distances itself from the Industrial Relations philosophy. The *HRD philosophy postulates*:

(i) An employee is an individual having his own vision, desire, ambitions.
(ii) He is amenable to "developmental" and virtues.
(iii) It is possible for an organisation to establish a direct relationship and rapport with him who is generally satisfied with the organisation.
(iv) The organisation is the sole custodian of the individuals' growth and development.
(v) The relationship of the organisation and the individual is homogenous, stable and cohesive.

2. Industrial relations scene in India

The evolution of industrial relations system is based on certain postulate such as:

(a) The employer-employee relationship is adversarial.
(b) Each of them struggle to get control over the work processes and economic gains.
(c) The relationship is politicised.
(d) The relationship is conficit ridden.
(e) The relationship is conditioned by legislative enactments, executive authority and judicial pronouncements.

3. Can HRD approach applied unionised to employees also?

The above postulates are given in the Indian context of Industrial Relations system as it has evolved over years. The question we have to consider is to what extent are the assumption of the HRD approach are valid. What constituents of the HRD approach can be adopted in the industrial relation system. The assumptions of HRD concept are subject of debate, and have to be carefully adopted in view of the fact that the industrial relations are subject to employer-employee relationship which have emerged in India, as contractual, legalistic, political and combative.

It is also noticed that in view of the above conditions existing, many HRD practitioners or for that matter the companies, organisations, generally practise the HRD concepts at the *managerial, supervisory* level only. In a few exceptional cases where the unions have willingly co-operated, some of these concepts are also applied at the worker level.

Though the HRD concept is certainly dynamic and having a greater potential to bring a qualitative change in the organisations, unless the employees' unions willingly agree to co-operate in implementing these, it is doubtful whether the concept can be fully applied at the workers' level.

However, it will take some time for the unions, who have a role to play, to understand and agree to at least some of the concepts, instruments of introducing HRD practices. The relationship is showing gradually change from reactive to proactive. Organisations would prefer to have an integrated approach to human resources management and development.

It would be advisable to consider the applications of HRD concepts, prescriptions to *individual, groups and organised entities,* i.e., at all levels of the organisation and after a dialogue with employees' representative. This process may take a longer time to introduce and apply HRD interventions but, it will be much easier to apply these with the support of the employees' representatives and unions.

There is shift in IR, based on dependency syndrome (disputes resolution under government agencies) to collaborative dialogue.

Historically industrial relations in the country have been based on a dependency syndrome, as the unions and employers have been depending on the dispute resolution machinery under the Government agencies and the judiciary. Currently the industrial relations are being treated in a reactive or which is known as fire fighting approach. Since the *HRD approach is proactive,* its practice as suggested above with the support of the employees' representatives and the unions should be able to help in changing the IR scenario. The focus of HRD approach being developmental, it would be possible to orient the reactive relationship to proactive relationship, by adopting a bilateral mutually acceptable dialogue and keep away from the dependency syndrome. The employers and employees should adopt a strategy which would permit employees to have: (a) their unions, (b) the unions should have access to corporate information, (c) employer should recognise the unions and their right to go on strike, and (d) employees and unions should be permitted and involved in the development of the organisation, increase productivity and allowed to participate in matters concerning their welfare and future progress.

It would also be necessary for the employers to allow employees and unions, by bilateral agreements to have stakes in ownership of the organisation and sharing power in the organisation. HRD process and interventions demand democratisation process.

The bilateral arrangements based on HRD approach postulates that the parties should agree for: (i) Human Resources Planning for better performance; (ii) Training and Development for improving performance, future growth of human resources; and (iii) Appropriate compensation, rewards, recognition systems to encourage better performance by employees.

The above three interrelated systems of HRD would certainly bring in a collaborative spirit in an atmosphere of mutual trust, progress and welfare.

7. IMPORTANCE OF ROLE OF THREE ACTORS IN IR SYSTEM

The three important constituents of the Indian IR system have to play an important role to support the HRD approach and interventions. *The government* will have to modify and amend labour legislation, in the light of its new economic policy of liberalisation. The employers will have to accept the fact that they would need their employees commitment, performances co-operation in the progress of the organisation. The employers will have to create conditions and working atmosphere so that employees are treated as contributors to the productivity and other organisational objectives.

The *employees* and their unions shall have to realise that unless they improve their attitudes, performance and extend whole-hearted co-operation in achieving the goals and objectives of the organisation, their future will be uncertain in the changed circumstances.

Reference

S.K. Bhatia, "Human Resource Management—A Competitive Advantage" (2006), Deep & Deep Publications, New Delhi-27.

8

Employee Relations Strategy

In this chapter the learned author, Michael Armstrong has highlighted the need for employee relations strategy as under:

1. Concept of employee relations strategy.
2. Difference between employee relations strategies and employee relations policies.
3. Coverage of employee relations strategy.
4. Approaches to employee relations.
5. The HRM approach to employee relations.
6. Policy options to be considered for developing employee relations strategy.
7. For formulating strategies—communicate common perspective.
8. Should employers manage with unions? (Box 1)

1. CONCEPT OF EMPLOYEE RELATIONS STRATEGY

Employee relations consist of all those areas of HRM that involve general relationships with employees, *through collective agreements* where trade *unions are recognized,* and/or through commonly applied policies for *employee involvement and communications.*

Employee relations strategies define the intentions of the organisation about what needs to be done and what needs to be changed in the ways in which the organisation manages its relationships with employees and their trade unions. Like all other aspects of HR strategy, employee relations strategies will *flow from the business strategy* but will also aim to support it. For example, if the business strategy is to concentrate on achieving competitive edge through innovation and the delivery of quality to its customers, the employee relations strategy may emphasize processes of involvement and participation, including the implementation of programmes for continuous improvement and total quality management.

If, however, the strategy for competitive advantage, or even survival, is cost-reduction, the employee relations strategy may concentrate on how this can be achieved by *maximizing cooperation* with the unions and employees and by minimizing detrimental effects on those employees and disruption to the organisation.

2. DIFFERENCE BETWEEN EMPLOYEE RELATIONS STRATEGIES AND EMPLOYEE RELATIONS POLICIES

Employee relations strategies should be distinguished from employee relations policies. Strategies are dynamic. They *provide a sense of direction,* and give an answer to the question, 'How are we going to get from here to there?'. *Employee relations policies* are more about the here and now. They express 'the way things are done around here' as far as dealing with unions and employees is concerned. Of course, they will evolve, but this may not be a result of a strategic choice. It is when a deliberate decision is made to change policies that a strategy for achieving this change has to be formulated. Thus, if the *policy is to increase commitment,* the strategy could consider how this might be *achieved by involvement and participation* processes.

3. COVERAGE OF EMPLOYEE RELATIONS STRATEGY

Employee relations strategy will be concerned with how to:

- build stable and *cooperative relationships* with employees that minimise conflict;
- *achieve commitment* through employee involvement and communications processes;
- *develop mutuality*—a common interest in achieving the organisation's goals through the development of organisational cultures based on shared values between management and employees.

Strategic directions

The intentions expressed by employee relations *strategies may direct the organisation* towards any of the following:

- changing forms of recognition, including single union recognition, or de-recognition;
- changes in the form and content of procedural agreements;
- new bargaining structures, including decentralization or single-table bargaining;
- the achievement of increased levels of commitment through involvement or participation—giving employees a voice;
- deliberately by-passing trade union representatives to communicate directly with employees;
- increasing the extent to which management controls operations in such areas as flexibility;
- generally improving the employee relations climate in order to produce more harmonious and cooperative relationships; and
- developing a 'partnership' with trade unions as described at the end of this chapter, recognizing that employees are stakeholders and that it is to the advantage of both parties to work together (this could be described as a unitarist strategy aiming at increasing mutual commitment).

4. APPROACHES TO EMPLOYEE RELATIONS

Four approaches to employee relations have been identified by Industrial Relations Services (1994) in USA:

(i) *Adversarial*: the organisation decides what it wants to do, and employees are expected to fit in. Employees only exercise power by refusing to cooperate.
(ii) *Traditional*: a good day-to-day working relationship, but management proposes and the workforce reacts through its elected representatives.
(iii) *Partnership*: the organisation involves employees in the drawing up and execution of organisation policies, but retains the right to manage.
(iv) *Power sharing*: employees are involved in both day-to-day and strategic decision-making.

Adversarial approaches are much less common. The traditional approach is still the most typical, but more interest is being expressed in partnership. Power sharing is rare.

Against the background of a preference for one of the four approaches listed above, employee relations strategy will be based on the philosophy of the organisation regarding what sort of relationships between management and employees and their unions are wanted, and how they should be handled. *A partnership strategy* will aim to develop and maintain a positive, productive, cooperative and trusting climate of employee relations.

5. THE HRM APPROACH TO EMPLOYEE RELATIONS

The philosophy of HRM has been translated into the following prescriptions which constitute the HRM model for employee relations:

- a drive *for commitment*—winning the 'hearts and minds' of employees to get them to identify with the organisation, to exert themselves more;
- on its behalf and to *remain with the organisation*, thus ensuring a return on their training and development;
- an *emphasis on mutuality*—getting the message across that 'we are all in this together' and that the interests of management and employees coincide (i.e. a unitarist approach);
- the organisation of *complementary form of communication*, such as team briefing, alongside traditional collective bargaining, i.e. approaching employees directly as individuals or in groups rather than through their representatives;
- a shift from collective bargaining to *individual contracts*;
- the use of employee *involvement techniques* such as quality circles or improvement groups;
- continuous *pressure on quality*—total quality management;
- increased *flexibility in working arrangements*, including multi-skilling, to provide for the more effective use of human resources, sometimes accompanied by an agreement to provide secure employment for the 'core' workers;
- *emphasis on teamwork*; and
- *harmonization of terms and conditions* for all employees.

The key contrasting dimensions of traditional industrial relations and HRM have been presented by Guest (1995) and are shown in Figure 1.

FIGURE I

The key contrasting dimensions of traditional industrial relations and HRM (based on Guest, 1995)

Dimension	*Industrial Relations*	*HRM*
Psychological contract	Compliance	Commitment
Behaviour references	Norms, custom and practice	Values/mission
Relations individual	Low trust, pluralist, collective	High trust, unitarist
Organisation design hierarchy, division of labour, managerial control	Formal roles, flat structure, teamwork/autonomy, self-control	Flexible roles

Guest notes that this model aims to support the achievement of the three main sources of competitive advantage, namely, innovation, quality and cost leadership. Innovation and quality strategies require employee commitment, while cost leadership strategies are believed by many managements to be only achievable without a union. Guest further contends that:

> The logic of a market-driven HRM strategy is that where high organisational commitment is sought, unions are irrelevant. Where cost advantage is the goal, unions and industrial relations systems appear to early higher costs.

Is HRM approach still possible?

An HRM approach is still possible if trade unions are recognized by the organisation. In this case, the strategy might be to marginalize or at least side-step them by dealing direct with employees through involvement and communications processes.

6. POLICY OPTIONS TO BE CONSIDERED FOR DEVELOPING EMPLOYEE RELATIONS STRATEGY

There are a number of policy options that need to be considered when developing an employee relations strategy. The following four options have been described by Guest (1995):

(i) The new realism

A high emphasis on HRM and industrial relations. The aim is to integrate HRM and industrial relations. This is the policy of such organisations as Rover, Nissan and Toshiba. New collaborative arrangements in the shape of single-table bargaining are usually the result of employer initiatives, but both employers and unions are often satisfied with them. They have facilitated greater flexibility, more multi-skilling, the removal of demarcations and improvements in quality. They can also extend consultation processes and accelerate moves towards single status.

(ii) Traditional collectivism

Traditional collectivism is priority to industrial relations without HRM. This involves retaining the traditional pluralist industrial relations arrangements within an eventually unchanged industrial relations system. Management may take the view in these circumstances that it is easier to continue to operate with a union, since it provides a useful, well-established channel for communication and for the handling of grievance, discipline and safety issues.

(iii) Individualised HRM

Individualised HRM means high priority to HRM with no industrial relations. According to Guest, this approach is not very common, except in North American-owned firms.

(iv) The black hole—no industrial relations

This option is becoming more prevalent in organisations in which HRM is not a policy priority for managements but where they do not see that there is a compelling reason to operate within a traditional industrial relations system. When such organisations are facing a decision on whether or not to recognize a union, they are increasingly deciding not to do so.

7. FOR FORMULATING STRATEGIES—COMMUNICATE COMMON PERSPECTIVE

Like other business and HR strategies, those concerned with employee relations can emerge in response to an evolving situation. But it is still useful to spend time deliberately formulating strategies, and the aim should be to create a shared agenda that will communicate a common perspective on what needs to be done. This can be expressed in writing, but it can also be clarified through involvement and communication processes. According to Michael Armstrong *partnership agreement* may well be the best way of getting employee relations strategies into action. (also see Box)

(i) Partnership agreements

In industrial relations a partnership arrangement can be described as one in which both parties (management and the trade union) *agree to work together* to their mutual advantage and to achieve a climate of more cooperative and therefore less adversarial industrial relations. A partnership agreement may include undertakings from both sides; for example, management may offer job security linked to productivity and the union may agree to new forms of work organisation that might require more flexibility on the part of employees.

(ii) Key values

Key values for partnership can be as under:

(a) Mutual trust and respect.

(b) A joint vision for the future and the means to achieve it.

(c) Continuous exchange of information.

(d) Recognition of the central role of collective bargaining.

Box I

Should Employers Manage with Unions?

We mention here the views of famous writer, Jeffrey Pfeffer in his book titled "Human Equation, Building Profits by Putting People First."

Managers need to be able to develop cooperative and positive working *relationships with labour unions* for several reasons and do not treat unions as relic of past and are out of place and in rapid decline in a world of global competition.

Most industrialized countries other than the United States have much higher rates of unionization. If a company is going to be a truly global player, it is better not only *get used to working with labour,* but actually develop some skill and may be even some comparative advantage in doing so.

(i) Unionization has never been simply about money; it has also been *about job security and control over the work environment.* A climate of economic insecurity potentially favours unionization.

(ii) Organisations that do not implement *high commitment work practices,* the attraction of unionization increases. If union density begins to recover, firms that work constructively with labour will enjoy an advantage over those labour relations are antagonistic.

(iii) Some contemporary *labour organisations actively advocate* and negotiate for the implementation of many elements of high *performance management practices.* Therefore, these organisations can be important allies in making the change to high commitment management.

(iv) Finally, and most basically, firms cannot be serious about "putting people first" if they are unwilling or unable to work constructively with employees' representative organisations.

But many managers and organisations have a long way to go to begin working constructively with labour organisations and profiting from doing so. A mind set or perspective obstructs their progress.

This negative reaction stems from the perception that labour unions are impediments to management control in the workplace and hindrances to achieving competitive levels of costs, quality and productivity. The conventional wisdom maintains that even if the labour movement had at one time been necessary to achieve socially useful gains in areas such as occupational safety, child welfare and protection at work, and obtaining higher wages and better benefits, those days are past. Today, many managers would argue, governments in the major industrialized countries enforce laws about wages and hours, work place safety, and child labour, and market forces should control wages in industries that increasingly compete on a worldwide basis. Unions are seen as industrial fossils, remnants of some bygone era. And, union effects on productivity are presumed to be deleterious.

However, there are some positive indicators. The implementation of cross-organisational learning requires either competitive pressure or other stimuli to overcome the internal organisational obstacles to work-place reform. A certain industries the unions have really taken the lead in fostering interfirm learning about new work arrangements and in stimulating, through contract negotiations, work-place innovation and change. Such positive effects are not guaranteed and require union leadership that understands the elements and the importance of high performance work arrangements for both the companies and the union members. But, enough instances show that unions have helped diffuse work place change and foster inter-company learning that this potential benefit should not be ignored.

Organisations can actually benefit the most from what unions have the potential to contribute to the effective management of people.

Source: Jeffrey Pfeffer, Human Equation Building Profits by Putting People First, Harvard Business School Press, Boston, USA.

References

Michael Armstrong, Strategic HRM, McGraw-Hill, Boston.

Jeffrey Pfeffer, Human Equation Building Profits by Putting People First, Harvard Business School Press, Boston.

9

Line Manager's Role in Building Industrial Relations at Workplace

The promotion of bilateral industrial relations through various methods such as—collective bargaining, mutual settlement of disputes and worker participation machinery between managements and employees is one of the most prominent objectives of industrial relations policy at the national level. However, industrial relations at the factory level are also influenced by the *labour department* as the two parties often tend to rely on third party intervention for the solution of the problems.

There are three main aspects of handling industrial relations at the factory level:

(1) Individual relations;
(2) Role of line managers in building industrial relations at work place level; and
(3) Collective relations.

(I) INDIVIDUAL RELATIONS

Certain items like grievance handling and matters of discipline fall under the category of individual relations.

(a) Grievance Handling

A prompt redressal of individual grievances is an important element in the handling of relations with the employees. These grievances may relate to the work at the shop floor, working conditions, supervisory style and in respect of service conditions. The companies have laid down grievance procedure under the code of discipline as evolved by the Indian Labour Conference. The grievance procedure provides for three steps including the establishment of a grievance committee, which comprises of both union and management representatives, where there is mutual goodwill and cooperation between unions and managements, the grievance committees are successfully redressing individual grievances.

(b) Disciplinary Action

The legal framework under the Industrial Employment (Standing Orders) Act, 1946, and the Industrial Disputes Act, 1947, require companies to lay down procedure for disciplinary action. The misconducts committed by employees and the detailed procedure to be followed for issue of charge sheet and conduct of domestic enquiry are prescribed. Such procedures reduce element of arbitrariness.

(c) Employee Communication Systems Help in Developing Better Understanding

2. ROLE OF LINE MANAGERS IN BUILDING INDUSTRIAL RELATIONS AT WORKPLACE LEVEL

Good management and union relations are no guarantee that relationship between individual worker and manager will also be good. Individual worker therefore need to become the centre of attention.

Much of the problems in industrial relations stem from our failure to understanding industrial relations as consisting of something much more than union and management relationship. It is important to focus on inter-personal relationship and low motivation levels of employees as industrial relations component.

Manager's relationship with employees determine the overall quality of industrial relations in an organisation.

As such managers are given more weightage in man-management skills as compared to functional or business skills.

Infact unions/government/courts issues are not within our control. Can we afford to sit and take a stand that nothing can be done by managers to improve the industrial relations? What factors are in manager's control—let them attempt to concentrate in those, i.e. management-employees relations.

WHAT ROLE LINE MANAGERS CAN PLAY?

Line managers should take action on following aspects:

(a) They should try to *understand the profile* of workers in their sections.
(b) Managers should understand what employees want from management?

Some of the *employees objectives* are as under:

- Job security;
- Fair (wages, treatment);
- Opportunity for advancement and self-improvement;
- Job satisfaction and doing worthwhile work which is not routine only but challenging; and
- Involvement and participation at workplace in performance of job.

(c) They should attempt to understand perceptions of workers about managers.

Some of the *perceptions of workers about managers* found after research studies are as under:

(i) They play favouritism in promotions and other matters such as appraisals, grant of leave, merit awards, etc.
(ii) They lack appreciation of meritorious achievements.
(iii) They do not condemn neglect of work as lethargy on part of employees.
(iv) They delay in settling of grievances/complaints.
(v) There is lack of communication between managers and workers.
(vi) Managers are unsympathetic in treatment of workers and emotional needs of workers are not met when workers have some accident or bereavement in their family.
(vii) They do not care about the work satisfaction of employees by providing challenging assignments.
(viii) These factors are leading to alienation of workers due to dissatisfaction.

(d) Managers should understand that *conflict is inevitable*: Can managers have collaboration and cooperation at workplace—through consultative problem-solving approach and developmental approach. More training is required to be imparted to managers on conflict resolving skills. The objective is to build mutual faith, trust, cooperation and understanding. They should adopt strategy of win-win game.

(e) Managers should introduce *quality of work programmes* for increasing job satisfaction—such as job-rotation, job enlargement, job enrichment, self-managing groups, etc.

(f) Managers should learn to live with unionised staff. They can gain cooperation through various measures. Some of these are mentioned below:

(i) *By augmenting communication*: Co-policies and philosophy goals are to be shared with employees. Managers to encourage upward communication to know their mind and problems. This is necessary as unions do not communicate what is not in their favour and distortions in communication create problems.
(ii) *Open-door policy*: Management should adopt approach of openness to solve problems of employees and not depend unless it comes through proper channels.
(iii) Effective grievance handling system to be introduced. It is to be ensured that grievances are promptly redressed.
(iv) *Adopt proactive approach*: To diagnose, identify problems, take preventive steps in advance.
(v) *Approach to managers*: They should be fair, just and firm. They should contain problems which arise in localised boundaries. They should not allow them to become company-wide issue by sorting these promptly at section or department level. Managers should not compromise on work and discipline matters. They should avoid vindictive action and must take action where point of discipline is involved—constructive discipline is to be favoured. Overall approach has to be of building trust.
(vi) *Dignity respect as a man*: Third generation of urban workers have to treated with dignity and respect. They want to be understood with empathy not sympathy. Right to manage has to be meshed with dignity of man. Managers to stick to principle.
(vii) *More consultation and persuasion will be effective* than command and punishment. Participative style.

Suggestion system to be encouraged.
Counselling to be used for handling emotional problems.

(viii) Without effective personnel policy, there cannot be good industrial relations:
Give feeling of justice and being fair.
To adopt consistency in decisions.
Common policy for all employees.

(ix) Direct participative forums such as quality circles, productivity groups, small groups for effective involvement of workers to be formed.

(x) Managers should lay thrust on individual development and personal growth of employees.
Focus has to be on change of attitude of employees.

(xi) De-centralise personnel administration activities.

(g) In order to avoid delay in dealing with personnel cases of employees from centralised personnel department, it is better to attach personnel staff with each line department.

3. COLLECTIVE RELATIONS

In production organisations, collective relations between employees and managements normally arise out of the employment terms and working conditions. Some significant collective relations are:

(a) Relations with trade unions and recognition of trade union;
(b) Negotiations with trade union(s), collective bargaining and arriving at agreements;
(c) Functioning of joint participative forums such as the suggestion committee, the canteen committee, works committee, workers' participation in management, safety committee, etc.
(d) Prevention and settlement of industrial disputes directly by two parties or through the intervention of the government machinery such as conciliation or voluntary arbitration or adjudication, etc.
(e) Compliance of labour laws by management unions and employees.
(f) The human resource function has now stabilised and have an enlightened outlook to base industrial relations on bilateralism. Attitude of confrontation is giving place to an attitude of genuine partnership on which the harmonious relations can be created and maintained.

10

Collective Bargaining

Collective bargaining is a technique adopted by the organisations of workers and employers collectively to resolve their differences with or without the assistance of a third party. Its ultimate aim is to reach some settlement acceptable to both the parties involved in labour-management relations.

In this chapter an attempt has been made to delineate the definition and concept of collective bargaining together with its main features. The chapter then proceeds to explain the importance of this vital instrument in resolving the differences and achieving better understanding as well as ensuring industrial harmony. Following aspects are covered:

1. Concept and definition of collective bargaining;
2. Features of collective bargaining;
3. Purpose and importance;
4. Process of collective bargaining;
5. Prerequisites of successful collective bargaining;
6. Obstacles in the growth of collective bargaining; and
7. Collective bargaining and productivity bargaining.

I. CONCEPT AND DEFINITION OF COLLECTIVE BARGAINING (CB)

The phrase collective bargaining is made up of two words—collective which implies group action through its representatives; and bargaining, which suggests haggling and/or negotiating. The phrase, therefore, implies 'collective negotiation of a contract between the management's representatives on one side and those of the workers on the other'. *Collective bargaining may be defined as a process of negotiation between the employer and the organised workers represented by their union in order to determine the terms and conditions of employment.*

2. FEATURES OF COLLECTIVE BARGAINING

The main features and characteristics of collective bargaining are:

(i) It is a *two-way process*. It is a mutual give-and-take rather than a take-it-or-leave-it method of arriving at the settlement of a dispute. Both parties are involved in it. A rigid, hard or inflexible position does not make for a compromise settlement. Collective bargaining is a 'civilised confrontation' with a view to arriving at an agreement, for the object is not 'welfare' but 'compromise'. The essence of collective bargaining lies in the readiness of the two parties to a dispute to reach an agreement and mutually settling it. It is concerned about the emotions of the people involved as well as with the logic of their interests.

(ii) It is a *continuous process*, which provides a mechanism for continuing an organised relationship between management and trade unions.

(iii) Collective bargaining is not a competitive process but it is essentially a *complementary process*, i.e. each party needs something that the other party has, namely, labour can make a greater production effort and management has the capacity to pay for that effort and to organise for the effort. It is based on give-and-take approach.

(iv) Collective bargaining is a *negotiation process* and is a device used by wage-earners to safeguard their interests. It is an instrument of an industrial organisation for discussion and negotiation between the two parties.

3. PURPOSE AND IMPORTANCE

(a) Collective bargaining is the technique that has been adopted by unions and management for *compromising their conflicting interests*. It plays a significant role in *improving the labour-management relations* and in ensuring industrial harmony. It helps a lot in better understanding of each other's points of view as well as problems. Through discussion and interactions, both the parties learn more about others and often misunderstandings may be removed. Collective bargaining helps in easing out many minor differences and there are many instances in which even major disputes are said to be settled without any work-stoppage or outside intervention. Accordingly, its role in conflict resolution is very significant. It builds up safety valves, allowing the opposite groups, excess stream to escape without blowing the whole mechanism to pieces.

(b) Labour legislation and enforcement machinery can only provide the setting in which an industry may function; the solution of common problems can only come from the parties which are directly concerned with them. In this context, "Collective agreements provide a *climate for smooth progress*."

(c) From the union's point of view, collective bargaining agreements ensure that managements do not take any unilateral decision. In other words, collective bargaining is an *employer-regulating device*, a method of guaranteeing the rights and immunities of the workers by limiting the employer's freedom of action. A collective bargaining agreement develops a sense of responsibility and of self-respect among the workers and is a guarantee towards wage protection, etc.

(d) In fact, a collective bargaining agreement *brings both labour and management together* to determine the conditions of employment which, till then, had been decided exclusively by an outside agency, and paves the way to the closing of the psychological and emotional gulf which divides labour and management.

Prof. Butler has viewed the functions of collective bargaining under three heads:

(i) Collective bargaining as a *process of social change*. Collective bargaining acts as a technique of long-run social change, bringing rearrangements in the power hierarchy of competing groups.

(ii) Collective bargaining has *served as a peace treaty* between two parties in continued conflict. The compromise is a temporary truce with neither side being completely satisfied with the results. Each would like to modify it at the earliest opportunity. Since the contract is almost always of short duration, each begins to prepare a new list of demands.

(iii) Collective bargaining creates a system of *"industrial jurisprudence."* It is method of introducing civil rights into industry, that is, of requiring that management be conducted by rule rather than by "arbitrary decision". It is *rule-making* or *legislative process,* in the sense that it formulates terms and conditions under which labour and management will cooperate and work together over a certain stated period.

The purpose/importance of collective bargaining are in Table 1.

4. PROCESS OF COLLECTIVE BARGAINING

TABLE I

Purpose of Collective Bargaining

- Brings parties closer.
- Develops better understanding, industrial peace, and industrial democracy.
- Resolves conflicts and differences.
- Guarantees the rights and responsibilities of the workers.
- Develops self-respect and fosters responsibility on both workers and employers.
- Brings social change through acceptable solutions.
- Formulates terms and conditions under which labour and management will work together.

Indian Institute of Personnel Management has suggested the following process for collective bargaining:

Composition of the Negotiating Team

The negotiating team should consist of representatives of both workers and employers, with adequate qualities, job knowledge and skill for negotiation. They should not only truly represent the two parties but also have full authority to speak for them and make decisions. A correct understanding of the main issues to be covered and intimate knowledge of operations, working conditions, production norms and other relevant factors in addition to the basic qualities of balanced views, even temper, analytical mind, and objective outlook are highly desirable in the members of the negotiating team. It is essential to include in the management team, executives who can talk authoritatively on personnel and production matters. If other functional heads, conversant with other aspects like costs or indutrial engineering, can be included, it would be much better.

Make a Good Beginning

It will be good to stress the need for mutual co-operation and for putting the members in the right frame of mind before the talks start. With a proper climate for mutual understanding and a common desire to reach agreement by objective assessment of facts, with a true spirit of "give-and-take", the process of negotiation has every chance of success.

Maintain Continuity of Talks

Collective bargaining is like any other negotiation and, there will on occasions be emotional outbrusts and road blocks. The important thing is never to reach a dead end but to keep talks continuing. Under the worst situations, breaking-off temporarily for cooling down and rethinking may be necessary. When the main issue gets confused in the dust and storm raised, bringing things to fundamentals will often help. It may at times be necessary to leave controversial points alone for the time-being and leap over to the next issues. As long as talks continue, a solution will be possible ultimately. To keep the discussion fluid is therefore very important.

Develop Problem-solving Attitude

The attitude of problem-solving on both sides will help in reaching at the agreement.

Right Type of Leadership

Growth of right type of leadership on the part of trade union is important management team may also associate members from production and other related departments. A composite team is important.

5. PREREQUISITES OF SUCCESSFUL COLLECTIVE BARGAINING

For the success of collective bargaining the following facts must be recognised. These are explained through a Figure 1.

FIGURE 1

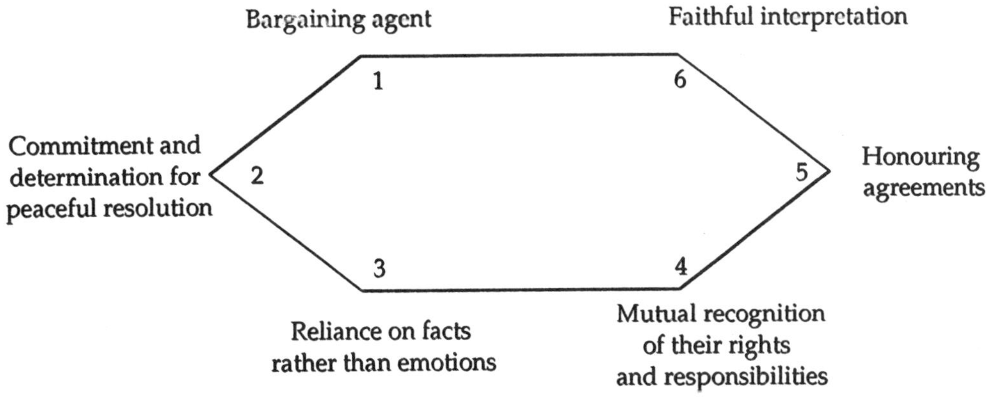

Bargaining agent
1
Faithful interpretation
6
Commitment and determination for peaceful resolution
2
Honouring agreements
5
3
4
Reliance on facts rather than emotions
Mutual recognition of their rights and responsibilities

(i) Collective bargaining is best conducted at plant level. It is imperative to have a recognised trade union which should be the sole *bargaining agent* of all the workers in an organisation. A responsible and strong trade union is vital. Statutory framework to provide mode of determining the sole bargaining agent on the workers' side.

(ii) Both the parties—representatives of employers and employees should be *committed and determined* to arrive at an agreed solution. The two parties should be determined to resolve their differences on their respective claims in a peaceful manner. They do not look to a third party say adjudication for the solution of their problems. Any refusal to negotiate on the part of either side should be looked upon as an unfair practice. Rigid attitudes are out of place in a collective bargaining system. The essence of collective bargaining lies in the readiness of both the parties, to regulate the working conditions and terms of employment together.

(iii) Negotiations can be successful only when the parties *rely on facts and figures* to support their point of view. Both the parties should adopt a constructive approach at the bargaining table rather than the present agitational or litigation-oriented approach. Unfair labour practices are to be avoided by both sides and negotiations conducted in an atmosphere of goodwill.

(iv) There should be unanimity between labour and management on the basic objectives of the organisation and of the workers, and a *mutual recognition of their rights and obligations*. There should be mutual accommodation.

(v) Once an agreement is reached, it should be put down in writing. It must be *honoured and fairly implemented*.

(vi) A *provision for arbitration* could be incorporated in the agreement, which could become operative when there is any disagreement on the interpretation of its terms and conditions.

6. OBSTACLES IN THE GROWTH OF COLLECTIVE BARGAINING

The progress of collective bargaining in India is not very encouraging, of course of late it has achieved some amount of success. T.N. Chhabra has given several factors which are responsible for this state of affairs. These are disucssed below:

(i) Multiplicity of Unions

There is a problem of multiplicity of unions in most of the industrial establishments. No union enjoys the support of the majority of workers in the plant. Moreover, rivalry among the trade unions does not allow to create the proper atmosphere for collective bargaining.

(ii) Non-recognition

There is a lack of definite procedure to determine which union is to be recognised to serve as a bargaining agent on behalf of the workers.

(iii) Political Interference in Trade Unions

There has been very close association between the trade unions and political parties. As a result, trade union movement has not encouraged collective bargaining.

(iv) Defective Laws

The law provides an easy access to adjudication. Under the Industrial Disputes Act, the parties to the dispute may request the government to refer the matter to adjudication which government agrees. Thus, faith in bargaining process is reduced.

7. COLLECTIVE BARGAINING AND PRODUCTIVITY BARGAINING

A lot has been said about the development of Collective Bargaining in India. But in fact, collective bargaining which is to be a two-way affair, has been used at present only as a one-way exercise in which the union, as the aggressive partner, makes the demands, and the management, as the passive partner, derives satisfaction merely by countering the extent to which it is able to minimise the additional burdens while meeting the union's demands. There are not many examples even now where the union as well as the management, as equal partners, have approached the process of collective bargaining with the objective and spirit that collective bargaining must bring concrete benefit to both the partners.

Considering this aspect, in this chapter an attempt has been made to bring to focus salient factors required for creating an environment where free and meaningful collective bargaining is possible so that it contributes to the benefit of employees and the organisation.

Collective bargaining should be approached from the point that it must bring concrete benefits to both the parties, i.e. workers and management as equal partners. It will be appropriate to examine this aspect in detail here. Amongst the various features of collective bargaining, two characteristics are of significant importance:

(a) That collective bargaining is a two-way process. It is a mutual give-and-take rather than a take-it-or-leave-it method of arriving at the settlement of a dispute. The essence of collective bargaining lies in the readiness of the two parties to a dispute to reach an agreement and mutually arrive at a compromising settlement. It is concerned about the emotions of the people involved as well as with the logic of their interests.

(b) The second and more vital point is that collective bargaining is essentially a complementary process, i.e. each party needs something that the other party has, namely, labour can contribute and cooperate in certain ways and management can compensate for that effort. In this respect behaviour scientists have made a distinction between *"distributive bargaining"* and *"integrative bargaining"*.

The former is the process of dividing the 'cake' which has been produced by the joint efforts of management and labour. In this process, if one party wins something, the other party has a relatively smaller size of it. So it is a 'win-lose' relationship. In other words, distributive bargaining deals with issues or an issue in which the two or more parties have conflicting interests. Here the parties have competitive behaviours that are intended to influence the division of limited resources such that one party's gain is the other's loss. In this situation the aim of bargaining is not so much to argue their own case but to destroy their opponents. Such bargaining may be characterised by acrimony and bitterness.

Integrative bargaining is a process where both the parties can win, each contributing something for the benefit of the other party. They are problem-solving behaviours. Such a process develops common objectives, a better understanding of each other's needs and capabilities, a better respect for each other and a greater involvement of commitment to the well-being and growth of the enterprise as a whole. To extend the metaphor of the cake, the integrative approach would be, "why not by our joint efforts increase the size of the cake so that each one can have a bigger slice of it?" This is in effect a cooperative approach to bargaining in which the agenda items are seen as common problems rather than divisive issues. Integrative bargaining makes a problem-solving approach. Both the parties have common concern with the problem, both make a positive effort to solve it to their mutual satisfaction. Both these characteristics mentioned (i.e., it is two-way process and it is complementary process) emphasise the fact that collective bargaining is meant for the benefit of both the parties.

Management's Charter

The two main headings under which most of the managements' demands on their unions can be fitted are:

(i) Higher Productivity/Efficiency

This can come either from activising sluggish human efforts and methods of work, or from freedom to modernise the machines or work methods. Productivity in its broadest sense is an attitude of mind. It is striving for employees excellence. Individual has the main role to play; every action of ours, wherein we operate on resources, including our own effort needs to be so well directed that the aggregate input produces the maximum output. Improvements can be primarily attempted by curbing waste on the one hand and improving utilisation of the resources on the other. Secondly, efforts could be directed towards development of new processes/services that may reduce the input requirement itself for activising the same or enhanced output. There are variety of productivity improvements which individuals/groups can bring about by critical examination of details of process through which the resources—men, machines, materials, money and time are processed. Similarly, various management processes play an important role in productivity enhancement such as—planning, systems and procedures with the aid of computers.

(ii) Removal of Restrictive Practices

Restrictive practice have the strange habit of stealthily creeping into every organisation in their weak moments when the managers or supervisors were either not vigilant enough to see the serious long-term implications of the seemingly innocent malpractices, or were too over-stretched to resist them. Some of the instances are—insistence on employees to take planned leave as irregular attendance and persistent absenteeism cause dislocation of planned and scheduled work; avoiding of poor time keeping; avoiding of unnecessary movements of employees in the factory; acceptance of redeployment depending upon the work requirements; requiring of multi-skills by workers through training; a code of discipline for union office-bearers so that they work and are at their work spot/duty.

Besides this, *procedure agreements* may be reached with the union by a process of collective bargaining. Normally, a procedure agreement relates to such matters as: machinery for consultation about terms and conditions of employment; machinery for consultation about other questions which may arise between an employer and workers; negotiating rights; facilities for officials of trade unions; procedures relating to matters of discipline or relating to grievances of individual workers. Anyway, one way of removing these restrictive practices is to 'decide' to do so (rather than face the rigmarole of notice of change, union's resistance to discontinuance of 'an established practice'. Another is to require the union to agree to the removal of such restrictive practices as a 'quid-pro-quo' for some other concessions. Apart from the fact that such removal of restrictive practices have been known to pay back considerable part of the additional costs of a settlement, they serve yet another very important purpose—they usher in a greater sense of responsibility in the union and its members, and an overall vigilance among the managers in the organisation against further creeping in of restrictive practices.

Productivity Bargaining

Productivity bargaining is the use of collective bargaining to revise inefficient working methods, by specifying changes in working practices in a collective agreement, the enforcement of which is seen as the joint responsibility of management and the trade union. Inducement to accept the changes and responsibilities involved is provided by considerable improvement in wage, incentives, bonus, etc., financed by the increase in effectiveness and productivity produced by more efficient working practices. Productivity bargaining has often been described as *integrative bargaining* because the parties appear to be more concerned with increasing the total sum available for distribution rather than with adjusting their respective shares of a static sum.

It may be mentioned that there is growing awareness to move from 'distributing bargaining' towards 'integrative bargaining'. Enlightened unions and managements are entering into productivity agreements.

Productivity bargaining has been the subject of much debate and varying interpretations. In the pursuit of industrial harmony and improved unit performance, productivity bargaining is a viable alternative to the traditional collective bargaining process. The characteristics that distinguish it from conventional collective bargaining, and its limitations are discussed in this chapter.

Productivity bargaining is the process of making a deal between two parties with the object of improving: (i) productive efficiency, and (ii) the rewards for work. Translated into action the settlement achieves higher efficiency, a reduction (or at least stabilisation) of unit labour costs, and higher earnings. The process attempts to achieve in the long-run an overall increase in the value of return on capital employed, and continuous application of industrial engineering, work study, job evaluation, feasibility surveys to identify areas which promise greater efficiency and more effective use of resources. The distinctive feature of productivity bargaining is its specificity, with respect to the nature of achievement and rewards, and also to the time period during which extra rewards and extra achievements are coupled.

Characteristics

Characteristics of collective bargaining and productivity bargaining are summarised in the Table 2.

CONCLUSION

Of late there is a definite shift in emphasis and reliance on collective bargaining. Collective bargaining has got a foothold as a primary method of settling industrial disputes. Conditions have to be created to promote collective bargaining. The most important among them is recognition of a representative union as the sole bargaining agent.

Collective bargaining is an essential component of industrial relations. It is the preferred

TABLE 2

Characteristics

Sl. No.	*Collective bargaining*	*Productivity bargaining*
1	*2*	*3*
(i)	Preoccupation is with wage rates, working conditions, concessions to labour. It is wage bargaining.	Preoccupation is with overall cost performance of unit. It is wage-work bargaining encompassing performance-related issues. Within the negotiation setting, all important elements of the work system and employment relationship are synthesised.
(ii)	Labour demands; employer resists; eventually settlement reached with/ without industrial action initiative with labour. Management perspective one of containing labour, i.e. what minimum can give to buy peace for a period.	Management initiative process; may/may not be as counterproposals to labour demands. Management develops strategy and structures the situation. Basis is what management wants to achieve in corporate performance and in return what it can give.
(iii)	One-way process; union takes, management gives; the giving is straight away. It is a will-lose situation.	Two-way process; has an input-output relationship. Concessions are granted against matching specific achieving. It is a win-win situation. Concessions follow achievements in phases.
(iv)	Bargaining over rights—labour's entitlements *versus* management prerogatives. Tendency to bargaining to one another. Management negotiates to keeping concessions low and workers respond with low efforts.	Principle of mutuality; participation of parties in generating gains and sharing equitably. Management offers high rewards to workers' response of higher effort, leading to lower or static unit labour cost.
(v)	Demands decided in terms of factors such as cost of living index, ability to pay, regional practices, rewards, precedents, dictates of union pressures, price to be paid to buy peace.	In taking decisions, parties find themselves discussing topics such as restrictions on output, flexibility in of man-power, work re-organisation, reducing time-wasting practices, elimination of worker resistances to desired changes, misuse of facilities. The negotiations place a premium on workers' cooperation with management in raising efficiency.

(vi) Disclosure of corporate information results more from the pressures at the collective bargaining table rather than from managerial initiative. The involvement is largely of the negotiating body at the top.	Process initiates a participative style of operation to achieve greater use of existing potentials, identified through rigorous exercises involves intensive management communication at all levels.
(vii) Fragmented; the negotiation process is initiated as and when demands are raised and agreements concluded. An *ad hoc* process.	Continuous process; negotiation of an agreement is the last stage of a long programme of management activity. The approach is comprehensive/integrated so that implications of issues are considered on a total organisational basis. It is not a one shot exercise but a planned sequential approach to change.
(viii) With reference to Herzberg's motivation-hygiene theory the focus here is only on putting the hygiene situation right. Dissatisfaction on wages and job-context factors are reduced.	Work itself gets analysed, discussed and negotiated. Job content factors get focussed attention. A mere positive motivational policy is established.

method of working out employer-employee relationship. Collective bargaining is considered one method to effectively integrate the interests of unions with the interests of the company. This is due to the fact that the process of bargaining often leads to better mutual understanding and flexibility in approach. Collective bargaining agreements provide a method for regulation of conditions of employment by those directly concerned. Collective bargaining thus helps the parties to adjust the abrupt and unforeseen change in the environment without disrupting either the existing arrangements or the production activity.

Collective Bargaining Strategies

In this chapter some collective bargaining strategies and system of facilitating union-management cooperation are discussed as under:

1. Three negotiating strategies.
2. Approaching to negotiating process.
3. Mutual respect and honest communication is key to effective employee relations.
4. Bargaining strategies.

1. THREE NEGOTIATING STRATEGIES

Human resource professionals may be aware of the three basic negotiating strategies used in union environment.

(a) Parallel bargaining

Parallel bargaining is also known as pattern bargaining or leap frogging. It means union negotiates with one employer at a time. Once a contract is reached with this employer, the union uses the gains made during the negotiations as a base negotiations with the next employer.

(b) Multi-employer bargaining

It is that the union negotiates with more than one employer in an industry or region at a time. This situation can occur when temporary workers are part of a client employer's bargaining unit and the union negotiates with *both the temporary agency* and the client employer on employment issues.

(c) Multi-unit bargaining or coordinated bargaining

This occurs when several unions represent different bargaining units in the company. An example of this occurs in the Airline industry, when employer negotiates with the unions representing pilots, flight attendants, or other classes. This allows the employer to coordinate negotiations on mandatory and permissive subjects while allowing the union to cooperate on issues that have meaning to their various members.

2. APPROACHES TO NEGOTIATING PROCESS

Collective bargaining positions can be taken and each position impacts the bargaining processes. There are two basic approaches to the negotiating process such as positional bargaining and principal bargaining.

(a) Positional bargaining

Positional bargaining is a strategy represented by demands by each party concentrates on "winning" the position. This makes the process an adversial and competitive one. It is also known as hard bargaining or distributive bargaining. It is win-lose situation.

(b) Principled bargaining

Principled bargaining as a negotiation strategy is characterised by parties who are *interested in solving a problem* than they are in winning a position. In this parties look to solution, brain-stroming for ideas and open coming up with an agreement that solves problem in an innovative way. The most common forms of principaled bargaining are: First, *integrative bargaining* (in this parties look at all issues and are able to trade-off between those issues). Second is *interest-based bargaining* means both sides have harmonious interests. For example, these days both management and union have an equal interest in the continuing viability of business, i.e. for management to earn profits and for union have continued employment.

(c) Bad faith in bargaining process

Bad faith in bargaining process can be evidenced by a lack of concession on issues, refusing to advance proposals to bargain, stalling tactics, or withholding information that is important to process. Evidence of bad faith by management in the bargaining process can be evidenced by attempts to circumvent the union representative by going directly to employees with proposals before they have been presented to the union. Another indicator of bad faith bargaining by management occurs when unilateral changes are made to working conditions.

(d) Avoid unionisation

The most effective way for management to avoid unionisation is to treat employees fairly and give them a voice in decisions that affect their day-to-day work. Effective management and employee relations are critical element of a successful business, where employees are treated with dignity and respect. Organisation culture and communication strategies determine (top-down or empowerment, etc.) the philosophy of good relations.

3. MUTUAL RESPECT AND HONEST COMMUNICATION IS KEY TO EFFECTIVE EMPLOYEE RELATIONS

An effective employee relations programme is based on mutual respect, open and honest communication, fair and equitable treatment, and mutual trust. These characteristics begin at the top management team. When executive team supports employees in making decisions and taking risks, it demonstrate trust in the competence of its employees who are empower to take ownership of the work they do, accepting the rewards of good work and consequences of errors are more productive.

4. BARGAINING STRATEGIES

Negotiators for an employer should develop a plan covering their bargaining strategy. To ensure adherence to the employer's course of action, this plan should be prepared as a written document. The plan should consider the proposals that the union is likely to submit, based on the most recent agreements with other employers and the demands that remain unsatisfied from previous negotiations. The plan should also consider the goals the union is striving to achieve and the extent to which it may be willing to make concessions or to resort to strike action in order to achieve these goals.

At a minimum, the employer's bargaining strategy must address these points:

- Likely union proposals and management responses to them.
- A listing of management demands, limits of concessions, and anticipated union responses.
- Development of a database to support management bargaining proposals and to counter act union demands.
- A contegency operating plan should employee's strike.

12

Negotiation Process

Negotiation means bargaining. Negotiation is an important component of collective bargaining. Collective bargaining may be defined as a *process of negotiation* between the employer and the organised workers represented by their union in order to determine the terms and conditions of employment.

In this chapter we shall discuss following aspects of negotiation process:

(i) Meaning of negotiation.

(ii) Types of bargaining.

(iii) Negotiation process:

1. Preparation and planning.
2. Defining the procedure of negotiation.
3. Clarification and justification of demands.
4. Bargaining and problem-solving.
5. Arriving at agreement and closure.

(iv) Techniques to help negotiate successfully.

(v) Seeking cooperation.

I. MEANING OF NEGOTIATION

- Negotiation is a *process* in which one party agrees to exchange a product or service with another party for something. Or negotiation is a process of arriving at mutual satisfaction through exchange of information.
- Negotiation is a *common practice* in organisations such labour and management, salesmen and customers, purchasers and suppliers, etc.
- Negotiation *involves bargaining* and then to arrive at an *agreement*.

2. TYPES OF BARGAINING

Broadly there are two types of bargaining:

2.1 Distributive bargaining (DB)

This approach involves dividing a fixed amount among negotiating parties. In this one party gains the other party suffers an equivalent loss, i.e. *win-lose situation*. It is very competitive bargaining.

In distributing bargaining (DB), each party has a target point which it hopes to achieve. It is the lowest point it would be willing to accept. (Figure 1)

FIGURE 1

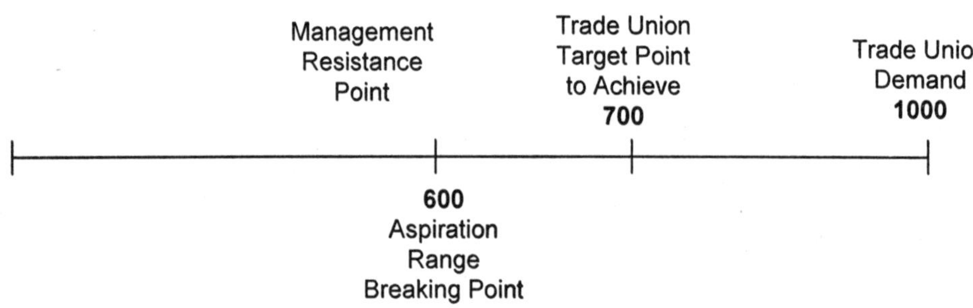

2.2 Integrative bargaining (IB)

It assumes there exist more solutions to problem which could result in a *win-win situation*.

(a) Advantages

- Integrative develops long-term relationship.
- Both parties end happily.
- Both task (result) and relationship issues are considered by both parties.

(b) Conditions for success of integrative bargaining are:

(i) Parties should be sensitive to each other's needs.
(ii) They should trust each other.
(iii) They should be willing to be flexible.

Integrative bargaining (IB) is always preferable way of negotiation, but it has limitations.

3. NEGOTIATION PROCESS

It has *five stages* as explained under:

3.1 Preparation and planning

- Negotiating team has to understand nature of conflict.

- Team should identify goals they want to achieve and also understand what other party goal is seeking to achieve.
- To collect information also related to opponents.
- Try to visualise BANTA (Best Alternative to be Negotiated Agreement). It is the limit below which both parties will not be satisfied.

3.2 Defining procedure of negotiation

- Identifying leader by each party.
- Clarity of issues/agenda of demands.
- Clarifying time limit for discussion.
- Lay strategy, to be adopted, if dead-lock is reached.
- To keep membership of negotiating teams small.

3.3 Clarification and justification of demands

- Clarify doubts on demands of other party at the beginning of negotiations.

3.4 Bargaining and problem-solving

- Normally initial demands list is long which include important and unimportant items.
- Each party gradually drops some demands in the form of concessions to the other party.
- Parties then find integrative solution.
- It is preferable to move to critical issues.
- Have breaks in meeting, i.e. gap to reduce tensions.
- Have joint lunch, etc. to have more informal conducive negotiations. This will give chance to modify strategy.
- Keep *humour, listen attentively* and maintain positive and friendly attitude.
- Give every member opportunity to speak
- Do not let negotiations reach *stalemate* stage. Suggest a solution.
- Keep *flexibility* and search for solutions. Continue dialogue.
- There is no place of ultimatums or confrontation during negotiations.
- Have *positive attitude*, have *consideration* for other party. Do not expose weaknesses of other party.

3.5 Arriving at agreement and closure

- Arrive at agreement that is mutually acceptable.
- Agreement to be formally written and signed by both parties.
- Lay procedure for implementation of agreement.

4. TECHNIQUES TO HELP NEGOTIATE SUCCESSFULLY

(i) Do establish rapport with other team. Reflect your *positive* attitude. State that you are after a *win-win* solution. Come prepared with some *conversational openers*.
(ii) Ask open questions to *explore* statements being made. Also observe *body language and tone of communication*.
(iii) Explain *reasons* when making your offer. Do not indicate 'take-or-leave-it' (offer).
(iv) Make concessions *gracefully* without implying any weakness.
(v) If deadlock is reached, focus on problem. Take a *break to rethink* and to reduce the gap.
(vi) Focus on areas of agreement and do come to mutually satisfactory conclusions on certain aspects.
(vii) What is crucial is creating and sustaining a good relationship with other party.
(viii) Winning a negotiation at the expense of other party may be a losing proposition in the long-run.
(ix) Avoid statement that initial demands are final.
(x) It is better to know background of opposite team members.

5. SEEKING COOPERATION

(a) *Cooperation* or *support* comes when both parties (management and union) perceive *goal is shareable*. The parties work together to achieve the goal and share it. Competitive behaviour results when the *goal* is perceived as attained by only one party.
(b) *Cooperation promotes*:
- Relationship of *mutuality* and *maximise* their contributions based on strengths.
- *Generate* alternatives/solutions to problems.
- *Reinforce* mutual support.
- *Develops collective actions* in solutions.
- Leads to better communication and coordination of efforts. Climate of friendliness.

(c) *How to develop cooperation*?
(i) All human beings have basic need to care and help others. *Strengthen* this motivation.
(ii) Develop *mutual norms* which are to be adhered by both parties.
(iii) If groups perceive *higher rewards*, then they repeat efforts.
(iv) With mutual strength, trust, parties are encouraged to take better risks in achievement of goals.

13

Strategies for Developing a Climate of Trust

- A strategy for building trust is the only basis upon which commitment can be generated.
- Trust should be regarded as social capital—the fund of goodwill in any social group that enables people within it to collaborate with one another. Trust is a 'unique human resource capability that helps the organisation fulfil its competitive advantage'—a core competency that leads to high business performance. There is thus a business need to develop a climate of trust, as there is a business need to introduce effective pay for contribution processes that are built on trust.
- Trust is an outcome of good management. It is created and maintained by managerial behaviour and by the development of better mutual understanding of expectations—employers of employees, and employees of employers. Herriot *et al.* (1998) argue, 'Issues of trust are not in the end to do with managing people or processes, but are more about *relationships and mutual support through change.*
- Trust is exemplified when management is honest with people, keeps its word (delivers the deal) and practises what it preaches.
- More specifically, *trust may be developed if management* acts fairly, equitably and consistently, if a policy of transparency is implemented, if intentions and the reasons for proposals or decisions are communicated both to employees generally and to individuals, if there is full involvement in developing reward processes, and if mutual expectations are agreed through performance management.
- Herriot *et al.* (1998) suggest that *if trust is lost, a four-step renewal strategy* is required:
  1. *admission by top management* that it has paid insufficient attention in the past to employees' diverse needs,
  2. a limited process of contracting that *takes individual needs into account,*
  3. *establishing 'knowledge-based' trust* based on a developing perception of trustworthiness, and

4. achieving trust based on identification by which *each party empathises with the other's needs*, employees confidence, self-belief and a self-perception which says that we are good enough to go but also happy to stay. A large part of the last piece is driven by environment which they are working in. It has got to be open, honest and straightforward and non-hierarchical. People must feel engaged and able to speak their minds. You have to have very clear signals from the top about these standards, and you have got to have managers who follow them. We have to make it very clear that no matter how good you are, if you get your business results by a climate of fear, then we don't want you. If you get there by creating leadership that is a different thing.

Reference

Michael Armstrong, Strategic HRM, Kogan Page, London.

14

Workers' Participation in Management: Industrial Democracy

In this chapter on 'Workers' Participation in Management" following aspects are covered:

1. Meaning.
2. Objectives of workers' participation in management.
3. Effects of participative decision-making (PDM).
4. Need for participation.
5. Scope of collective bargaining and workers' participation in management.
6. Nature of workers' participation in management.
7. Forms of workers' participation in management.
8. Background of workers' participation in India and government policy.
   8.1 Scheme of workers' participation in management.
   8.2 Workers' participation in Management Bill, 1990.
9. Essential conditions for success of workers' participation in management.
10. Barriers in workers' participation in management.
11. Quality circles.
    11.1 Self-managing teams.

1. MEANING

Workers' participation in management is mental and emotional involvement in group situation which encourages workers to contribute to group goals and share responsibility. Participation has three ideas:

(i) First, participation means mental and emotional involvement, rather than mere muscular activity. A person's self is involved rather than his body. It is more psychological than physical.

(ii) Second idea in participation is that it motivates persons to contribute to achievement of organisational goals by creative suggestions and initiative.

(iii) Third area is that it encourages people to accept responsibility. They are ready to work with the manager, instead of against him.

To put it briefly, it is team working together for a common purpose. It is a notion of industrial democracy. Workers have greater say over their work situation.

2. OBJECTIVES OF WORKERS' PARTICIPATION IN MANAGEMENT

(i) To raise level of motivation of workers by closer involvement.

(ii) It is an opportunity for expression and to provide a sense of importance to workers.

(iii) It forges ties of understanding leading to better effort and harmony.

(iv) It is a device to counter-balance powers of managers.

(v) It recognises human dignity.

(vi) It is panacea for solving industrial relation problems.

3. EFFECTS OF PARTICIPATIVE DECISION-MAKING (PDM)

Figure 1 shown on next page traces the mechanisms through which participative decision-making (PDM) is said to affect employee behaviour and attitudes and, in turn, organizational results. It suggests that participation improves both employee ability and motivation. Ability is improved primarily through communication and information sharing, which results in more informed employees who are better able to contribute creative ideas to the success of the enterprise. Motivation is improved in part because employees tend to set higher goals participatively than management does unilaterally and in part because the process causes individuals to become ego involved and committed and to exert pressure on themselves and their co-workers to ensure that their decisions are sound and their goals are met. The act of participating can also increase employees' sense of trust and control, which may lower their resistance to new ways of doing things. On the attitudinal side, some find that participation (like job enrichment) meets their needs for challenge and accomplishment (growth), causing satisfaction.

4. NEED FOR PARTICIPATION

The union and the management relationship can be of any of the three patterns:

(a) Hostility/conflict/fight.

(b) Neutral-hostility replaced by desire to negotiate/resolve problems.

(c) Cooperation and participation which is beneficial to all.

FIGURE I

Effects of Mechanisms of Participative Decision-Making

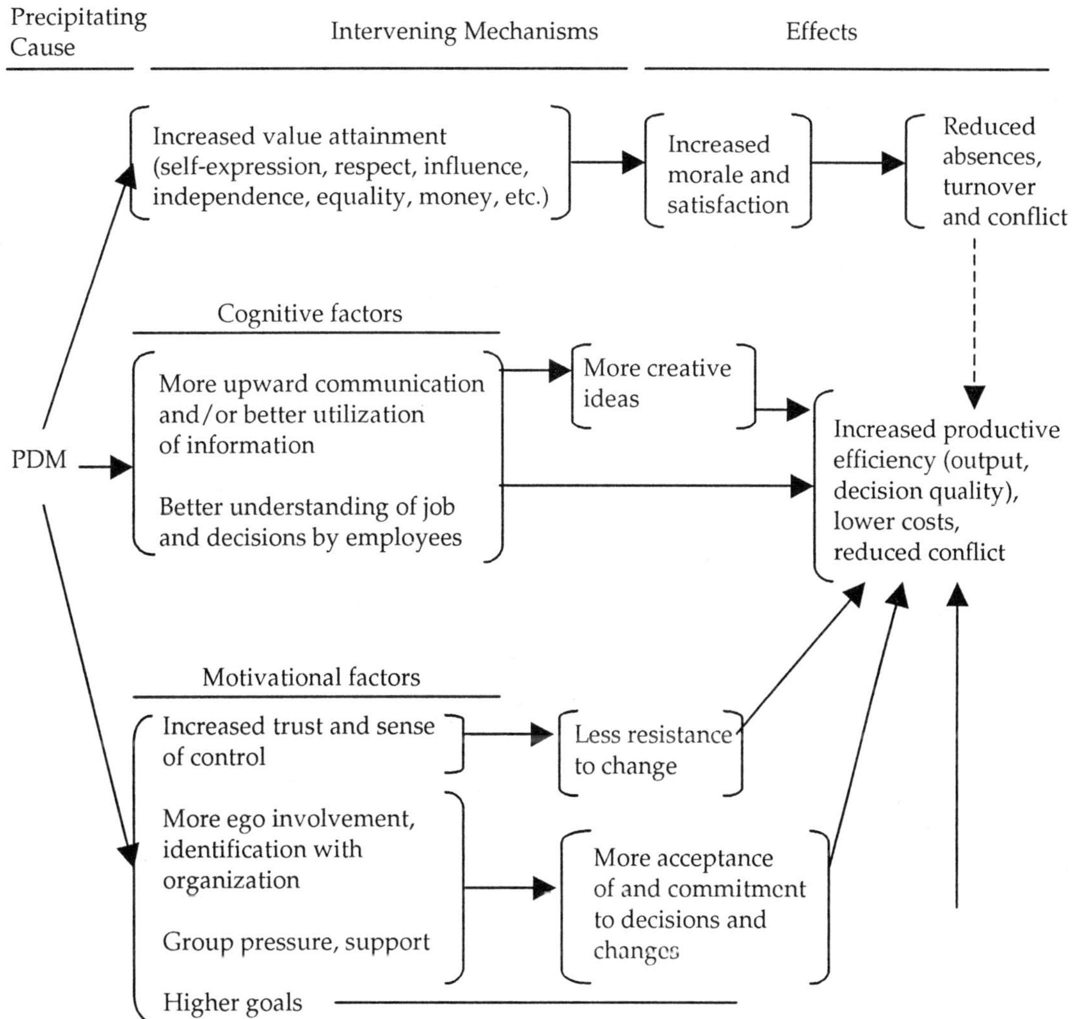

Source: E.A. Locke and D.M. Schweiger, "Participation in Decision-making: One More Look", in *Research in Organizational Behaviour*, ed. B.M. Staw (Greenwich, Conn.: JAI Press, 1979), p. 279.

5. SCOPE OF COLLECTIVE BARGAINING AND WORKERS' PARTICIPATION IN MANAGEMENT

This is explained as under:

(a) Collective bargaining relates to interest-related issues in bilateral union negotiation, i.e. economic issues—compensation, welfare, security, etc.
(b) Workers' participation in management relates to other areas where unions want to have say in decision-making (basically management functions). Work-related issues are production, quality, productivity, safety, working conditions, training of workers, etc.

6. NATURE OF WORKERS' PARTICIPATION IN MANAGEMENT

Workers' participation can vary in different forms, such as:

(i) *Sharing of information*: It is about the decisions taken by the management. This information is about policies and its changes, through meetings, newsletter, etc.
(ii) *Consultation*: It relates to securing opinions and views of workers' representatives before a decision is taken about work and working conditions.
(iii) *Joint decision-making/collaboration* on work-related issues.
(iv) *Co-determination/self-management* on all issues to provide workers' greater autonomy and control over production process.

7. FORMS OF WORKERS' PARTICIPATION IN MANAGEMENT

Employee participation in management can take two forms:

(a) *Indirect participation through representatives*, e.g. schemes of workers' participation in management, suggestion scheme, grievance committee, worker director, co-partnership, works committee.
(b) *Direct participation of employees* in their own area on work-related problems, such as, i.e. quality circles, productivity groups, problem-solving groups, self-managing teams. These are mentioned at the end of this chapter.

8. BACKGROUND OF WORKERS' PARTICIPATION IN INDIA AND GOVERNMENT POLICY

(i) Workers' participation philosophy was pioneered by TISCO in India as early as 1947 in the form of general wage settlement mechanism, through informal joint consultations.
(ii) Though the Royal Commission on Labour felt the need for an internal machinery called Works Committee in 1931, the suggestion did not receive any attention till the Industrial Disputes Act, 1947 has provided for setting up Works Committees in all undertakings employing 100 workers or more in order to remove friction between the employer and the employees.

(iii) The Industrial Policy Resolution of 1956 has further emphasised the role of joint consultation of workers and management as a means of industrial peace. Government took great interest in setting up Joint Management Councils, particularly during the Third Five Year Plan. The study group set-up by the Central Labour Ministry to study the working of JMCs in 1962 stressed the need for workers' education for making any participation meaningful.

(iv) Government's commitment to workers' participation was stressed when a scheme for participation at the shop floor level and plant level was introduced on 30th Oct. 1975 which was applicable to the manufacturing and mining units in the public, private and cooperative sectors, which employed 500 or more workers.

(v) Government's determination was further established when Article 43(A) was inserted as a Directive Principle of State Policy in the Constitution of India by the Constitution Amendment Act, 1976. Article 43(A) reads as: "The state shall take steps by suitable legislation or in any other way, to secure the participation of workers in the management of undertakings, establishments or other organisations engaged in any industry." In January 1977, Government decided to extend the scheme to the public sector commercial and service organisations.

8.1 Scheme of Workers' Participation in Management

A scheme of Workers' Participation in Management was introduced in 1983, which was applicable to *public sector undertakings*. Brief details are as under.

The scheme provided for shop level councils (department) and plant (unit) level councils. We give here brief role of these councils:

(i) *The Shop Councils*: These are to deliberate on:
- production facilities;
- operational problems;
- waste control—cost reduction;
- safety;
- quality;
- cleanliness;
- welfare measures in the shop; and
- monthly targets of production.

(ii) *The Plant Councils (Unit)*: These are to deliberate on:

(a) Operational Areas:
- productivity schemes;
- planning and review of monthly targets;
- house keeping;
- quality matters;
- machine utilisation;
- review of working of shop councils; and
- material and inventories.

(b) Financial Areas:
- profit and loss of unit;

- cost reduction; and
- performance of the plant.

(c) Personnel Matters:
- absenteeism reduction; and
- training of workers.

(d) Welfare Matters:
- welfare schemes;
- medical and transport facilities;
- safety;
- sports; and
- housing/canteens.

(e) Environmental Areas:
- pollution control; and
- community development work by the enterprise.

8.2 Workers' Participation in Management Bill, 1990

So for workers' participation in management has been of voluntary form except in public sector undertakings where it is as per the central government directives. It is non-statutory. Prof. B.R. Virmani has pointed out in "Workers' Participation in Management", 1978, "as in Britain, in India too, such joint committees have failed because of their purely consultative and advisory character on peripheral issues, disabling them to consider substantial issues in which workers are interested."

The government introduced a bill in the Parliament on 25 May, 1990 titled "Workers' Participation in Management Bill", 1990 which provided:

(a) Participation at shop floor level, establishment level and board of management level in industrial establishments.
(b) Procedure to lay for representation of employees at three levels.

However, bill could not be passed.

9. ESSENTIAL CONDITIONS FOR SUCCESS OF WORKERS' PARTICIPATION IN MANAGEMENT

Some pre-requisites are as under:

(i) Determination and will to work together in all circumstances is essential.
(ii) Mutual trust, faith and confidence in each other.
(iii) Mutual recognition of each other's rights and responsibilities.
(iv) Constructive and positive problem-solving approach and arriving at decision process through consensus.
(v) Training in developing proper knowledge, behaviour/attitudes for management and workers relating to concept and approach towards workers' participation in management.

10. BARRIERS IN WORKERS' PARTICIPATION IN MANAGEMENT

(a) Lack of proper attitude towards consultative bodies due to militant attitude, negative attitude—due to past efforts on workers' participation have failed. Line managers also do not like as they feel their authority is checked.

(b) Lack of genuine faith in the workers' participation system and willingness to work together, such as—
- apathy and even hostility,
- lack of trust and suspicion,
- lack of understanding of concept, purpose and benefits of scheme, and
- joint committees have become ritualistic bodies.

(c) Lack of peaceful atmosphere as there are strikes/lock-outs.

(d) There are number of joint bodies, e.g. works committee, production committee, suggestion committee, canteen committee and safety committee. As such there is confusion and duplication of activities.

(e) Difference between workers' participation and collective bargaining is not kept. Participation is treated as complementary to collective bargaining.

(f) Sometimes trade unions are not associated in workers' participative forums and there is problems of inter-union rivalry. Besides, criteria for recognition of representative union is not defined under the law.

(g) Gap in two-way communication and tendency to hide the real problems.

(h) Lack of proper leadership style. It is authoritarian. As such proper training is required for management personnel.

(i) Normally, there is delay in implementing the decisions and absence of follow-up of action taken on decisions.

(j) Political interest of trade unions is a hindrance in arriving at consensus.

11. QUALITY CIRCLES

Quality Circles (QCs) are groups of employees that meet regularly to work on problems affecting a work area. They exist outside the normal organizational hierarchy, and their powers are to recommend but also implement solutions after approval by the management. It is a form of direct participation of employees.

Some typical characteristics of Quality Circles are as under:

Objectives

- To attain employee involvement in the identification and solution of problems relating to such issues as productivity or costs, quality, and conditions of work, (e.g., housekeeping, safety).
- To improve results in these areas.

Organization

- Each QC consists of a leader or coordinator, who is usually not from management, and 3 to 13 other employees (the average is around 9) from a single work unit or section.

Comparison of Quality Circles and Self-Managing Work Teams

Characteristic	*Participation Concept*	
	Quality Circles	*Self-Managing Teams*
Implementation	Most in nature plants	Most in new, "greenfield" sites
Ease of start-up	Moderate in ease and speed	Much more difficult and lengthy
Participation	Usually totally voluntary	Usually not voluntary, but individual participation levels vary
Membership	Subset of work group	The entire work group
Leadership	Initial leader, frequently a supervisor, may be elected or appointed by management	Internal leader elected; external leader appointed by management
Type and frequency of problems	One at a time, usually a larger issue for a long period, selected from a wide range	Many small day-to-day issues, selected from a wider range
Implementation authority	Usually recommended; sometimes implement	Usually implement
Motivational impact	Moderate to strong.	Stronger
Relationship to existing organization	An overlay	Largely replaces existing organizations

- An organization may have many QCs that are assisted by one or more facilitators, usually a professional who is trained in group process skills.

Membership

- Participation is voluntary.
- Most QCs are in manufacturing operations and involve blue-collar employees, although increasingly they are being adopted in service industries and are involving white-collar (but not managerial) employees.

Scope

- QCs usually select the problems they will work on (within the scope of their own work area) although sometimes they are formed to tackle a particular issue.
- QCs have no budgets and no direct control over any organizational resources, although often their recommendations involve the expenditure of funds.

Training

- QC leaders or coordinators receive training in group facilitation skills.
- QC members receive training in group process, problem-solving and communication skills and may receive training in specialised areas such as statistical quality control techniques. Ten to 20 hours of training per individual is common.

Meetings

- QCs meet weekly or biweekly for an hour or two, although the meetings may become more frequent or lengthy as they become immersed in a particular issue or involved in preparing a presentation to management.
- Meetings take place on company time, although some may be scheduled for after hours.

Rewards for Participation and Performance

- Monetary rewards beyond normal compensation are rare.
- Non-monetary rewards—awards, plaques, banquets—are common. Often a lot of publicity—team names, emblazoned caps and t-shirts, etc.—accompany QC formations.
- The big reward, however, is the satisfaction that comes from successfully tackling significant problems, making presentations to management, and having suggestions adopted, implemented and (it is hoped) succeed.

11.1 Self-Managing Work Teams

Self-Managing Work Teams (SMWTs) are groups of employees given responsibility for managing and operating their own particular pieces of a business. The development of SMWTs is analogous to job enrichment, but at the group level. SMWTs are responsible for planning the work to be done, organizing themselves to get it done, selecting team members and assigning them to jobs, providing their own "supervision" (traditional supervisors, if present, usually serve as group facilitators).

References

H.P. Sims, Jr. and J.W. Dean, Jr., "Beyond Quality Circles: Self-managing Work Teams", *Personnel*, January 1985, pp. 25-32.

E.E. Lawler, III, *High Involvement Management* (San Francisco: Jossey-Bass Publishers, 1986), pp. 46-50.

B.R. Virmani, "Workers' Participation in Management", 1978.

Managing Grievances

1. MEANING

Grievances means any discontent or dissatisfaction expressed by an employee which is connected with the organisation.

Features

- It is connected to the policies, procedures and operations of the organisation.
- Discontent is expressed or implied.
- Is legitimate and not based on emotions like anger, fear, envy.
- Employee feels injustice done to him.
- Grievance is of individual nature. It is not of collective nature, e.g. bonus, wage increase or hours of work which are taken by the union in collective bargaining.

2. CAUSES OF GRIEVANCES

A grievance is violation of rights on-the-job in several forms:

(a) Conditions of work, e.g. safety, hazards, non-availability of tools.
(b) Service conditions, e.g. non-promotion, denial of increment, or transfer, leave, etc.
(c) Managerial decisions, e.g. job allocation.
(d) Style of leadership.

3. EXPRESSION OF GRIEVANCE IS IMPORTANT

- Where people work together their will inevitably be grievances off and on. There is nothing to get alarmed, if people/aggrieved express their grievances. Rather, it is matter of concern, if they do not express blocked individual grievances which may lead to industrial conflict.

- If grievance level is an organisation is too low, this could mean either one of the two things:
  (i) The level of frustration may have created relationship of apathy among employees and supervisors, and
  (ii) The need of employees towards search for satisfaction has gone too low.
  Both are harmful for the organisation.

4. GRIEVANCE PROCEDURE

A prompt and effective of grievances is essential for industrial harmony. This requires for a procedure for handling of grievances promptly and satisfaction of employees. There are two types of grievance procedures for redressal of the employees. These are:

(a) Stepladder Procedure

This grievance procedure is based on Model Grievance Procedure which was formalised in a tripartite committee in 1958. This was formulated in pursuance of code of discipline adopted in the 15th session of the Indian Labour Conference, 1957.

The Industrial Disputes Act, 1982 provides for the reference of certain individual disputes to grievance settlement authorities. Section 9C of the Act stipulates that in every establishment in which one hundred or more workmen are employed, the employer shall set-up a time-bound grievance redressal procedure.

Essence of Model Grivance Procedure

The three cardinal principles of grievance settlement, under the procedure are:

(i) settlement at the lowest level and line of appeal clear to employees;
(ii) settlement as expeditiously as possible; and
(iii) settlement to the satisfaction of the aggrieved.

Like justice, grievances must not only be settled but also seem to be settled in the eyes of the aggrieved.

The Model Grievance Procedure has a three-tier system for the settlement of grievances at the levels of the immediate supervisor; departmental head; and a bipartite grievance committee representing the management and the union, with a provision for arbitration or appeal to the organisation head, and a specified time-limit for the resolution process. See Figure 1.

The procedure has successive time-bound steps, each leading to the next steps in case of lack satisfaction. Under the procedure, an aggrieved employee would first present his grievance to a designed officer, who would give a reply within 72 hours. If the worker is dissatisfied with the decision or fails to get an answer within the stipulated time, he would, personally or accompanied by his departmental representative, present his grievance to the head of the department. If the department head fails to give a decision within 3 days or if the decision is unsatisfactory, the aggrieved worker can seek relief through the grievance committee, consisting of nominees of management and workers. This committee would communicate its

FIGURE I

Steps or Stages in Grievance Procedure

	Employee submits grievance to ↓	
Stage I	Supervisor	Reply to employee
		If not satisfied ↙
Stage II	HoD (Manager) (Can take representative)	Reply
		If not satisfied ↙
Stage III	Grievance Committee (Management and union representatives) Recommendations to ↓	
	GM	Reply

Note: Successive time bound stages.

recommendations to the general manager within 7 days of the grievance reaching it. If the recommendations are not made within this time, the reasons, therefor, would be recorded, and if an unanimous decision is not possible, the relevant papers would be placed before the general manager for decision.

Further, a grievance procedure should be evolved in consultation with the union in the organisation.

(b) Open Door Policy

In this aggrieved employees are free to meet the top executive of the organisation on Sundays and get their grievances redressed. Each grievance is processed and redressed. However, it has certain disadvantages such as, lower level executives feel by-passed, complicate boss-subordinate relationships, lack of follow-up of such grievances.

5. BENEFITS OF GRIEVANCE REDRESSAL SYSTEM

(i) Grievance procedure brings problems to open and is source of upward communication. Management can assess the health of the organisation and know impact of its policies. Management can initiate corrective action.

(ii) Grievance redressal system helps in preventing grievances in future by taking action.

(iii) It provides change to employees for emotional release of their dissatisfaction. It builds emotional security that a system exists for redressal of grievance.

(iv) Grievance procedure establishes procedure for ventilation of grievances.
(v) System acts as a check on arbitrary management action.
(vi) Grievance procedure encourages climate of trust and mutual concern.
(vii) In the absence of grievance redressal system, the day-to-day grievances get piled up and accumulated discontent of workers culminates in industrial disputes.

6. MANAGERIAL APPROACH IN DEALING WITH GRIEVANCES EFFECTIVELY

Some basic points for dealing with aggrieved employee are as follows:

- Way you treat a man with the grievance matters a lot. Show concern for the employee.
- Attend to him with promptness.
- Listen to grievance well.
- Understand the true nature of grievance and decode the message.
- Get the facts so as to identify the problem. In this process try to avoid emotional overtones of the employee.
- Deeper analysis of grievance may help identify real the causes.
- Take action best suited to the situation immediately and communicate to the employee.
- If grievance is imaginary or unfounded, attempt may be made to counsel the employee.
- Follow-up of employee to ensure whether he is satisfied or not.
- In brief, call employee, listen him, solve the problem and explain him.
- This is problem-solving approach on day-to-day basis and to avoid formal grievances.

7. ROLE OF SUPERVISORS IN HANDLING GRIEVANCES OF EMPLOYEES

Some guiding points are as under:

- All supervisors should know how to handle grievance. Then we can do something about preventing grievances.
- Supervisor not pass the buck to some body else.
- If he cannot do any thing he should bring to attention of his superior.
- Handling grievance encourage facts rather than perceptions.
- Have problem-solving approach not a battle to be won.
- Role of first line supervisor is important as his findings last.
    - o Immediacy of action.
    - o Show concern for employee.
- Employee may be seeking satisfaction or recognition or attention out of process.

An emphathetic approach by supervisor encourages a climate of trust, openness and mutual concern.

16

Managing Discipline

Maintenance of discipline is a prerequisite for the attainment of maximum productivity in an organisation. Discipline is also essential for promotion of harmonious human relations in an organisation.

1. CONCEPT OF DISCIPLINE

Simply stated, discipline means obeying the orders of supervisors or orderly behaviour. It is behaviour according to rules, regulations and procedures, which are deemed to be necessary for the effective functioning of an organisation.

It is a form of employee *self-control* to meet organisation standards. It is *willing acceptance of norms* of behaviour of the organisation. Central core of discipline is self-discipline. Discipline is described as willing cooperation and observance of the regulations of the organisation. See Figure 1 inculcate self-discipline.

If people always do what they ought to do, then no discipline is required to be imposed. But this is not the case. So discipline is required to be imposed by the supervisor. In case of failure to maintain positive discipline, punitive approach is employed. Object of disciplinary procedure is to correct the employee and not to weed him out of the organisation.

Promotion of discipline is essential for the progress and growth of an organisation. If employee is dissatisfied—grievance procedure for redressal. Management dissatisfied with conduct of employee, it is management's duty to use disciplinary procedure to correct employee.

2. HOW TO MAINTAIN AND IMPROVE DISCIPLINE IN AN ORGANISATION?

Some basic steps are maintaining and improving discipline in an organisation are:

1. Prof. Douglas McGregor has suggested the *hot-stove rules* for maintaining discipline. Hot-stove rule as features are:

FIGURE 1

Inculcate Self-Discipline

(a) *Communicating the rules of discipline*: As advance warning. Management to specify the *rules* and *penalties* clearly and made known to employees and managers which should serve as code of conduct.

(b) *Immediacy of action*: Stove burns *immediately* if warning is not headed, so management should initiate disciplinary action promptly after the misconduct of the employee. Delayed disciplinary action can do harm and effect morale of other employees.

(c) *Impartiality or Consistency*: Stove burns alike child or old person. No favour/under identifical situation. If two employees have done same misconduct, the disciplinary action should be consistent in the interest of fairness. Discipline should be progressive.

(d) *Impersonality/objectivity*: Stove does not have personal feelings in inflicting pain whoever touches it. Stove has no felling of revenge or pleasure. We want to correct the behaviour and not personally attack the personality of the employee. We are penalising the rule violation, not the individual. Supervisor to treat the employee in the same manner as had prior to the infraction. It is relevant to mention the 'the discipline process' laid by Kenneth Blanchard. See Figure 2.

2. Discipline as a kind of *warning to others*: Some management's give publicity in their news letters, etc.

FIGURE 2

The Discipline Process

The One Minute Reprimand works well when you:

1. Tell people beforehand that you are going to let them know how they are doing and in no uncertain terms.

the first half of the reprimand:

2. Reprimand people immediately.
3. Tell people what they did wrong—be specific.
4. Tell people how you feel about what they did wrong—and in no uncertain terms.
5. Stop for a few seconds of uncomfortable silence to let them *feel* how you feel.

the second half of the reprimand:

6. Shake hands, or touch them in a way that lets them know you are honestly on their side.
7. Remind them how much you value them.
8. Reaffirm that you think well of them but not of their performance in this situation.
9. Realise that when the reprimand is over, it's over.

Source: "The One Minute Reprimand", from *The One Minute Manager* by Kenneth Blanchard.

3. A strong *representative union can* be ally if sounded about the misconduct and disciplinary action.
4. Tackle *conduct outside* the workplace also, e.g. employee committed misconduct in a public place, gambling, commission of crime, etc.
5. *Leadership* role is critical to set an example in following rules. This has salutary effect on employees.
6. Periodic *review of rules* and procedure of the organisation as a part of enlightened personnel policies.
7. Prompt *attention to grievances* of employees and there should be suitable grievance procedure for such redressal.
8. Supervisory staff to adopt a practice to *reprimand in private* and do commendation in open in presence of other colleagues.
9. An effective *two-way communication* system where supervisory personnel listen to employees' problems.
10. Scheme for *employee participation* in management is useful.
11. Supervisors may be imparted *training in dealing with employees* in fair manner.
12. Disciplinary action should stress on prevent recurrence of indiscipline in future. Negative or punitive approach to discipline which means employees are forced to observe rules and regulations on account of fear of punishment to resorted only when essential.
13. Positive approach or *constructive discipline* or self-discipline to be encouraged by the supervisors. It means that employees believe in and support discipline and

follow the rules, regulations and desired standards of behaviour. Supervisors may educate the employees the value of discipline, as it is the highest form of discipline in any organisation. Discipline in the context of modern management process needs to be viewed as a behavioural control mechanism.

14. *Participative system* of formulation goals and standards of performance.

To sum up, the purpose of disciplining is to correct a particular behaviour that is misaligned. We do not attack the personality of people when disciplining, but instead address some aspect of their work behaviour.

3. FACTORS WHICH DISTURB DISCIPLINE

(i) Term and conditions of employment, e.g.:
- Lacking external parity in wages.
- Hire and fire policy.
- Favouritism in implementation of benefits.

(ii) Grievance syndrome:
- Not proper redressal of grievance leading to alienation and low morale of employees.
- Habitual late coming and absenteeism.
- Dishonesty, e.g. stealing, false punching of another's time card.

(iii) Politicalised trade unions and inter-trade unions rivalry:
- Internal fighting and indiscipline.
- Failure to observe safety rules.
- Subversive activity.

(iv) Supervisory and managerial personnel—style of expressions—attitude of supervisory personnel may provide resentment among employees.

(v) Some behaviour on the part of supervisory personnel which causes damage in overall indiscipline, e.g.
- In the form of power struggle and group intrigue and thus supervisors *criticising colleagues* in presence of employees.
- Supervisors *supporting negative behaviour* of trade unions.
- Managers grumbling all the time in *presence of employees* about company policies. Such men erode their leadership.
- Supervisors avoiding reporting of serious misbehaviour and initiating disciplinary action.

(vi) Socio-economic factors, e.g. related to pressure of rising prices leading to fall in real wages.
- Down-sizing of organisation and consequent reduction of employees.

17

Disciplinary Action

1. OBJECTIVES OF DISCIPLINARY POLICY

The organisation has to provide environment, formulate policies, programmes and procedures in such a way that employees behaviours are conditioned to be disciplined. In case of failure to maintain positive discipline, punitive approach is employed by the management. The objective of any disciplinary procedure adopted should be to correct the employee and not to weed him out.

2. DISCIPLINARY ACTION

With the dwindling sense of discipline, emergence of indiscipline takes place which manifests itself in form of behaviour in breach of accepted norms of conduct codified. After the constructive, preventive, educative and corrective efforts prove futile to inculcate the sense of discipline, disciplinary action is to be taken against the delinquent for the acts of omission and commission which constitute misconduct.

2.1 What is a Misconduct?

A behaviour which is in breach of the accepted or excepted norms of conduct constitutes misconduct. It however, presupposes a *wrongful intention* and not merely an error of judgement. It is in the former case, disciplinary action is called for. Acts of omission and commission such as habitual absenteeism, dishonesty with the affairs of the company, etc. are misconducts. These are laid in standing orders of the company. Similarly, the various penalties to be imposed as punishments are also mentioned in the rules.

2.2 Right to take Disciplinary Action

Right to take disciplinary action emanates from employer-employee relationship and is regulated by contract of employment, standing order of the company (for workers) or conduct and discipline (appeal) rules (for supervisory staff) of the organisation promptness in disciplinary cases is essential. It has to be ascertained which disciplinary rules are applicable to the delinquent employee for taking action.

2.3 Disciplinary Action Procedure

- To start with, based on any misconduct committed by the employee or complaint, a preliminary enquiry is called for. Then disciplinary authority has to initiate action.
- The following authorities are laid by the organisations for various levels of employees:
  (a) Disciplinary authority;
  (b) Appellate authority; and
  (c) Reviewing authority.
- Based on judicial pronouncement, elaborate procedure have been evolved which has to be followed to avoid infirmities in the disciplinary action. Various stages involved are briefly indicated as under:
  (i) preliminary enquiry,
  (ii) framing and serving of charge sheet,
  (iii) holding of domestic enquiry,
  (iv) report of the enquiry officer,
  (v) consideration of the report of the enquiry officer by disciplinary authority,
  (vi) order of punishment and its communication, and
  (vii) appeal.

Stages of Disciplinary Proceedings are explained through flow chart in Figure 1.

2.4 Principles of Natural Justice

The principles of natural justice, require:

(a) *Punishing authority should not be same as enquiring officer.* No man shall be a judge in his own cause.

(b) Obligation of affording every *reasonable opportunity* to delinquent to *depend himself*, i.e. opportunity to deny charges and establish innocence by:
  (i) clearly informed of the charges levelled against him,
  (ii) to answer the charges,
  (iii) no evidence is recorded in absence of delinquent employee,
  (iv) opportunity to defend by cross-examining witnesses produced against him, and
  (v) by examining himself and his witnesses in support of his defence.

(c) Domestic enquiry is conducted *fairly* and methodically. Enquiry officer to record his findings with the reasons in his report.

(d) *Penalty* imposed must be *commensurate with charge established.*

(e) Justice should not only be done, but should be seen to be done.

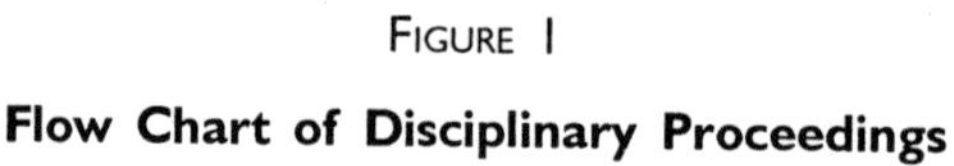

FIGURE I

Flow Chart of Disciplinary Proceedings

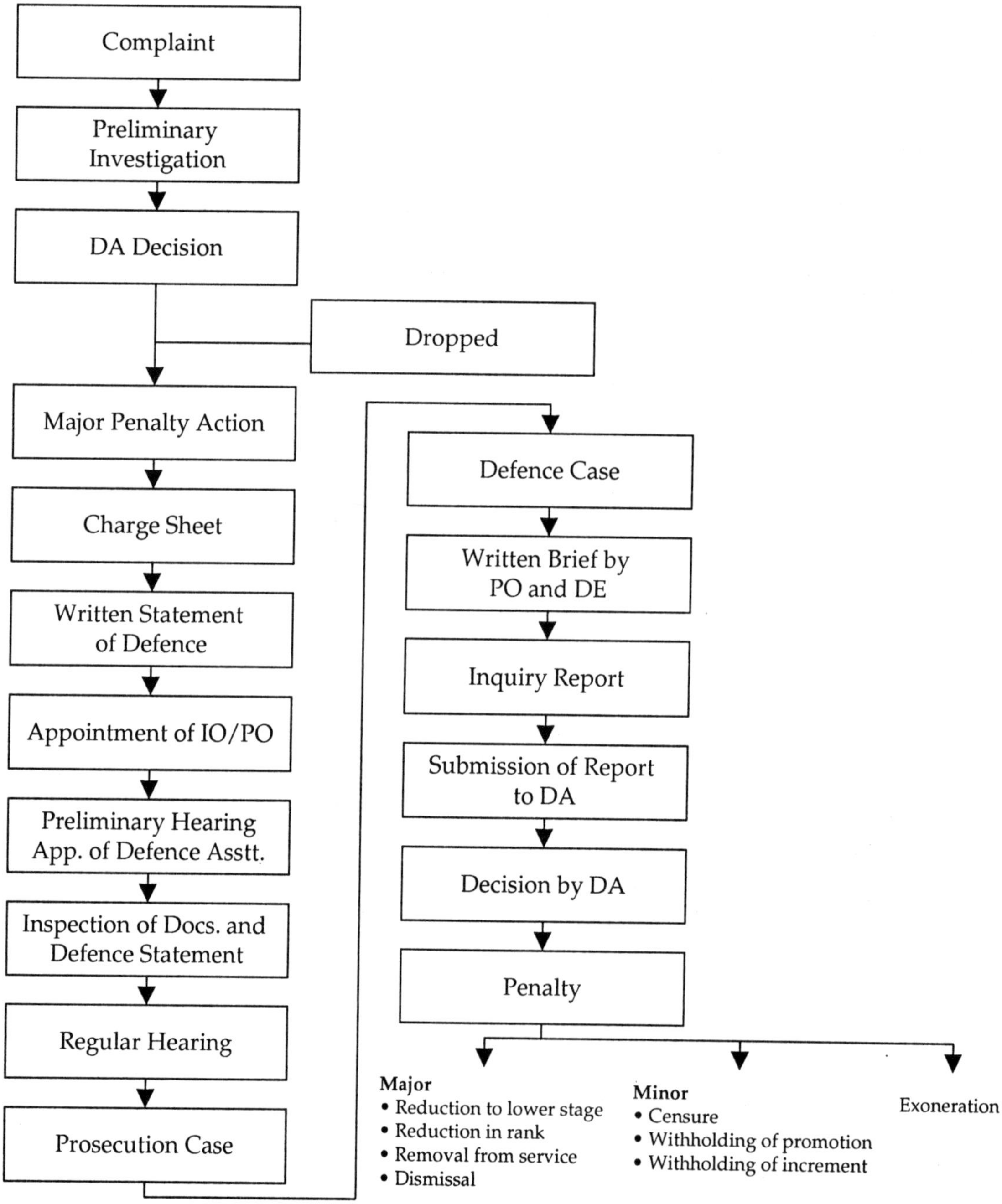

Complaint
↓
Preliminary Investigation
↓
DA Decision
→ Dropped
↓
Major Penalty Action
↓
Charge Sheet
↓
Written Statement of Defence
↓
Appointment of IO/PO
↓
Preliminary Hearing App. of Defence Asstt.
↓
Inspection of Docs. and Defence Statement
↓
Regular Hearing
↓
Prosecution Case
↓
Defence Case
↓
Written Brief by PO and DE
↓
Inquiry Report
↓
Submission of Report to DA
↓
Decision by DA
↓
Penalty

Major
- Reduction to lower stage
- Reduction in rank
- Removal from service
- Dismissal

Minor
- Censure
- Withholding of promotion
- Withholding of increment

Exoneration

3. STAGES OF DISCIPLINARY ACTION PROCEEDINGS

3.1 Issue of the Charge-Sheet

Delinquent employee is to be issued a charge-sheet call him to submit his explanation within a specified period of time. This charge-sheet should be drafted in a clear and unambiguous language so that the workman does not have any difficulty in understanding the charges that he has to answer. Wherever possible, the relevant clause of the company's standing orders should be mentioned in a charge-sheet. If the charge relates to an incident, the date, time and place of the occurrence should be mentioned. Proper care should be taken in framing the charge-sheet, for the validity of the punishment would depend on the enquiry of the misconduct mentioned in the charge-sheet. The charge-sheet should be in the local language.

The charge-sheet framed against delinquent employee and duly signed by the disciplinary authority should be served on him personally if possible and acknowledegment to the effect should be obtained from him. In case the workman is absent, of if he refuses to accept the charge-sheet when presented to him, the same should be sent to his local and home addresses by post under-registered cover with acknowledgements due, after getting his refusal attested by two witnesses. In case the charge-sheet is returned unserved with the remarks of the postal authorities, the same should be kept intact without opening. In such a case, the employer should display the charge-sheet on the notice board or act in accordance with the provisions of the standing orders. In some cases, it may be necessary to publish the contents of the charge-sheet in a local newspaper having wide publicity.

3.2 Suspension Pending Enquiry

In a case where the charges levelled against—a workman are of serious nature and it is considered by the disciplinary authority that his physical presence might endanger the safety of other workmen, or if it is apprehended that he might intimidate others or tamper with the evidence, he may be suspended. During the period of suspension pending enquiry, the workman will get subsistence allowance as per rules.

3.3 Consideration of the Explanation

After a charge-sheet has been served on a workman for reply he may submit his explanation:

(i) admitting the charges and requesting for mercy, or
(ii) denying the charges and requesting for an enquiry, or
(iii) not submitting any explanation at all, or
(iv) requesting for more time to submit explanation.

- In a case where the workman admits the charge which is of a minor nature and begs for mercy, no enquiry is held and decision is taken accordingly on the charge-sheet. If, however, the misconduct is serious enough to warrant discharge or dismissal, the management should still arrange to hold a proper enquiry, the admission of the charges not withstanding.
- In a case where the workman submits an explanation mentioning that the charges levelled against him are false, baseless, motivated, concocted, etc. A proper enquiry as per procedure should be held before awarding any punishment.

- When the workman fails to submit any explanation within the specified time limit, the management should take steps to hold a proper enquiry
- When the workman concerned makes a *bonafide* request on reasonable grounds for extension of time to submit explanation, the same should be granted.

3.4 Notice for Holding the Enquiry

After consideration of the explanation of the charge-sheeted workman or when no reply is received within the specified time limit, the disciplinary authority should issue an order appointing an enquiry officer or an enquiry committee to hold the enquiry of the charge-sheet. The enquiry officer can be an official of the company, or even an outsider, but care should be taken to appoint only such a person as enquiry officer who is neither a witness nor is personally interested in any way in the matter for which the charge-sheet has been issued. It should also contain the name of the management representative.

Thereafter, the enquiry officer should issue a notice of enquiry. This notice of enquiry should clearly mention the date, time and place of enquiry. It should ask the workman to present himself with his witnesses/documentary evidence, if any, for the enquiry. It should also be mentioned in the notice of enquiry that if the workman fails to attend the enquiry on the appointed date and time, the same will be held *ex-parte*. A reasonable period of time should be given to the workman for preparing his defence before the enquiry is held.

3.5 Holding of the Enquiry

The object of holding an enquiry is to find out whether the workman is guilty of the charges levelled against him in the charge-sheet, or not. In doing so, the enquiry officer gives the workman a reasonable opportunity to defend himself by cross-examining the witnesses/ documentary evidence/exhibits produced against him and by examining the witnesses/ documentary evidence in his defence. The workman concerned can also make statement in his defence apart from what is stated in reply to the charge-sheet. It should be clearly understood that it is for the management's representative, i.e. presenting officer to prove the charges against a workman by adducing evidence during the enquiry and it is not the workman who has to prove his innocence. Unless management side has been able to prove the case against the workman, he should not be considered guilty.

3.6 The Enquiry

On the appointed date and time, fixed for the enquiry, the following persons should be present apart from the enquiry officer.

(a) Presenting Officer

He is the person who will lead the case from the management's side by producing witnesses and relevant documentary evidence in support of the charge. He may himself be a witness, in which case he is the first person to be examined. The presenting officer has a right to cross-examine a charge-sheeted workman as well as the witness/documentary evidence produced by him.

(b) Delinquent Employee

No enquiry can be said to have been held as per procedure in the absence of the charge-sheeted employee. If however, he refuses to take part in the enquiry after presenting himself, or when he does not report for the enquiry despite receiving the notice sent to him, the enquiry may proceed *ex-parte*, provided in the notice of the enquiry a specific mention to that effect had been made. Also, if during the enquiry, the delinquent employee withdraws himself, the same may be held *ex-parte*. In such a case, it is advisable to postpone the enquiry and give another opportunity to the delinquent employee rather than holding *ex-parte* enquiry. In a case, where the delinquent employee turns up for the enquiry after some witnesses have been examined, it would be proper for the enquiry officer to allow him to participate in the enquiry after recording this fact in the proceedings. The enquiry officer should recall the witnesses who have already been examined in the absence of the delinquent employee so that he gets an opportunity to cross-examine such witnesses.

(c) Representative of the Delinquent Employee

If the delinquent employee writes in reply to the charge-sheet or makes a subsequent request that he should be allowed to take a knowledgeable co-worker of his choice to assist him in the enquiry, the same should normally be allowed. In some companies, union committee member of the recognised trade union is allowed to attend an enquiry on the specific request of the workman, to either assist him or play the role of an observer as per procedure.

(d) The Procedure of Enquiry

At the commencement of the enquiry, if the delinquent employee is present, the enquiry officer should record the date, time and place of enquiry, names of the persons present and obtain their signatures on the order-sheet. Thereafter, he should proceed as follows:

- Read out and explain the charges and the reply of the charge-sheet to the delinquent employee and get his confirmation to that effect. In case the delinquent employee has not accepted the charge in reply to the charge-sheet, he should be asked if he pleads guilty of the charges. If the charges are admitted, that should be recorded and signatures of all concerned, with date, should be taken. A full-fledged enquiry need not be held if the misconduct is of a minor nature. In case the charge, if proved, is serious enough to warrant discharge or dismissal, the proper course is to hold the enquiry.
- Explain to the delinquent employee concerned the procedure to be followed in the enquiry, viz., that the presenting officer will produce witnesses/documentary evidence/exhibits in support of the charge and the delinquent employee will have opportunity to cross-examine. Thereafter, the delinquent employee should be given opportunity to produce his witnesses and the management representative will have a right to cross-examine them. The delinquent employee will have further opportunity to make statement, if any, in his defence. At any stage of the enquiry, the enquiry officer can seek clarification from any witness or the delinquent employee by puffing questions to him. Neither the presenting officer nor the delinquent employee can put leading questions to their respective witnesses.
- Witnesses in support of the charge are to be examined one by one in the presence of the delinquent employee.
- The charge-sheeted workman is to be given an opportunity to cross-examine management's witnesses. In case he declines to cross-examine any witness, an endorsement to that effect should be recorded by the enquiry officer.

- The delinquent employee should be asked to produce his own witnesses one by one and the presenting officer will be allowed to cross-examine them. The delinquent employee should be asked to give his statement after his witnesses are examined and cross-examined. He may also produce documentary evidence, if any. In case the delinquent employee declines to produce any witness/documentary evidence or declines to give any statement, the enquiry officer should make a record to that effect in the order-sheet and obtain signatures of all concerned. If the enquiry remains incomplete in the first sitting and some more witnesses are required to be examined, it may be continued on any other day mutually agreed by both sides. In such a case, the enquiry officer should make a suitable endorsement in the order-sheet and obtain signatures of all concerned.
- On each page of the enquiry proceedings, the signature with date of the charge-sheeted workman, his representative, if any, the concerned witness and the management representative should be taken. The concerned witness should sign on each page of his statement only. The enquiry officer will sign on each page of the proceedings after endorsing that the statement has been recorded by him and explained to the parties in their language before they were asked to sign. If the delinquent employee refuses to put his signature even after he had been asked to do so, the enquiry officer should make an endorsement to that effect and get it attested by others present

(e) Ex-parte Enquiry

If, on the day fixed for the enquiry, the delinquent employee does not turn up, an *ex-parte* enquiry may be held by following the usual procedure. In such an enquiry, the presenting officer has to lead the evidence against the charge-sheeted workman. The enquiry officer, by putting questions to the witnesses, gets facts to come to reasonable conclusion about the validity or otherwise of the charges. As stated earlier, it is advisable to fix another date of enquiry, instead of holding an *ex-parte* enquiry on the first sitting itself.

The Enquiry Report

After the enquiry is over the enquiry officer makes an appreciation of the evidence on record and comes to his conclusion. If there is no corroborative evidence on a particular point, the enquiry officer has to give his own reasons for accepting or rejecting the evidence of such a witness. The enquiry report is a document which should clearly indicate whether the charges levelled against the delinquent employee are proved or not. The conclusion of the enquiry officer should be logical and based only on evidence brought out during the enquiry. The enquiry officer may record clearly and precisely his conclusions with reasons for the same. There is no place for any conjecture or surmises in the enquiry report. It should be such that as per the evidence on record, any impartial man, not connected with the case, should be able to come to the same conclusion as that of the enquiry officer.

3.7 Final Decision of the Disciplinary Authority

The enquiry report is submitted to the Disciplinary Authority. Before he takes a decision on the findings of the enquiry officer, he is required to furnish a copy of the enquiry officer's report to the concerned employee. If he agrees with the findings of the enquiry officer, after considering the gravity of the misconduct and the past record of the delinquent employee equitable treatment with precedents of action taken, etc., he may pass an order on the quantum of punishment after recording his reasons for the same in writing. An order in writing is passed to that effect and is communicated to the delinquent employee.

A letter communicating the order of discharge/dismissal should set out clearly the charge(s) proved against the delinquent employee and the date from which the order is to become effective. Normally, the order of discharge/dismissal should be effective from the date of the order, unless there is an express provision in the standing orders to the contrary.

3.8 Appeal

An employee can appeal against an order imposing upon him any of the penalties. The appellate authority may confirm, enhance, reduce or set-aside the penalty.

3.9 To Conclude

It is the employer's right to direct its internal administration and maintain discipline. However, before passing an order of discharge or dismissal, the employer has to arrange for a fair and proper enquiry in consonance with the principles of natural justice. The reason is that its decision may not be reversed by the adjudicator at a later date, if the workman raises an industrial dispute challenging the order.

A domestic enquiry need not be conducted in accordance with the technical requirements of a criminal trial but they must be fairly conducted and in holding them, considerations of "fair play" and "natural justice" must govern the conduct of the enquiry officer. A domestic enquiry must be conducted with an open mind, honestly and *bonafide*, with a view to determine whether the charge framed against the delinquent employee is proved or not.

In today's context, no employer can discharge or dismiss a delinquent workman even for a serious misconduct without following an elaborate procedure for taking disciplinary action. An employer can be guilty and penalised if the adjudicator finds that there was want of good faith; or there was victimisation or unfair labour practices; or the management was guilty of a basic error or violation of a principle of natural justice; or on the grounds that the finding was completely baseless or perverse.

4. LEGAL PROVISIONS RELATING TO DISCHARGE OR DISMISSAL (UNDER INDUSTRIAL DISPUTE ACT, 1947)

(i) Individual Dispute

Individual disputes are not covered by The Industrial Disputes Act, 1947, except dispute of an individual workman relating to his discharge, dismissal, retrenchment and termination from service, which is to be considered as an industrial dispute under the Act (Sec. 2a).

(ii) Prior to Introduction of Sec. 11A

In 1971, an employer could discharge or dismiss a workman for misconduct as per standing orders after following the procedure for conducting a domestic enquiry. The management's decision could not have been challenged before labour court, if enquiry was fairly and properly conducted as per the principles of natural justice. The court could not interfere with quantum of punishment. However, court had powers to interfere only when:

(i) there was want of good faith, or
(ii) there was victimisation or unfair labour practice, or
(iii) violation of principles of natural justice, or
(iv) findings was completely baseless or perverse.

(iii) Position under Sec. 11A

If labour court is satisfied that order of discharge or dismissal was not justified, it may set aside the order of discharge and direct reinstatement of the workman or award lesser punishment. Thus, court has been empowered to act as an appeal.

(iv) Industrial Dispute (Amendment) Act, 1982

An employer may be held guilty of unfair labour practice, in case court finds dismissal/ discharge is to be (i) on account of victimisation, or (ii) not in good faith, or (iii) in utter disregard of natural justice, and (iv) for patently false reasons or disportionate punishment. Apart from the remedy of reinstatement of workman, the employer is liable for the penalty under Sec. 254.

18

Voluntary Retirement Scheme (VRS)

In this chapter we share some salient features of VRS, now often talked about in corporate and government sector as under:

1. Need for VRS due to impact of liberalisation and modernisation;
2. Meaning of voluntary retirement;
3. Legal aspects of VRS;
4. Steps and procedure for VRS;
5. Disadvantages and advantages of VRS; and
6. Pink slips and facing them.

I. NEED FOR VRS DUE TO IMPACT OF LIBERALISATION AND MODERNISATION

Due to liberalisation and on-set of fast competitive economic environment, corporations are trying to survive and remain competitive. In this process companies are resorting to cost cutting and modernisation. Reduction of surplus staff has become necessary. Most of the corporations which have adequate funds have started the process of restructuring by adopting innovative schemes of voluntary retirement. Some other *factors for reduction* of employees are:

- Recession in business.
- Changes in technology, new product lines, re-engineering of process.
- Takeovers and mergers.
- Joint-ventures with foreign collaboration who bring latest technology.
- Restructuring of business due to market conditions. Leaner organisation structure and more delegations to business units.
- Out-sourcing of staff and more services are provided by outside supplier.

2. MEANING OF VOLUNTARY RETIREMENT

H.L. Kumar, noted legal advisor states 'voluntary', means without compulsion-willingly. Voluntary is an act on the part of the employee to give up employment willingly and without compulsion from the employer. It is a unilateral act on the part of an employee to cease the contract of employment with the employer. The word "voluntary retirement" received legislative recognition in 1953, when section 2(oo) was engrafted, in the Industrial Disputes Act. The said Section 2(oo) asserts that retrenchment does not include voluntary retirement of the workmen.

3. LEGAL ASPECTS OF VRS

(a) Notice of change under ID Act. H.L. Kumar, further states that there is no explicit clause in Section 9-A (i.e. Notice of Change) of the ID Act which states that VRS does not attract Section 9A. Since VRS must necessarily result in decrease in the existing strength of workers, therefore, *prima facie* it must result in reduction of post. Hence, VRS would be covered by item 11 of Schedule IV to the ID Act. Such an approach has been taken by unions in litigation and this approach was upheld on 17th April, 1998 by Bombay High Court. The judgement was set aside on 9th October, 1998 when consent terms were signed by both the parties and accepted by the High Court of Judicature at Mumbai. However, the case-law on this is still not settled and is still a point for litigation by unions. Companies are avoiding for "notice of change", as it entails delays and litigation.

(b) Impetus in Voluntary Retirement Schemes in the Wake of New Industrial Policy in 1991 of Government of India. Reduction of manpower through VRS by companies was prevalent in the past but the process speed up after New Industrial Policy in 1991. The Government of India amended in 1992, the Income Tax Act wherein compensation had under Voluntary Retirement Schemes for both private and Public Sector Employees does not get taxed. The companies are not required to get the scheme of VRS approved from the Income Tax Department as was earlier.

The Government in 2002 decided to exempt the Voluntary Retirement Scheme (VRS) income from tax for employees who have completed 10 years of service or 40 years of age. This has been done to provide relief to those opting for early retirement.

4. STEPS AND PROCEDURE FOR VRS

(a) H.L. Kumar further emphasises that before embarking on a Voluntary Retirement Scheme (VRS), companies must work out other alternatives for improving performance. VRS should be the last alternative because it is a painful process and has social implications on the departed employees and the society.

(b) The strategy to be develop will be dependent on the history of labour management relating to the company, the role of internal and external trade union leaders, the profile and capability of the human resource and company's financial ability to bear the cost of compensation under VRS. The reduction process should match with strategic corporate plan.

(c) The effect of down-sizing, i.e. post-reduction operations should be planned such as redeployment, training, etc.

(d) The management has to notify through a circular decision to VRS which should cover:

(i) The reason for right-sizing.
(ii) Eligibility, i.e. who can apply for VRS.
(iii) The age limit of employee who is 40 and above and those who have completed minimum 10 years of service in the establishment.
(iv) The benefits that employees who offer to retire voluntarily are entitled as per law and rules the benefits of Provident Fund, Gratuity and salary for balance of privilege leave upto the date of their retirement, besides the voluntary retirement benefits. Management's are offering lucrative separation benefits which are much above the retrenchment compensation under ID Act. One public sector has offered the terms as under:
  (a) 60 days salary for each completed year of service.
  (b) Monthly salary for remaining period of service before normal retirement, whichever is less. This is subject to maximum of 60 months salary.
  (c) Continue to avail medical facilities as applicable to their retired employees.
(v) The right of an employer to accept or reject any application for voluntary retirement.
(vi) The date upto which the scheme is open and applications are received for consideration by the employer.
(vii) To indicate income tax exemption on voluntary retirement benefits upto of Rs. 5 lakhs, which is maximum tax free benefit.
(viii) If the company is public sector undertaking obtain approval of the government.
(ix) If there is a union of employees in the establishment involve the union by communicating to them the reasons, the target group and the benefits to be offered to those who opt for the scheme.
(x) Motivate the managers and employees. The VRS should be made attractive and no pressure should be made to ease out persons. There should be transparency.
(xi) Provide professional assistance to employees who accept VRS to plan their post-retirement activities and financial management.

5. DISADVANTAGES/DRAWBACKS OF VRS

(i) It is seen that good, capable and competent employees normally apply for separation which may cause embarrassment to the managements. Some safeguards to be provided as was done by some banks and PSUs in respect of not having required qualifications, non-promotion for two years when eligible, long absence of 90 days impairment due medical problems, business unit declared as shrinking and enviable were allowed to opt for VRS.
(ii) To certain extent it create fear, a sense of uncertainty among employees.
(iii) Trade unions sometimes protests the operation of such schemes put obstructions.

Advantages/Merits of VRS

(i) We may overcome the above merits, so as to smoothen the whole process of VRS.
(ii) It offers to the employee an attractive financial compensation than what is permitted under retrenchment law.
(iii) It allows flexibility and can be applied only to certain divisions and departments where there is excess manpower.

(iv) It allows overall savings in the employee costs thus lowering the overall costs.

(v) Voluntary nature of the schemes precludes the need for enforcement which may give rise to conflicts and disputes.

(vi) There is no legal obstacle in implementing VRS—as it predominantly encountered in retrenchment under the labour laws.

6. PINK SLIPS AND FACING THEM

Down-sizing is handled in the most unprofessional manner, without caring about the sensibilities of the employees. Some call it a pink slip because that is the colour of the wound it leaves on one's ego and self-esteem. Being pink-slipped is an awful experience.

Aziz Haider suggests, often isomnia, social withdrawal, lethargy and decline in libido are results of sudden joblessness. You may develop a negative attitude towards yourself that reflects in your relationship with kids, wife and friends. You may become more irritable, lose interest in household activities, and start taking solace in solitude.

(a) In such a scenario, cultivating a positive attitude is the key.

(b) The single most effective tool for preempting maladaptive stress response is self-confidence.

(c) Talk to your friends or loved ones and to those you can trust. Tell them what you are going through and actively seek their advice. Else, seek professional help.

(d) Focus on activities you still enjoy—playing games, working in garden, reading books—and try to keep depression at bay. Strong familial bonds and joint family system, safety valves of religion and tradition, and the collective rituals of our society can remedy the situation to some extent.

(e) Relaxation exercises, yoga, meditation and activities as mundane as watching TV or spending constructive time with the family. Further, sleep well, eat a balanced diet with plenty of fruits and vegetables. And don't fall pray to alcohol or drugs that may bring newer problems.

(f) A different solution to bring your mind and thoughts out of this siege of crisis can be achieved through a re-look at your ability and past achievements. Keep your skills going, while you are marketing for a job to get.

(g) Create work for yourself. Otherwise look at entrepreneurship as an option, even if one a small scale. Else go for retraining, thus developing skills that may help you in future.

(h) Besides this, if there is a time when you are severely stressed, go for the instant reliever. Take three slow, deep breaths. Each time, breathe in through your nose until your lower abdomen is full (about four counts), pause the eight counts to let the air circulate, then slowly exhale, pulling in your abdomen as you do.

References

H.L. Kumar, "Designing and Implementing: An Innovative VRS", *Human Capital*, November 2002, New Delhi.
C.B. Memoria and S.V. Ganekar, Himalaya Publishing House, Mumbai.
Aziz Haider, *HT Careers*, June 13, 2002.

19

Social Security

The term 'social security' originated in USA and was used to establish schemes of unemployment and old-age insurance in 1935. In 1938, the same term was used by New Zealand when it created social security system—a measure of income security for all citizens.

According to ILO, "Social security is that security that *society* furnishes through appropriate organisation against certain risks to which its members are exposed. These risks being sickness, maternity, invalidity, old-age and death. It is for contingencies that affect the ability of working man to support himself and his dependents in health and decency."

The concept of social security is essentially related to the high ideas of human dignity and social justice. It has become a major aspect of public policy in most countries. It yields benefits in the long-run.

Three *characteristics of social security* are common, though social security schemes differ from country to country. These are:

(i) They are established by law;

(ii) They provide some form of cash payment to individuals to compensate part of loss of income due to contingencies such as old age, widowhood, orphanhood; and

(iii) The benefits or services are provided in three ways:

   (a) *Social insurance,* i.e. benefits are provided to contributors during old-age, sickness unemployment, etc.

   (b) *Social assistance,* no contributions are made but government gives benefits to invalids, aged, disabled, mothers, children, etc., as minimum needs could be met.

   (c) *Public service financed by government,* such as national health service in government hospitals, pensions for aged, etc.

SOCIAL SECURITY IN INDIA

India is a welfare state as envisaged in her constitution. Article 41 of our constitution lays down, "The state shall *within limits* of its economic capacity and development make effective provision securing the right to work, to education and to public assistance in case of unemployment, old-age, sickness, etc.

Several laws enacted are:

(i) *Employee's State Insurance Act, 1948 (ESI).* Some benefits to contributors are:
- Sickness benefit and medical benefit,
- Maternity benefit and disablement benefit, and
- Dependents benefit (widow and children), funeral benefit.

(ii) *Employees Provident Fund Act, 1952 (PF).* Pension, deposit linked insurance scheme.

(iii) *Payment of Gratuity Act, 1972.*

(iv) *Workmen's Compensation Act, 1923* (employer to pay for accidental injury, occupational disease and death).

(v) *The Maternity Benefit Act, 1961*:
- 12 weeks maternity leave (paid) in pregnancy.
- 6 weeks miscarriage leave (paid) in pregnancy.

(vi) Old-age pensions by state governments.

(vii) Public health facilities by government.

(viii) Social security to unemployed workers by ESIC.

(ix) *Employment Guarantee Act, 2005.*

20

Labour Welfare

CONCEPT

(i) Labour welfare is to promote the welfare of workers in a variety of ways. Any kind of service will come under the purview of labour welfare, if it aims at helping the workers to work better in a more meaningful manner, physically, socially, morally, economically and intellectually.

A significant definition describes labour welfare as "the voluntary effort of the employer to improve the living and working conditions of his employees." The first essential to the welfare of the employees are steady work, a fair wage and reasonable hours of work. Besides employees pay regard for the comfort, health, safety and well-being of employees.

(ii) Labour welfare is an important facet of industrial relations. It gives satisfaction to the worker in a way which even a good wage cannot. With the growth of industrialisation and mechanisation, it has acquired added importance. Labour welfare, contribute to efficiency in production, but is expensive. Each employer depending on his priorities gives varying degrees of importance to labour welfare. It is because the Government is not sure that all the employers will provide basic welfare measures that it introduces statutory legislation from time to time to bring about some measure of uniformity in the basic amenities available to industrial workers. Today, welfare has been generally accepted by employers.

OBJECTIVES OF LABOUR WELFARE

There could be multiple objectives of having a labour welfare programme. The concern for improving the lot of the workers, a philosophy of humanitarianism. Such an overture of caring is supposed to build a sense of loyalty on the part of the employee towards the organisation.

The humanitarian approach has given way to a more practical utilitarian approach. The utilitarian approach views investment in welfare through an economic framework where the possible cost benefit to the organisation gains greater concern through improved or quicker services from the employees.

LABOUR WELFARE

It is useful to consider welfare benefits under two basic categories, viz., inter-mural and extra-mural. The following categorisation is used by ILO:

Inter-mural	*Extra-mural*
• Drinking water	• Social insurance (gratuity, pension, PF, etc.)
• Toilets	• Benevolent fund
• Creche	• Maternity benefits
• Washing facilities	• Health and medical facilities
• Occupational safety	• Education facilities
• Uniforms and protective clothing	• Housing facilities
• Shift allowance	• Recreation facilities
• Canteen	• Leave travel facilities
	• Worker cooperatives
	• Vocational training
	• Transport to and from place of work

These facilities and benefits can be further classified into those provided by legislation and those provided voluntarily by management or as a result of bipartite settlements between the management and the trade unions.

Statutory Welfare Matters

Provisions relating to health, welfare, safety, working hours, annual leave with wages and conditions on employment of women and children have made in various labour laws:

(a) The Factories Act, 1948;
(b) The Shops and Establishment Act;
(c) The Plantations Labour Act, 1951; and
(d) The Mines Act, 1952.

Non-Statutory Welfare Amenities

These relate various matters such as:

(a) Provision of housing facilities to workers.
(b) Provision of recreation, sports and cultural activities.
(c) Transport services for commuting of workers.
(d) Education facilities for workers' children are available in industrial townships in the form of schools, colleges, reimbursement of cost of textbooks, scholarships, sports, etc.
(e) Exgratia payment of distress relief and cash benefits in case of death, injury, sickness, marriage or as a facilitation grant.

CONTEMPORARY WELFARE FACILITIES

In addition to traditional statutory and non-statutory amenities mentioned above, certain contemporary welfare facilities are provided these days. These are summarised as under:

(i) Quality of Work Life (QWL).
(ii) Control of drug abuse and alcoholism.
(iii) Precautions against AIDS.
(iv) Accidents prevention and safety.
(v) Coping with stress.
(vi) Managing turnover.
(vii) Managing absenteeism.
(viii) Managing alienation.
(ix) Providing good working environment.
(x) Vocational guidance.
(xi) Job satisfaction improvement programmes.
(xii) Employee counselling.

These are explained below:

(i) Quality of Work Life (QWL) Programmes

QWL seeks to create a work commitment in organisations and society at large so as to ensure higher productivity and greater job satisfaction of the employees. It is a process by which an organisation attempts to unleash the creative potential of its personnel by involving them in decisions affecting their work lives. "QWL is a process of work organisations which enables its members at all levels to participate actively and efficiently in shaping the organisation's environment, methods and outcomes. It is a value-based process, which is aimed towards meeting the twin goals of enhanced effectiveness of the organisation and improved quality of life at work for the employees."

Quality of Working Life is the degree to which members of a work organisation are able to satisfy their personal needs through their experience in the organisation. Its focus is on the problem of creating a human work environment where employees work cooperatively and contribute to organisation objectives. The major indicators of QWL are job involvement, job satisfaction and productivity.

Areas of Quality of Working Life are as under:

(a) Compensation

The reward for work should be above a minimum standard for life and should also be equitable.

(b) Health and Safety

The working environment should reduce the adverse effects of pollution that can adversely affect the physical, mental and emotional state of employees.

(c) Job Security

Employees should not have to work under a constant concern for their future stability of work and income.

(d) Job Design

The design of jobs should be capable of meeting the needs of the organisation for production and the individual for satisfying and interesting work.

(e) Social Integration

The elimination of anything that could lead to individuals not identifying with the groups to which they belong. This includes the elimination of discrimination and individualism, whilst encouraging teams and social groups to form.

(f) Protection of Individual Rights

The introduction of specific procedures aimed at guaranteeing the rights of employees at work.

(g) Social Relevance of Work

Initiatives to increase the understanding among employees of the objectives of the organisation and the importance of their part in them.

(h) Respect for Non-work Activities

Respect for the activities that people engage in outside the workplace. The impact of work activities on private life should also be recognised.

Methods to Improve QWL

In order to improve the quality of working life, the following steps may be followed:

(a) Job Enrichment and Job Enlargement

These attempts to provide a person with exciting, interesting, stimulating and challenging work. In other words, it improves the quality of the jobs. These motivate the employees with higher level needs and overcome problems of monotony in the jobs.

(b) Autonomous Workgroup

Under this, each group of workers is given freedom of decision-making on production methods, distribution of tasks, selection of team members and leaders, work schedules and so on.

(c) Flexibility in Work Schedules

Employees demand more freedom at the workplace, especially in scheduling their work. Among the alternative work schedules capable of enhancing the quality of working life for some employees are:

- *Flexitime.* A system of flexible working hours.
- *Staggered hours.* Different groups of employees begin and end work at different intervals.

- *Compressed work-week.* It involves more hours of work per day for fewer days per week, e.g., five days a week.

(d) Job Redesign

Job redesign based on participative system helps in better job satisfaction.

(e) Opportunity for Growth

Opportunity for growth is important for achievement-oriented employees. If the employees are provided opportunities for their advancement and growth and to develop their personality, they will feel highly motivated. Their commitment to the organisation will also increase.

(f) Employees' Participation

People in organisations have a need for participation in matters affecting their lives. So they want participation in the decision-making process. Employees' participation in the form of suggestion system, management by objectives (MBO), workers' participation in management, etc. provides psychological satisfaction to the employees.

(ii) Drug Abuse and Alcoholism Control Programmes

Drug abuse and alcoholism are major problems of employees these days. Absence rates of such employees are very high even four times those of other employees. Employees personal habits and problems are major contributors.

However, they fabricate excuses for absences. The company programmes treat alcoholism and drug abuse as illness and provide both medical help and psychological support for alcoholics. These seek to rehabilitate the affected employees. These are both preventive and treatment of the problems so as to enable such employees to retain self-image as a useful person in society and at work.

(iii) Precautions against Acquired Immune Deficiency Syndrome (AIDS)

In recent years, AIDS, i.e., Acquired Immune Deficiency Syndrome has received significant media attention because of its serious consequences. Employees fear about contracting the HIV or AIDS disease has made many employers to develop AIDS programmes and policies.

Dealing with the infected workers at the workplace is a very complex problem. It has been made clear by the government policies that the infected workers have right to equal treatment, freedom from discrimination and access to normal rehabilitation and invalidity retirement processes. The World Health Assembly resolution relating to HIV-infected people and people with AIDS, urges member-states:

(a) to foster a spirit of understanding and compassion for HIV-infected people and people with AIDS;
(b) to protect the human rights and dignity of HIV-infected people and people with AIDS and to avoid discriminatory action against and stigmatisation of them in the provision of services, employment and travel; and
(c) to ensure the confidentiality of HIV testing and to promote the availability of confidential counselling and other support services.

Consistent policies and programmes are to be developed at national and enterprise levels through consultation between employees and unions, and where appropriate, governmental agencies and other organisations. National Aids Control Organisation (NACO) has been set-up which creates awareness among the general public about the need to take adequate precautions against AIDS through mass media. It also provides financial assistance to State AIDS control societies set-up in various states to fight against AIDS.

(iv) Accidents Prevention and Safety

Industrial accidents mainly cause loss of man-days apart from other losses. Industrial accidents are also due to various human reasons such as carelessness of workers, absence of proper education and training to workers, alcoholism and drug-addiction among workers, defective plant layout, limited space for movement of workers and so on. The industrial accidents which are due to human errors can be avoided.

Impact of Accidents

Accidents have disastrous effects on the organisation, the employees and the society at large. Accidents prove costly for the organisation as workers have to be compensated and machinery has to be repaired. Besides, lost man-days of the affected workers and cost of training of new workers further burden the cost of production.

Employees also suffer adversely from accidents. They face mental and psychological shock, more so when they or their colleagues become physically disabled. Accidents have demoralising effect on the workers. Their morale is lowered. Moreover, the rates of absenteeism and labour turnover go up.

Sometimes they also affect the general public adversely. The Bhopal Gas leak tragedy in 1985 is a case in point. Thousands of people were killed and several thousands became disabled in this accident. Thus, efforts should be made to avoid industrial accidents in the interest of workers, employers and the society at large.

Measures for Ensuring Industrial Safety

The basic objective of the safety programme should be safety and security of the lives, health and welfare of the workers employed therein. The following precautionary steps may be adopted to prevent accidents in the industries:

(a) Imparting of Safety Training

The supervisors should train the new employees in safety methods. The possible causes of accidents should be explained to the new employees and they should be taught habits and motions that will keep them out of danger. Training programmes should also be designed for the Supervisors.

(b) Installation of Material Handling Equipments

Material handling equipments should be installed to carry bulky materials from one place to another. No worker may be required to lift or carry heavy loads which may cause injury.

(c) Maintenance of Plant

The plant should be maintained in good condition. All objects likely to obstruct the passages meant for movement by workers should be removed. Passages should not be used to store goods or materials.

(d) Guarding of Machines

Safety guards should be constructed and used to provide positive protection, prevent access to the danger zones during operations, avoid inconvenience in operation and give protection against unforeseen contingencies.

(e) Provision of Protective Items and Clothing

The workers should be provided with proper protective items such as hand gloves, masks, helmets, safety footwear, etc. while at work. Chemicals should be carefully handled.

(f) Floors Free from Oils

There should be no trailing of telephone cables on the floors. Floors, passages and stares must be kept clear of obstructions.

(g) Period of Inspection

There should be periodic inspection of machines and equipment and electricity cables to check any leakages.

(h) Equipment Redesign

Industrial engineers should be engaged to improve the man-machine system. Equipment, machinery and work procedures should be redesigned to cut down accident rate.

(i) Formation of Safety Committee

Safety committee may be constituted in every plant. It should consist of the representatives of both the management and the workers. All the safety programmes should be implemented through the safety committee.

(j) Safety Campaign

Safety programme must be given a wide publicity through posters and hoardings. Safety contests may also be held between the plants as a part of the safety campaign. Plant with lowest accident rate may be given some reward.

(v) Coping with Stress

Randall S. Schuler has stated, "Stress is a dynamic condition in which an individual is confronted with an opportunity, constraint or demand related to what he or she desires and for which the outcome is perceived to be both uncertain and important."

This definition has three features:

(a) *Stress is not necessarily bad in itself.* It also has positive value when it offers potential gain.

(b) *Stress is associated with constraints and demands.* The former prevents you from doing what you desire. The latter refers to the loss of something desired. So when you undergo your annual performance review at work, you feel stress because you confront opportunity, constraints, and demands. A good performance review may lead to a promotion, greater responsibilities, and a higher salary. But a poor review may prevent getting the promotion.

(c) Two conditions are necessary for potential stress to become actual stress. There must be *uncertainty* over the outcome and the outcome must be *important*. Regardless of the conditions, it is only when there is doubt or uncertainty regarding whether the opportunity will be seized, the constraint removed, or the loss avoided that there is stress. That is, stress is highest for those individuals who perceive that they are uncertain as to whether they will win or lose and lowest for those individuals who think that winning or losing is a certainty. But importance is also critical. If winning or losing is an unimportant outcome, there is no stress. If earning a promotion doesn't hold any importance to a person, he would have no reason to feel stress over having to undergo a performance review.

(d) Stress is body's reactions, physiological and psychological to any demand made upon it that requires more of us than usual. Our reception of events, activities stress. It is an individual matter. Certain events may be quite stressful to one person but not to other. Our imagination creates muscular tensions. Thinking process interferes with body. One's mind has substituted physical danger when it is not there. When one sits in an interview, chemicals are produced in the body.

(e) Stress is not undesirable. Mild stress actually improves performance. If stress is severe and persists for long period person is not able to cope with anxiety, mention and nervousness. It lowers performance it can be harmful. This is explain in Figure 1.

FIGURE I

Stress and Job Performance Relationship

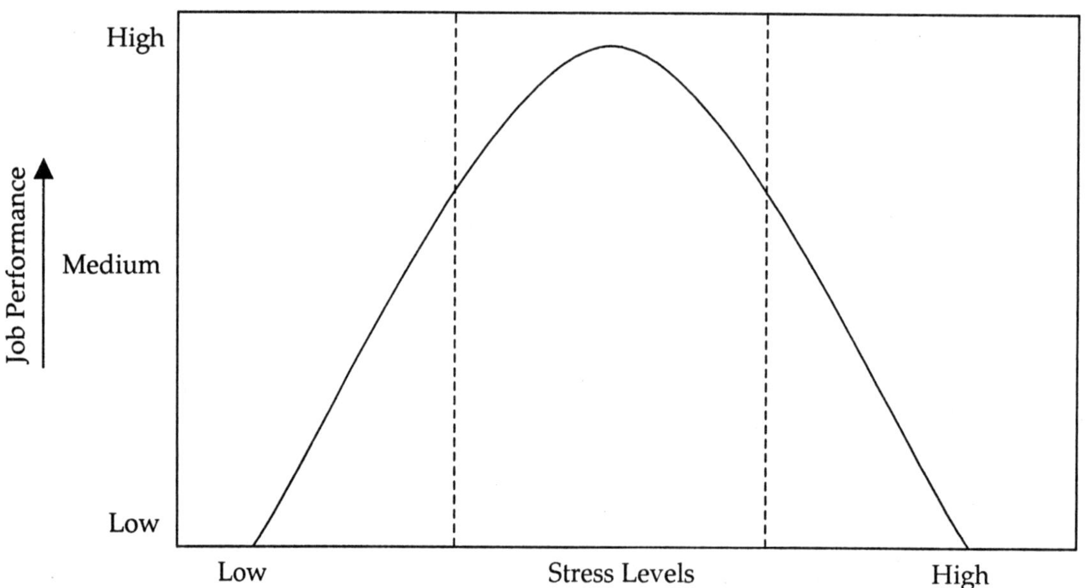

Sources of Stress

The potential stressors in a person's life can be divided into three categories:

(i) Environmental Stressors, which include technical, social, political and economic changes.
(ii) Organisational Stressors, comprises organisational characteristics and conditions, job demands and role characteristics.
(iii) Individual Stressors, which consists of personal characteristics, strengths and weaknesses, personal situation and events and coping efficiency.

A model based on the above classification is shown in the Figure 2.

FIGURE 2

Sources of Stress and Consequences

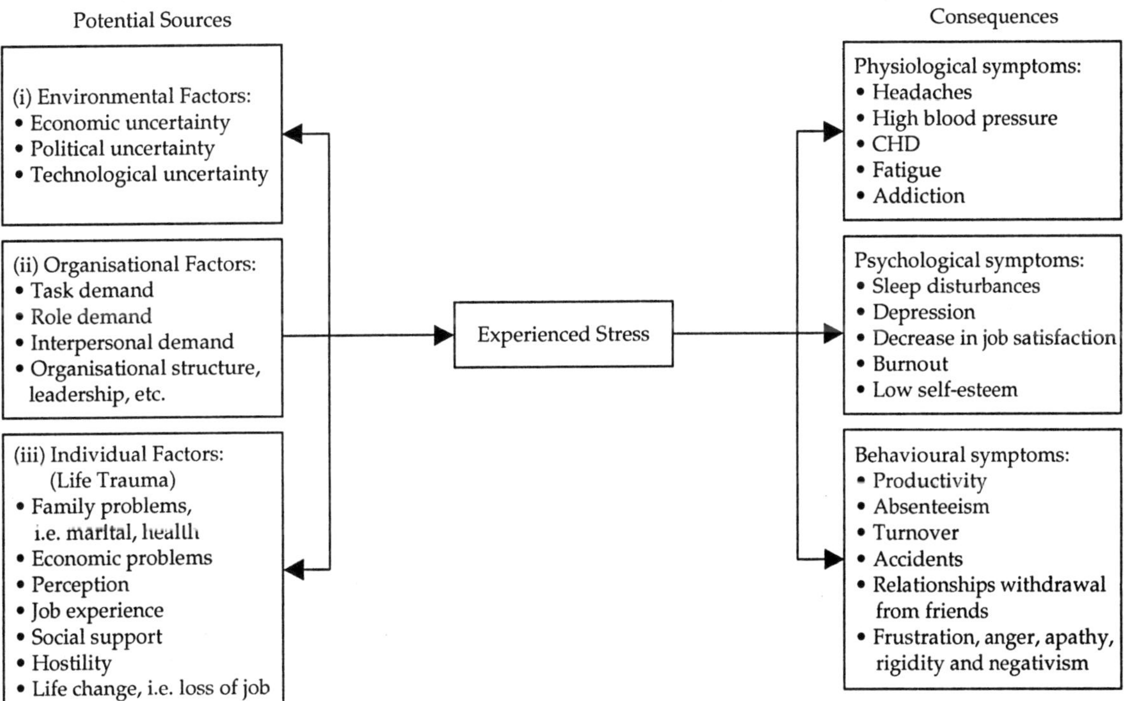

Individuals do not exist in isolation, but are part of an environment, the two most important of which are the organisational and the non-organisational environment. If both of these environments contain many stressors along with stressors within an individual at the same time, there is likely to be an increased level of stress. Stress levels would also vary according to the degree of interaction between the three types of stressors.

Nature of the Stressors

(i) Environmental Stressors

Environmental stressors include:

(a) Economic Changes

Economic change include inflation or fluctuation in interest rates, which can decrease the purchasing power of individuals and in these circumstances people find it difficult to plan ahead financially. This can create uncertainties in people's lives and result in stress. Similarly, decreasing levels of investment may lead to increasing levels of unemployment, which is another major cause of stress.

(b) Political Changes

Political changes in a country can also cause stress for individuals especially if people are not very clear about what to expect from a new political situation. Sometimes political changes can be so dramatic that the level of uncertainty can create a huge amount of stress for certain groups.

(c) Social Changes

Social changes also cause stress. It was expected that through the "Hong Kong Handover" the long established "American Values" in Hong Kong would change to "Asian Values" in terms of culture, sport and style, which resulted in uncertainties and created a great deal of stress prior to handover.

(d) Technological Changes

Technological changes are not only part of organisational life but are an inevitable part of daily life, and they have become another environmental stressors. Systems in banking, communication and shopping have become highly dependent on rapidly changing technology and depending on person's acceptance of technology, the facilities provided by such change can create stress.

(ii) Organisational Stressors

Organisational characteristics and processes can vary dramatically between organisations and, if not designed correctly, can cause stress. Characteristics can be analysed in terms of organisational policies, structure and processes. Some stress-related factors are shown in Figure 3.

Recent studies have focused on the effects of organisational polities on reviewing stress at work. Life in a highly centralized organisation, where control is concentrated at the top level of the organisation, people at the operating level have little control over their work behaviours and activities and thus becomes a source of stress.

(a) Job Demands and Role Characteristics

Taken together, job-demands and role characteristics constitute another set of stressors in an organisational environment. Job demands include repetitive work, time pressures and deadlines, low skill requirements, responsibility for people and underemployment. Role characteristics are more complicated and consists of:

FIGURE 3

Organisational Characteristics as Stress Factors

Aspects of Organisational Characteristics	*Resulting Stress Situation*
1. *Organisational Policies*:	
• Inequitable performance or inappropriate appraisal • Pay inequities • Idealistic job description	Feelings of unfairness or lack of clarity about personal goals or objectives.
2. *Organisational Structure*:	
• Centralisation of authority of decision-making • Not enough opportunities for growth and advancement • Increased organisational size and lack of participation. • Interdependence of organisational units	Lowered feelings of self-efficiency.
3. *Organisational Process*:	
• Poor communication and lack of information • Poor feedback on performance • Ambiguous or conflicting needs • Poor training programmes	Ambiguity and feelings that the worst is about to happen

(i) *Role perception:* Role perception represents an individual's view of how he is supposed to act in a given situation.

(ii) *Role expectation:* Role expectation are defined as how others believe one should act in a given situation. Mismatch between perception and expectation leads to stress.

(iii) *Role conflict*: When an individual is confronted by divergent role expectations, the result is role conflict. It exists when an individual finds that compliance with one role requirement may make compliance difficult with another. This develop stress.

(v) *Role Overload*: Role overload is experienced when an individual or employee is expected to do more than time permits.

(vi) *Role ambiguities*: It is created when role expectations are not clearly understood and the employee is not sure what he or she is to do.

(b) Other Organisational Stressors

(i) Air Quality

"Sick building syndrome" is a condition in which an office building or office segment puts polluted air into the worker's environment. This can be caused by solvents in the carpets and furniture, air-conditioning, moths and fungi and so on. If the pollution is bad enough, it can make individual sick and boost stress.

(ii) Excess Noise

Noise pollution can lead to significant work stress and if it is loud enough, can damage one's hearing over long-term. It is loud enough to interfere with one's concentration and raise one's stress level. The sound of people talking and laughing, office printers, computers, ringing phones, faxes and copy machines or meetings going on all combine to raise the stress level.

(iii) Uncomfortable Office Furniture

When an individual is staggering under files, papers and report, the stress level may be compounded if the desk, chair or lighting is not first rate. An individual's own posture is also important. Sitting—especially slouching—puts continuous pressure on lower back muscles and discs.

(iv) Computer Comfort

One of the prime sources for work stress involves the computer—its screen, proper placement of the keyboard and so on.

Organisations go through a cycle. They are established, they grow, become mature, and eventually decline. An organization's life stage, i.e. where it is in this stage cycle—create different problems and pressures for employees. The establishment and decline stages are particularly stress prone. The foundation stage is characterized by a great deal of excitement and uncertainties while the decline stage requires cutbacks, layoffs and different set of uncertainties. Stress tends to be least in maturity where uncertainties are at their lowest ebb. Information technology is particularly facing stress-related problems in a big way and considerable amount is being spent to develop coping strategies.

Stress Coping Strategies

The term 'coping' is used to denote the way of dealing with stress. "It is the process of managing demands (external and internal) that are appraised as taxing or exceeding the resources of the person". People use a combination of three approaches to cope stress.

The first is *control strategy* to directly anticipate or solve problems, it is to take charge and tackling the problem.

Second is the *escape strategy* which amounts to running a way when they fail to confront.

Thirdly, *symptom management strategy* consists of using methods such as relaxation, meditation, or medication to manage the symptoms of occupational stress.

Personal Strategy

Basically meeting stress is individual responsibility. He should have accurate information about stress. Some steps are:

- Learn to *recognise its symptoms*. Take symptoms seriously and slow down pace.
- *Change perceptions* which create stress. Do not carry demons in your mind. So minimise stress by changing your attitude. Avoid guilt feeling and share your anxieties. Improve communication and develop relationship of trust and caring of others.
- Learn to *realign goals* which are realistic and attainable. Restructure your job to make it less stressful. Try activities that capture interest and give satisfaction. Pursue some higher values of life.

- Maintain *positive attitude* toward self-development and self-improvement. Overcome stress as it is life long battle avoid obsolescence.
- Practice *relaxation techniques* such as yoga, meditation, biofeedback, intense exercise. Body is a great self-healer such as ability to withstand grief. Play games and avoid competition. Avoid bottling up anger within you.
- Cutback on *excessive hours* of work to overcome burnout. Keep balance between work and home life. Enjoy holidaying.

Organisational Programmes

The management may pursue the following strategies to reduce job stress:

- Setting clear *objectives* for the organisation. Departments and individuals so as to minimise scope for job conflicts and ambiguity among the employees.
- *Enriching* jobs for the employees.
- Developing *career plans and development* taking into consideration individual capabilities and aspirations, on the one hand, and the organisational requirements, on the other.
- Employee assistance programmes such as engaging of counsellors to guide on matters of career planning and opportunities, tackle alcoholism, drug addiction, etc.
- Training and development programmes.
- Organisation development or transformation programme so as to improve communication, innovation, participation, trust, openness, quality of work life, infact a concept of learning organisation.
- Strengthen process of placement, i.e. matching jobs and individuals and role clarity.
- Compensation to ensure equitable reward system.

(vi) Managing Absenteeism

1. Concept

Absenteeism is said to be there when an employee fails to come to work when he is scheduled to work. It is an important problem in many enterprises. Excessive absenteeism involves a considerable loss to the enterprise because work schedules are upset and delayed, and management has to give overtime wages to meet the delivery dates. The rates of overtime wages are double than the normal rates of wages. Therefore, analysis of causes of absenteeism is essential to deal with the problem.

Absenteeism means absence which is avoidable and wilful. Unauthorised absence from regular duty is absenteeism. However, absence on account of strikes, lock-outs, etc. does not constitute absenteeism.

The rate of absenteeism is expressed as the percentage of mandays lost through absence to the total number of mandays scheduled in a given period.

$$\text{Absenteeism} = \frac{\text{Number of mandays lost through absence}}{\text{Number of mandays scheduled to work}} \times 100$$

The number of mandays scheduled to work is calculated by multiplying the average number of workers by the number of working days during the given period.

2. Laws of Absence Prone Behaviour

Absenteeism is a universal problem in industry. It disturbs the production schedules and creates many problems. Studies done by S.K. Bhatia and G.K. Valecha have further revealed some general guidelines of absence proneness:

(i) The days before and after a holiday are liable to higher rate of absenteeism.

(ii) Women are absent more often than men.

(iii) Absence increases with marital status and family responsibilities.

(iv) Absenteeism increases when workers have relatively poor relations with their immediate supervisor.

(v) Men on continuous work have more absence.

(vi) A small group around 10 percent of employees (chronic absentees) account for large percentage of absenteeism (70%).

(vii) The people who have a high absence record in their academic life continue to be absence prone in their working life. There tends to be a correlation in such cases.

(viii) Absenteeism is more an attitude of mind and attributing it to other factors has no meaning. It is entrenched in the psychology of an individual.

3. Causative Factors of Absenteeism

At the micro-plant level, the causative factors are summarised in Figure 4.

FIGURE 4

Model for Causative Factors of Absenteeism at Plant Level

(a) Managerial style: • Quality and style of supervision. • Selection, induction and placement. • Recognition, communication and morale. • Job satisfaction and challenges. • Wages and incentive. • Overtime. • Leave rules and procedures. • Role of Unions.	(c) Technological environment: • Conditions of work and hours of work. • Accidents. • Occupational diseases and medical care. • Recreational facilities. • Work group.
(b) Personal factors: • Marital harmony. • Family size and responsibility. • Work orientation, leisure orientation. • Bad habits. • Emotional health. • Community obligations. • Educational level. • Standard of living. • Transport. • Housing. • Indebtedness.	(d) External factors: • Level of unemployment. • Social, religious and cultural aspects. • Time of the year and day of the week. • Climatic and related conditions. • Recreational facilities (local). • Transport facilities (local). • Housing (local).

4. Adverse Effects of Absenteeism

Labour absenteeism is harmful to both the employers and the workers as follows:

(i) Normal work-flow in the factory is disturbed.
(ii) Overall production in the factory goes down.
(iii) Difficulty is faced in executing the orders in time.
(iv) Casual workers may have to be employed to meet production schedules. Such workers are not trained properly.
(v) Overtime allowance bill increases considerably because of higher absenteeism.
(vi) When a number of workers absent themselves, there is extra pressure of work on their colleagues who are present.
(vii) Workers lose wages for the unauthorised absence from work.
(viii) Habitual absentees are constant drain on the organisation.

5. Remedial Measures for Control of Absenteeism

Management has to understand what kind of absence is occurring and try to devise effective measures to reduce the same. A model for managing absenteeism at plant level is explained in Figure 5.

FIGURE 5

Model for Managing Absenteeism at Plant Level

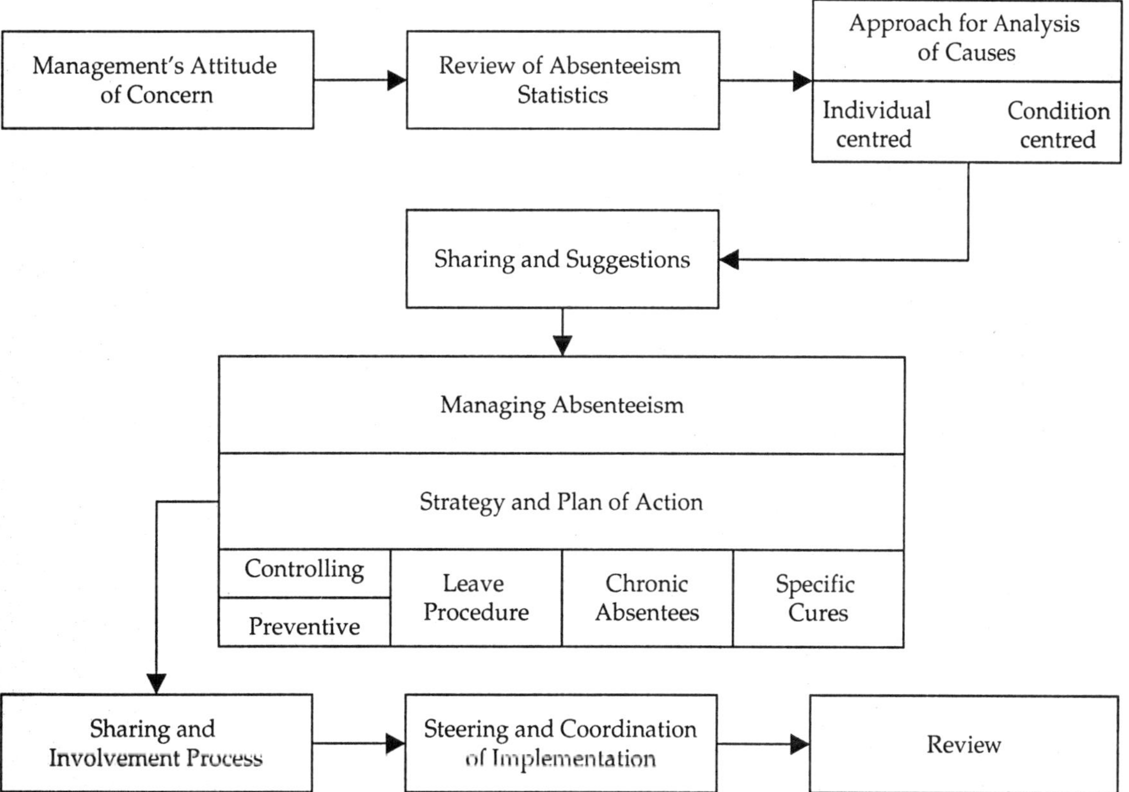

For effective control of absenteeism, the employees must necessarily be involved, as the real solution of the problem depends upon the joint acceptance of objectives by both parties, viz., the employees and management.

(i) Attitude of the Management

The attitude of the management towards absenteeism is of utmost importance. All too often, one senses an atmosphere of resigned despair which does nothing to improve matters. Such an attitude can contribute little towards dealing effectively with the problem of absenteeism. So commitment to absence control through the creation of a committee or department to coordinate programme for absence control.

(ii) A Strategy for Absence Control Programme

Formulation of an appropriate strategy and plan of action with time-bound objectives is necessary. The approach should be to maintain an improvement in controlling absence rate in contrast to a sudden and drastic clamp down. The emphasis is to be placed on reduction of discretionary and avoidable absences and also bringing about an improvement in procedural aspects of leave system. It is likely that the greatest scope for reducing absenteeism exists in reducing non-sickness absences. We have to recognise the need and value of long-term and ongoing programmes. These programmes should cover steps for control of absenteeism particularly relating to identified or identifiable problems and factors effecting absenteeism, through systematic analysis.

The efforts should be directed towards departments with high absence rates. Wherever absence is predominant, management action should be aimed towards alleviating the causes of it rather than towards symptomatic correction of the problem.

(iii) Establishing an Attendance Policy

It is essential to devise an employee attendance policy. Establishing clearly worded policy statement and making it known, as also periodically reminding employees about it, could reduce the number of absences caused by ignorance or misunderstanding of standards.

(iv) Rehabilitation of Chronic Absentees

Statistics show that employees fall into three groups with respect to absenteeism: (i) rarely or never absent, (ii) occasionally absent, and (iii) frequently absent. The latter account for the largest percentage of absence. The real problem rests with these apparently irresponsible absentees who take-off quite often, a day here and a day there. It is this group that must be studied to diagnose the reasons and determine possible specific cures. Rehabilitation of these persons and proper follow-up is imperative. Alcoholics also contribute to industrial absenteeism. A chronic alcoholic may feel that work itself is one of his problems and this interferes with his drinking, which is his only solace. The influence of alcoholics on the habits of other absentees is also deleterious. The importance of identifying alcoholics and providing help to them cannot be overstressed. Provision of professional counselling services in the organisation can help absence-prones in becoming self-directed, adjusted and changed for better.

Unions and management are to work together in dealing with chronically absent employees and in dealing with absenteeism in general. Disciplinary measures may be sometimes necessary in dealing with chronic absentees. Disciplinary action and discharge are effective weapons but cooperation and support of union is very necessary in this respect.

(v) Need for Supply of Adequate Statistics

Proper maintenance and supply of information on absenteeism to appropriate levels in the organisation is necessary as a control mechanism. A periodic statement, department-wise, of those who take leave frequently on loss of wages may be carefully scrutinised by the supervisors.

(vi) Supervisor has a Vital Role

Individual workers fail to turn up for work largely for their own individual reasons and the "cures" must be individual. In this direction, a supervisor can play an important role.

The supervisor is the key-man in absence control by ensuring proper working conditions, supervision, interpersonal relations and contributing towards providing necessary motivational factors on the job. It has to be impressed upon the new employees that unwarranted absences are regarded as a serious matter. All supervisors should be personally concerned with the absences in their sections and not abdicate their responsibility related to it. Punishment for unwarranted frequent absenteeism should exist.

It is important for the management to "humanise" jobs and make them more appealing and interesting and to create a cooperative atmosphere within the organisation. Modern management research related to studies on job rotation, job enrichment, group assignment and participative management indicate that these measures can contribute towards reduction of absenteeism.

(vii) Care in Selection and Placement

Absenteeism is also a matter of recruitment policy. These people who have a high absence record in their academic life may continue to be absence-prone in their working life. There may be a definite correlation in such cases. The only way to guard against this kind of persons is to carefully investigate school attendance record at the time of initial employment interview.

(viii) Preventive Health Programme

Sickness is probably the one major reason people give for absence. Ongoing health programmes can offer such preventive measures as vaccination and inoculation, TB & cancer detection, medical examination for employees returning to work after long and repeated illness, and making available complete medical check-up for all employees when they reach a certain age (say 50 years). Such programmes can definitely reduce time lost from work by preventing serious illness. These preventive health programmes are invaluable as an aid to morale of the employees and to their personal well-being; they can be regarded as indicative of management's concern for the employees.

(ix) Attendance Bonus Schemes

The Attendance Bonus scheme is one of the very common devices being introduced by several organisations for decreasing absenteeisms. However, this scheme does not involve any competition for getting the bonus. It only involves the mere physical presence of the individual. Under Indian conditions we may be able to ensure the presence of the employee but not commensurate productivity. Therefore, in order to introduce a healthy element of competition, the individual bonus system has been modified by some firms in the form of introduction of group bonus plans. Under this system there is a bonus guaranteed for the group which has the best production record. It has been observed that when such a scheme is introduced in a proper fashion, there is a concerted effort on the part of the group to pressurize the individuals specially those who have a tendency to be habitually absent to be regularly present because they need regular presence of all the members to attain best records. It has also been observed that when some employees still continue to remain habitually absent, the group takes steps in attempting to eliminate him, i.e. transfer him from their group to another group.

As another example of the use of positive incentive for coming to work there is a practice being followed quite commonly in the western world and, to some extent, in India of enabling the employees to accumulate sick leave over a period of years. This serves as an insurance or buffer available to the employee when he is rather advanced in age and when he may have greater need of utilising this leave; also there are provisions made for encashing the same on retirement just as we have encashment of earned leave.

(x) Absence Control Requires Sustained Efforts and Continuous Improvement in Techniques

There is no magic formula available to work as panacea for absenteeism in various organisations under different circumstances and conditions of work. None of the techniques of absence control can be guaranteed as effective in every situation. With so many factors affecting absence rates, it would be unrealistic to expect to find any one simple answer to the problem of industrial absenteeism. Success in keeping absenteeism under control will always require sustained efforts. Control of absenteeism can be exercised by continually trying to improve the combination of controlling and preventive measures. Any long-term programme should prove for change in the outlook, policy and approach to the problem.

(vii) Managing of Employee Turnover

Concept

Employee turnover means as "the rate of change in the working staff of a concern during a definite period." It means movements, shifting or migration of employees from one organisation to another. Upto a certain percentage, say 5% employee turnover is reasonable, but beyond this it becomes a serious problem, which requires investigation.

Employees turnover may be expressed as performance of employees left turning a specific period say one year out of the total employees.

$$\text{Employee Turnover (Separation) Rate} = \frac{\text{Number of Separations in a year}}{\text{Average Number of Employees in a year}} \times 100$$

A high rate of employee turnover is a warning to the management that something is wrong with the health of the organisation. However, employee turnover can merely give a warning. It cannot give reasons of the problem. A high rate of turnover is also an indicator of low morale. To control high rate of employee turnover, it is important to consider the causes for persons leaving.

High labour turnover is not desirable as it affects both managements and workers adversely. Both have to suffer in the following manner:

Effects on Managements

(i) As a result of higher rate of separations, management have to spend more time and money on advertisement, interviewing, selection, physical examination, preparation of service records and so on. This is expensive.

(ii) The expenditure incurred on the training of workers goes waste when workers leave their jobs after completing their training. Additional expenditure for training newly recruited workers in place of those who have left has to be incurred.

(iii) Delay in filling of vacancies results the smooth working of the production unit and also the quality of production. In addition, the overtime costs increase considerably.

(iv) The team spirit among the workers is disturbed due to high labour turnover as newly recruited workers need some time to develop friendly relations with the existing workers.

(v) High labour turnover leads to higher rate of industrial accidents as new or untrained workers are recruited very often.

(vi) The market reputation is adversely affected due to high labour turnover if orders are not executed in time.

Effects on Workers

(i) Due to changing of employment, a worker might have to sacrifice the benefits of his previous service. Such benefits include pension, provident fund, yearly increment, and so on.

(ii) A worker develops special skills and ability due to long and continuous service in an enterprise. These skills are his personal asset. However, these may become meaningless if the worker leaves the present job and joins a new one.

(iii) The worker may not be able to adjust on a new job in a new organisation. This might put tremendous mental pressure on him.

(iv) A worker who changes his job quite often may be looked upon by others (including employers) with suspicion.

(v) The work environments change when a worker shifts from one unit to another. He may find it difficult to adjust to the new environments.

Steps for Control of Labour Turnover

Remedial measures should be taken after ascertaining the exact reasons for leaving. Action should be taken to reduce the labour turnover which is avoidable. Other remedial measures involve the following:

(i) Improvement in recruitment policy and practices.

(ii) Use of proper tests and interviews while employing the personnel.

(iii) Provision of adequate training to the new as well as existing employees.

(iv) Introduction of security of service.

(v) Impartial promotion and transfer policies.

(vi) Introduction of a satisfactory wage policy.

(vii) Introduction of proper incentive system.

(viii) Provision of reasonable amenities and welfare measures.

(ix) Redressal of grievances and setting-up grievance machinery.

(x) Provision of social security benefits.

(xi) Augmenting communication with the employees to improve motivation and morale.

(viii) Managing Alienation at Work

Alienation refers to the detachment of the person from his work role. The concept of alienation at work is associated originally with the views of Marx. He saw the division of labour in pursuit of profit, and exploitation by employers, as a denial of the workers' need for self-expression. Workers became estranged from the product of their work. Work no longer provided a satisfying experience in itself, but represented a means to satisfying other external demands.

The concept of alienation was explained by Blauner. He described alienation in terms of four dimensions: powerlessness, meaninglessness, isolation and self-estrangement as stated below:

(i) Powerlessness

This denotes the workers' lack of control over management policy, immediate work processes, or conditions of employment.

(ii) Meaninglessness

It stems from standardisation and division of labour. It denotes the inability to see the purpose of work done, or to identify with the total production process or finished product.

(iii) Isolation

It means not becoming to an integrated work group or to the social work organisation, and not being guided by group norms of behaviour.

(iv) Self-Estrangement

It means failure to see work as an end itself or a central life issue. Workers feel depersonalised detachment, and work is seen solely as a means to an end. Blauner suggested that:

- (i) All *bureaucratic* organisations have inherent alienating tendencies and found most manual workers were alienated to some degree.
- (ii) The extent of alienation experienced is likely to be a function of the *nature of technology*:
  - (a) Assembly line technology was found to be most alienating.
  - (b) Machine minding and automated processess were in the middle.
  - (c) Craft technology was the least alienating.
  - (d) Workers in jobs involving a high degree of mass production lead to work stress and workers dislike it.

(ix) Providing Good Working Environment

It is essential to ensure favourable working conditions so that the workers can perform their tasks without experiencing physical or mental strain. Productivity can be increased simply by improving the working conditions. Bad or unfavourable working conditions mean loss of time, waste of materials and loss of output. Some of the conditions surrounding a worker as he does his job and affecting his physical well-being and thus his efficiency, are as under:

(i) Cleanliness

It is essential for health. Dirt should be removed daily from all rooms, passages and staircases.

(ii) Lighting

Good lighting can facilitate higher production. It is essential to the health, safety and efficiency of workers. Without proper lighting, eye damage will occur, accidents and spoilage of material will increase and production will slow down. The efficiency of light depends on both its quantity and quality. Factors determining quality of light include glare, uniformity of distribution and brightness. A good system of lighting should provide: (i) the right degree of intensity of light according to the job to be done; (ii) the light is well diffused and is spread uniformly over all parts of the workplace; and (iii) protection from any glare, either directly or indirectly.

(iii) Temperature and Ventilation

The employees must be provided tolerable temperature if they are to work efficiently. Their efficiency is bound to suffer if the temperature of the workplace is either too low or too high. Steps should be taken to ensure flow of fresh air having right temperature and humidity. Coolers can be used during the summer; and heaters can be used during the winter.

Air-conditioning may be used to regulate and control: (i) circulation, (ii) temperature, (iii) humidity, and (iv) purity of air.

(iv) Freedom from Noise

It has an adverse impact on the minds of employees tells upon their efficiency. It is a source of disturbance to the employees and does not allow them to work with concentration. Therefore, it is essential to keep noise under control. For general absorption of noise, sound absorbent materials may be used for four walls and ceilings. Machines producing noise may be installed in a separate shed and carpets may be spread on the floors to reduce noise caused by movement of the employees.

(v) Dust

It affects the health of the employees adversely. Dust also reduces the life of various machines and equipments. Therefore, it is essential to check the entry of dust into the factory premises. Dust should be cleaned quite regularly because it not only pollutes the environment but also has an adverse impact on the intensity of light. Big offices install air-conditioning systems which help in checking entry to dust into the office to a great extent.

(x) Vocational Guidance

In big concerns, vocational guidance programme is a part of the selection process. It is of utmost importance that the right man is selected for the right job. According to Dale Yoder, "Vocational guidance refers to the inevitable direction given to the case of new employees in the selection process and in their assignment to particular type of work." If the young person is not guided properly, he may choose a wrong occupation and feel dissatisfied after that. Thus, the role of vocational guidance is very important in the modern industrialised society.

Vocational guidance by an organisation leads to the following benefits:

(i) The candidate will have job satisfaction if the job really suits his temperament, aptitude and interest.

(ii) Since the employee is satisfied with his job, his *productivity* will increase.

(iii) Properly placed employees will be *less prone* to absenteeism. Moreover, labour turnover in the organisation will be reduced.

(iv) The employees will be *self-motivated* because of job satisfaction. Their morale will also be high which will lead to better human relations in the enterprise.

(xi) Job Satisfaction Improvement Programmes

Concept of Job Satisfaction

In the words of Feldman and Arnold, "Job satisfaction is the amount of overall positive effect or feelings that individuals have towards their jobs."

According to Andrew, J. DuBrins, "Job satisfaction is the amount of pleasure or contentment associated with a job. If you like your job intensely, you will experience high job satisfaction. If you dislike your job intensely, you will experience job dissatisfaction." Job satisfaction is an individual's emotional reaction to the job itself. It is his attitude towards his job.

Factors Affecting Job Satisfaction

The level of job satisfaction is affected by a wide range of variables relating to individual, social, cultural, organizational and environmental factors as stated below:

(i) Individual Factors

Personality, education, intelligence and abilities, age, marital status, orientation to work.

(ii) Social Factors

Relationships with co-workers, group working and norms, opportunities for interaction, informal relations, etc.

(iii) Cultural Factors

Attitudes, beliefs and values.

(iv) Organisational Factor

Nature and size, formal structure, personnel policies and procedures, industrial relations, nature of work, technology and work organisation, supervision and styles of leadership, management systems and working conditions.

(v) Environmental Factors

Economic, social, technical and governmental influences.

These factors affect job satisfaction of certain individuals in a given set of circumstances but not necessarily in others. Some workers may be satisfied with certain aspects of their work and dissatisfied with other aspects. Thus, overall degree of job satisfaction may differ from person to person.

Job Satisfaction and Productivity or Work Performance

(a) The old view that *'a happy worker is a productive worker'* does not clarify the complex relationship between job satisfaction and productivity. It was traditionally said that high job satisfaction leads to improved productivity, decreased turnover, reduced accidents and less job stress in the long-run. But the relationship between job satisfaction and productivity is not definitely established.

The content theories of motivation assume a direct relationship between job satisfaction and improved performance. The expectancy theories of motivation, however, recognise the complexity of work motivation and consider in detail the relationship between motivation, satisfaction and performance.

(b) Job satisfaction does not necessarily lead to improved work performance. For example, from the results of twenty studies, Vroom found no simple relationship, and only a low median correlation (0.14) between job satisfaction and job performance.

Porter and Lawler found that job performance leads to job satisfaction and not the other way round. They argued that performance leads to two kinds of rewards—intrinsic and extrinsic. The intrinsic rewards such as growth, challenging job, etc. stem from the job itself and extrinsic rewards are under the control of management such as salary, bonus, etc. Intrinsic rewards are more closely related to satisfaction. For instance, if a person performs well on a challenging assignment, he gets an immediate feeling of satisfaction.

(c) Argyle suggested a probable relationship between satisfaction and productivity for highly skilled workers, or for those workers involved deeply with their work. However, individual differences cloud the position. The 'average' workers do work hard when satisfied. But some workers may work hard in order to forget their lack of contentment, and other workers are more content when their work requires modest or little effort as shown in Figure 6.

Thus, the relationship between job satisfaction and performance is an issue of continuing debate and controversy. However, three distinct points of view have emerged. According to Fred Luthans:

(i) Satisfaction leads to performance, a view associated with the early human relations approach.
(ii) The relationship between satisfaction and performance is moderated by a number of variables, a view which is reflected in research studies.
(iii) A more recent view that performance leads to satisfaction.

Steps to Improve Job Satisfaction

Several elements contribute to job satisfaction. These are discussed as under:

(i) Aptitude for the Job

Job satisfaction is related to the aptitude of the employee. If the employee is given a work for which he has no aptitude, the job will provide no attraction to him. Hence, the question of contribution, creativity or motivation does not arise. It is for the management to design jobs in such a manner that each worker gets the job of his own choice.

(ii) Style of Supervision

The employee-centred supervisory style enhances job satisfaction as the leader looks after subordinates carefully, displays friendship, respect and warmth, etc. towards them.

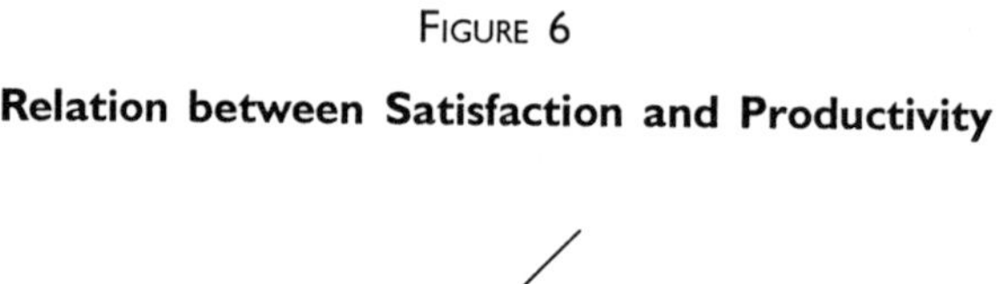

FIGURE 6

Relation between Satisfaction and Productivity

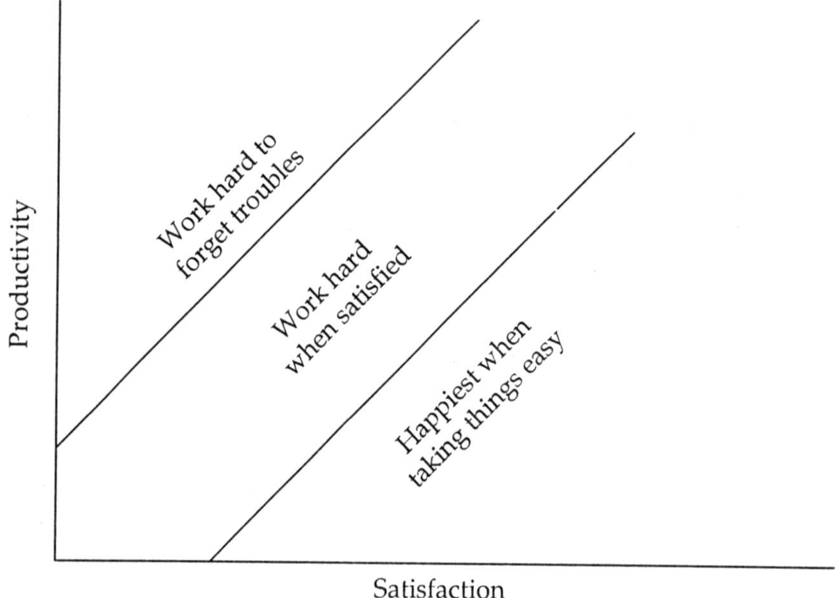

(iii) Congenial Working Environment

Job satisfaction is related to working conditions also. The work will be more attractive if working conditions are congenial to the task a worker proposes to accomplish. Good working conditions involve such facilities as adequate light, comfortable temperature, attractive surroundings, etc.

(iv) Financial Rewards

Monitory rewards play a significant role in influencing job satisfaction. This is because of two reasons. First, money is an important instrument in fulfilling one's needs; and secondly, employees often see pay as a reflection of management's concern for them. Employees want a wage pay system which is simple, fair, and in line with their expectations. When pay is seen as fair, based on job demands, individual skill level, and community pay standards, satisfaction is likely to result. What needs emphasis is that it is not the absolute amount paid that matters, rather it is one's perception of fairness.

(v) Opportunities for Advancement in Career

Promotional opportunities affect job satisfaction considerably. The desire for promotion is generally strong among higher level employees as it involves change in job content, pay, responsibility, autonomy, status and the like. It is no surprise that the employee takes promotion as the ultimate achievement in his career and when it is realised, he feels extremely satisfied.

(vi) Cooperative Work Group

It is the work-group that fulfils the need for social interaction of the members. If the worker has good relations with the fellow employees and the supervisor, he will feel satisfied. If the work-group enjoys a higher status, his job satisfaction will increase further.

(vii) Employee Morale

If the employee morale in an organisation is higher, satisfaction with job is likely to be higher and *vice-versa*. The workers will be loyal to the organisation if their morale is higher. The rates of absenteeism and labour turnover will also be low because of psychological satisfaction from the job.

(xii) Employee Counselling

Meaning of Counselling

Keith Davis has defined counselling as *'discussion of an emotional problem with an employee with the general objective of decreasing it.'* The implications of this definition are as under:

(a) Counselling Involves Discussion or Communication

Successful counselling depends upon communication skills of the counsellor to share the emotions of the depressed person.

(b) Counselling is Concerned with Emotional Problem or Disorder

It has no concern with other problems like technical, methodological, job inconvenience or occupational. But any emotional problem will require *'counselling'*. The main purpose of counselling is to understand and check an employee's emotional disorder.

(c) Objective is to Reduce the Emotional Problem

The origin of counselling can be traced back to the work of Freud. Freud's method of psycho-analysis dominated the field of psychotherapy for half a century which emphasised the relationship between the therapist and the client (or doctor and patient). Carl Rogers appeared a little later on the scene and worked extensively towards understanding counselling process. He was a pioneer in advocating the counselling method and showed that a constructive approach to the patient brings about a change in personality. He advocated a strong relationship between the client and the counsellor by developing and expressing attitudes of congruence, acceptance and empathy.

Functions of Counselling

The general objective of counselling is to help the employee in dealing with their emotional problems so that they can work well for the accomplishment of common goals and gain self-confidence, self-control, understanding and ability to work effectively. This objective can be achieved through performance of the following counselling functions:

(i) Reassurance

Reassurance is a way of giving courage to a worker to face a problem or to pose a confidence in himself that he is following the right path. Sometimes, supervisors are heard saying, *'Well, you are making good progress'* or *'don't worry, go ahead'* or *'You are right'*. These are all reassurances.

(ii) Release of Tension

One of the important functions of counselling is to release the employee's emotional tension. It is also called *'emotional catharsis'*. People tend to get an emotional release from their frustration and all other problems as soon as they tell these to some sympathetic listener. They feel relaxed. The release of tension does not necessarily solve the problems, but it removes mental blockade and gives courage to the individual to face the problem boldly and think constructively.

(iii) Reorientation

Reorientation involves a change in the employee's psychic self through change in basic goals and values.

(iv) Clarified Thinking

Facilitation of realistic thinking is also an important function of counselling. Counselling encourages clarified thinking because mental blocks are cleared and the counsel is made to think rationally.

Thus, counselling through the above noted functions improves the organisational climate by solving the emotional problems of the workers in the organisation.

Why Need for Counselling?

Counselling may be required in any situation, both on-the-job and off-the-job. The need for counselling is required because of the following factors:

1. Conflict

Emotional disorder may be caused by interpersonal and inter-group conflicts. The conflicts are due to different backgrounds, points of view, values, needs and personality of the fellow men or due to organisational change. Thus, conflicts are inevitable in an organisation, sometimes substantial. Counselling assists conflict resolution by reducing emotional blockages.

2. Frustration

Frustration is the result of motivation drive being blocked to prevent one from reaching a desired goal. For example, a worker while on work is interrupted time and again and his goal for the day remains unfulfilled, he will feel irritated and frustrated. The situation becomes more serious when it is long-run frustration such as blocked opportunity for promotion. Reaction to frustration such as irritation, uneasy feeling or some other reactions are known as defence mechanism. Reactions of frustrated behaviour are aggression, apathy, withdrawal, resignation, fixation, physical disorders, substitute goals and compromise. These reactions are in no way favourable to the individual or the organisation; so it is desirable to reduce the frustrating conditions in the organisation.

3. Stress

Stress is a condition of strain on one's emotions, thought processes and/or physical conditions that seem to threaten one's ability to cope with environment. Excessive stress or stress over a long period of time may result in physical and emotional disorders and lowered effectiveness. Stress is also affected by the tolerance power of the person concerned.

Stress may be on-the-job and off-the-job. The main causes of stress on- the-job are job itself (work overload, pressure of work, tension and insecurity), role conflicts and role ambiguity, conflicts with people (mainly when it is with the supervisor or any other authority), etc. Off-the-job stress may be caused by family and financial problems.

Stress is a major contributor to emotional disorder of employees. It leads to physical disorder such as stomach disorder, bodyache or headache and much permanent disorder. Counselling is necessary to disperse the emotional disorders caused by stress.

Counselling System in Organisations

(i) Manager's Role in Performance Review Counselling

It requires manager to allow participation of subordinate in performance review discussions and goal-setting process. This has almost become a part of performance appraisal system in the organisations.

(ii) Supervisor to Help Employees

In guidance and coaching on-the-job, assisting them in their efforts to grow and develop, improve their interpersonal relations at work. He can also help in dealing personal problems of employees such as alcoholism, indebtedness, family relations, children vocational guidance, etc.

(iii) Human resource department can also organise counselling through experts to help employees on various aspects:

(a) To gain knowledge about his *potential,* strengths and weaknesses, career opportunities and guidance. Emphathetic atmosphere can enable him to freely discuss and share his views with counsellor. He can seek guidance for improving performance, etc.

(b) To release *emotional tension* and feel relaxed.

(c) To obtain feedback and gain an insight into his *behaviour* for developing better inter-personal relationships.

(d) To seek help on personal problems such as family disharmony, children problems, indebtedness, alcoholism, absenteeism, etc. Counsellor provides emphathetic listening support which helps individuals to find solutions to the problems.

References

Bhatia, S.K., Management of Absenteeism, Asian Publication Services, New Delhi, 1981.

Bhatia, S.K. and Valecha, G.K., Absenteeism—An Industrial Malady, An Empirical Study of Factors Associated with it, Integrated Management, Bangalore, 1978.

Filippo, Edwin B., Principles of Personnel Management, McGraw-Hill, New York, 1989.

Blauner, R., Alienation and Freedom, University of Chicago Press, 1964.

Chhabra, T.N., Human Resource Management, Dhanpat Rai & Co. (P) Ltd., Delhi.

Feldman, D.C. and Arnold, H.J., Managing Individual and Group Behaviour in Organisations, McGraw-Hill, New York, 1983.

Andrew, J. Dubrins, The Practice of Supervision, Universal Bookstall, New Delhi.

Vroom, Victor H., Work and Motivation, Wiley, New York, 1964.

Porter, L.W. and Lawler, E.E., Management Attitudes and Performance, Richard D. Irwin Inc., Homewood, Ill., 1968.

Argyle, M., The Social Psychology of Work, Penguin, Oxford, 1974, pp. 238-39.

Luthans, Fred, Organisational Behaviour, McGraw-Hill, New York, 1989.

21

Wage Policy

R.S. Dwivedi (Human Resource Management, Galgotia Publishing Company) has highlighted that "wage policy forms a highly sensitive and complex dimension of labour policy in view of a widespread impact of wages on the status of workers, their commitment to industry and their level of motivation, morale and productivity and standard of living. It is not merely an economic phenomenon but also a social issue which is of interest to consumers, the state and the society as a whole."

Immediately after independence in view of the industrial unrest, the Industrial Truce Resolution, 1947 was adopted. Then Industrial Policy Resolution, 1948 was evolved. It stressed:

(i) Fixation of statutory minimum wages in sweated industries, and
(ii) Promotion of fair wage agreements in the more organised industries.

I. THE CONCEPT OF MINIMUM WAGE

- The Minimum Wages Act, 1948 does not define minimum wage.
- Definition of *minimum, fair* and *living* wages is given by Fair Wages Committee, 1948 which consisted of representatives of the government, employers and worker's organisations.

(a) The Concept of Minimum Wages

The committee asserts that:

(i) Minimum wage must not merely provide for *bare subsistence* of life, but for the preservation of the *efficiency* of worker.
(ii) It must provide for education, medical and amenities.
(iii) Providc for risc in cost of living index.
(iv) Employer cannot plead inability to pay minimum wage.

(v) There is to be paid weekly off after 6 days of working.
(vi) Payment of over time beyond 48 hours per week.

The Concept of need-based minimum wage (laid by 15th Session of Indian Labour Conference, 1957) certain norms were laid to ensure minimum human needs.

1. Working *class family* to comprise of three consumption units for one earner.
2. *Minimum food* requirements to be calculated on the intake of 2700 calories for an average adult.
3. *Clothing* requirements are to be based on 18 yards per annum per person, 72 yards per annum for four members.
4. *Rent* as charged by the central government.
5. Fuel, lighting and other basic items to be calculated as 20% of total minimum wage.

(b) The Concept of Fair Wage

For fair wage *lower limit* is the minimum wage; and the *upper limit* is set by the *capacity* of industry to pay.

Between the two, actual wage will depend on following factors:

(a) Productivity of labour,
(b) Prevailing rates of wages in similar occupation in the same or neighbouring localities,
(c) Place of industry in the economy, and
(d) National income and its distribution.

It is a standard adopted by the government for Wage Boards.

(c) The Concept of Living Wage

It should enable the male earner to provide for *himself and his family* not merely the bare *essentials of food, clothing and shelter,* but a measure of *frugal comfort;* including *education* for his children; protection against *ill health;* requirements of *essential social* needs; and a measure of *insurance* against the misfortunes including old-age.

The Constitution of India adopted in November 1949 stressed the "living wage" as the aspiration and included in the *Directive Principles* of State Policy of the Constitution.

2. FIVE YEAR PLANS AND WAGE POLICY

The First Plan (1951 to 1956) suggested that pre-war levels of real wages should be restored as a first step towards "living wage" through increased productivity. It further suggested various measures for making wage adjustments. These measures included: reduction of disparities in income, reduction of gap between the existing and living wages, standardisation and maintenance of wage differentials to provide incentives.

The Second Plan (1956 to 1961) stressed improvement in wages through increased productivity stemming from efficiency on the part of the workers, improved layout of plants and improvement in management practices. It suggested a wide application of the system of payment by results with due safeguards such as protection against fatigue and undue speed-up. Specifically, the plan recommended settlement of industry-wise wage disputes through tripartite wage boards. Significant development during this period relates to the recommendation of the fifteenth Indian Labour Conference with respect to the need-based minimum wage. Another major development was the report of the Second Pay Commission for central government employees. The concept of need-based minimum wage generated public controversy.

The Third Plan (1961 to 1966) reinforced the wage policy of the preceeding two plans with respect to minimum wage fixation, reduction of disparities and wage differentials and stressed the role of productivity in raising the living standard of workers.

The Fourth Plan (1969 to 1974) did not provide a fresh direction or any shift of the government's wage policy.

The Fifth Plan (1974 to 1979) recommended that the reward structure of the industrial employees in terms of wage and non-wage benefits must be related to performance records in industrial enterprises. The plan suggested that it was necessary to build up over a period of time a national wage structure to narrow down disparities within the organised sector itself, including both public and private sectors. Committee on Wage Policy released its report at the end of 1975. The report relates to the problems of wage policy in the organised sector of the economy including the government sector. The committee felt that the objectives of a wage policy cannot be accomplished if wage fixation is left to the forces in the labour market. According to the committee, the objectives of wage policy include provision of minimum wages not below the poverty line to ensure health and efficiency of workers, distribution of due share in the fruits of growth, rationalisation of wage differentials and minimisation of disparities, removal of unjustified wage differentials between the organised and the unorganised sector, provision of compensation for health and life hazards and other disadvantages, provision of compensation for rising cost of living, provision of incentives for productivity and skills, reduction of wage disputes, removal of malpractices in wage payments, etc.

The Sixth Plan (1980 to 1985) pointed out that there were marked disparities with respect to wages between the organised and unorganised and urban and rural sectors. Specifically, it observed that wage levels in the organised sector varied not only between regions and industries but among even units in the same industry. These levels were related neither to the nature of occupations nor to the level of skills. The anomalies and disparities have resulted in social tensions and industrial unrest. Therefore, the plan stressed the need for bringing about a greater rationalisation of wage structure and linking of wages at least in some measure to labour productivity. The plan also realised an urgent need to generate a climate conducive to modernisation in industry, and adoption of new techniques which help in increased productivity without being detrimental to employment.

The Seventh Plan (1985 to 1990) asserted that an important aspect of labour policy related to the formulation of an appropriate wage policy. The basic objectives of the wage policy as visualised by the plan were a rise in the levels of real income in consonance with increases in productivity, promotion and productive employment improvement in skills, sectoral shifts in the desired directions and reduction in disparities.

The Eighth Plan (1992 to 1997) laid focus on formulation of wage policy relating to child labour, bonded labour, rural labour, women labour and inter-state migrant labour.

The new wage policy for public enterprises should generate their own resources to meet wage revision and enhanced liabilities.

22

International Labour Organisation (ILO)

I. BACKGROUND OF ILO

International Labour Organisation (ILO) was formed on 19th April, 1919, as a result of peace conference at the end of World War I, it has continued first under the League of Nations and now under the United Nations Organisation (UNO) as labour wing.

2. OBJECTIVES OF ILO

1. To achieve full *employment* to raise standard of living.
2. To provide facilities *for training* to member-countries.
3. To formulate *policies* in regard to minimum wages, bonus, etc.
4. To get recognition of the *right of collective bargaining* for member-countries and improvement of productivity, collaboration of workers and employers.
5. To extend *social security* measures and protect the health of workers.
6. To provide *child welfare and maternity protection.*
7. To assure *equality* of educational and vocational opportunity.

3. ILO ORGANISATION SET-UP

ILO headquarters are at Geneva.

(a) Director General is Head of ILO.
(b) It has governing body which is tripartite of 56 members as under:
  - 20 members represent governments.
  - 14 members employers.
  - 14 members workers.

  Members are for a period of three years term.

(c) An International Labour Conference is held every year and it has tripartite representation from each member-country (i.e. government, labour unions and employers' representatives).
(d) ILO has regional headquarters to concentrate on area-wise labour issues/problems.
(e) ILO's role is to formulate international labour standards:
   - To fix contribution by member-state.
   - To select members of ILO governing body every three years.
   - To elect its president.

4. FUNCTIONS OF ILO

Some important functions of ILO are as under:

1. To pass *conventions* and make recommendations on labour matters. Also to formulate international labour codes.
2. To render expert *advice* to member-countries to make plans for improving labour conditions.
3. To carry research studies on labour problems. To set-up institutes of labour studies.
4. To arrange training on solving labour problems.
5. To organise regional conferences.
6. Promotion of collective bargaining (CB) in member-countries which occupies an important place in ILO's mandate.

India has ratified about 25% of the ILO conventions. ILO has helped India in:

- To implement scheme of training within industry (TWI) in early 1960's.
- Apprenticeship training scheme.
- Improving productivity in cotton mills and engineering industry in West Bengal in 1960's.
- Development of cottage industries.

5. INTERNATIONAL LABOUR STANDARDS

(a) Major concern of trade unions has been to focus on accepting certain standards like freedom of association, abolition of forced labour, discrimination between sexes, and child labour. ILO conventions ratified by Government of India are 38 as per list in Annexure I. (at the end)
(b) An area influencing MNC labour practices contained in *codes of conduct* on IR issued by ILO.
(c) Another is *social charter*, a non-binding statement of intent by European Union (EU) headquarters. Although codes and charter are voluntary, they may signal future transnational regulations of MNC's activities.
(d) Trade union have been anxious to get interpretations of the guidelines and make them legally enforceable.
(e) ILO guiding principles on CB are given in Annexure II. (at the end)
(f) Indian MNCs are now participating in the global compact principles of the United Nations. Bharat Heavy Electricals Ltd. is participating in this. See Annexure III. (at the end)

Theoretical Framework of Industrial Relations

Following theories/approaches are there in industrial relations all examined here:

(a) Approaches in industrial relations perspectives
(b) The system model of national industrial relations
(c) A modified version of the industrial relations system model
(d) Different perspectives in industrial relations
(e) Industrial relations strategy
(f) Contexual and constitutional framework in industrial relations in India

(A) APPROACHES IN INDUSTRIAL RELATIONS PERSPECTIVES

1. Environmental or External Theories or System Model

This approach is developed by economists. This is 'systems' approach developed by John Dunlop. He views industrial relations system as a sub-system of society. According to Dunlop, the core elements of the systems model of industrial relations are actors, *certain contexts, an ideology which binds* the industrial relations system together and body of rules created to govern the actors at the workplace. (see Figure 1)

2. Internalists or Implant Theories

These theories were contributed by behavioural scientists who were concerned with the patterns of human behaviour at work situations.

(i) Human Relations School represented by E. Mayo during 1927-32 which conducted Hawthorne studies in Western Electric Co., USA. The central argument of human relations school is that key to worker morale, high productivity and industrial peace lies in the *quality of human relations* in industry.

FIGURE 1

Dunlop's System of Model of National Industrial Relations

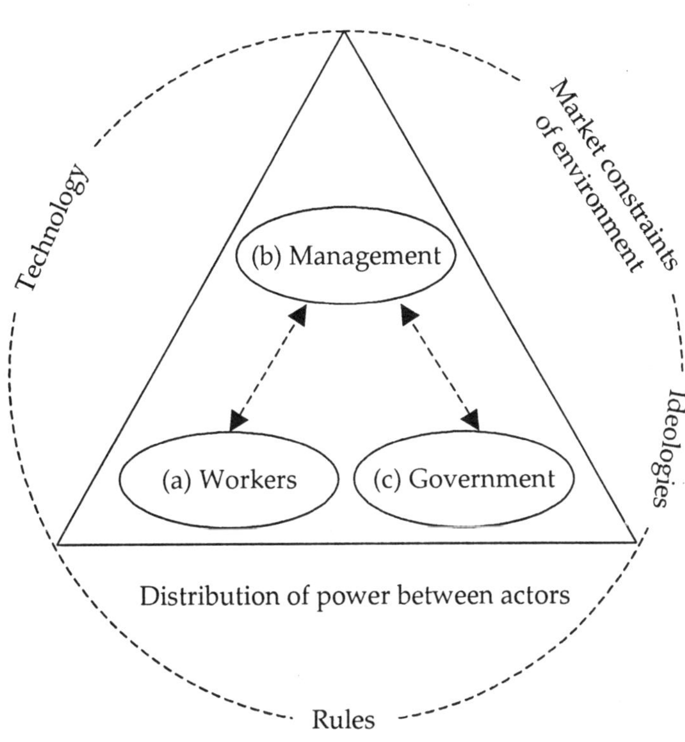

(ii) Behaviour School. According to this school worker's degree of attachment to work and their morale are closely linked with *fulfulment of the basic motives* of *security* and *participation.*

The conflict between workers and managers is caused by *lack of understanding* of interpersonal factors such as personality differences and irrational behaviour arising out of frustration and poor communication.

Effective communication would help the parties to develop accurate perceptions and understand each other's needs—such as safety and social needs (Maslow) even though their physiological needs are met.

McGregor also mentioned that employees should get opportunities at work to satisfy higher level needs, otherwise their behaviour will be affected. D. McGregor has developed the principle of integration in respect of participative management whereby individual workers can achieve their goals by directing their efforts to the success of the organisation.

According to behaviour scientists, the issues in industrial relations have their origin in the *differences in the perceptions* of management, unions and workers. The differences arise due to personalities and attitudes. Similarly, factors like motivation, leadership, group goals *v.* individual goals, etc. are responsible for industrial conflicts.

3. The Pluralist Approach

Flanders (1970) is yet another industrial relations theorist who evolved his Pluralist approach to union-management relations. In this *approach job regulation through collective bargaining* becomes a major preoccupation. The entire thrust of this approach is oriented to the containment of conflict through institutionalisation and regulation of the structure and process of union-management relations. Fox made a distinction between unitary and pluralist concepts of industrial organisations, the former recognising only one source of legitimate authority whereas the latter concept accepts the reality of several interest groups invested with power. Fox, however, recognised an unequal distribution of power within and without the enterprise because unlike the pluralist, the radical does not see collective organisation of employees into trade unions as resorting a balance of power.

4. Weber's Social Action Approach

Weber's approach gives importance to "control" work organisation—a *power struggle* in which all actors in the industrial relations are caught up. The orientation of approach is to analyse the impact of techno-economic and socio-political changes on various actors and also to analyse the power of various components of the industrial relations environment—government, employees, trade unions and political parties.

5. Gandhian Approach to Industrial Relations

M.K. Gandhi advocated trusteeship, i.e. peaceful coexistence of capital and labour. Trusteeship implies cooperation between capital and labour. He advocated the following rules to resolve industrial conflicts:

(i) Workers should seek redressal of demands through collective bargaining.
(ii) Strikes to be avoided and only resorted to as last measure and non-violent methods to be used.
(iii) Workers should take recourse to voluntary arbitration where direct settlement fails. (See also Mahatma Gandhi's views on Industrial Relations in Annexures)

(B) JOHN DUNLOP (1958)—THE SYSTEM MODEL OF NATIONAL INDUSTRIAL RELATIONS (IR)

The core of this framework is that industrial relations can be viewed as a system or sub-system of society; just as we speak of political or economic sub-systems.

In Dunlop's view, the system of industrial relations consists of four basic components:

(1) Actors or parties;
(2) The rules;
(3) An ideology; and
(4) An environmental context.

(1) The Actors

The actors are:

(a) Employees and their organisations (Trade unions);
(b) Employer's and their associations (Chambers); and
(c) The government.

(2) An Environment

These three actors *maintain relations with one another* within an environment made up of three tightly inter-woven contexts:

(a) the *technological features of work situation* (technological context),
(b) the market *opportunities or limitations* (the economic context), and
(c) the relative *distribution of power* between the actors (the political context).

These *contexts should be understood as dynamic forces* which bring about constant change in the relationships and the results of the interactions between the actors.

(3) The Rules

The most important objects of study in industrial relation are the rules, which are in effect the product of mutual cooperation and opposition between the actors. These rules are substantive and procedural in nature. *Substantive rules* are the *requirements* and conditions for the application of labour, whereas *procedural rules* involve the way in which the parties actually arrive at and formulate these rules.

(4) An Ideology

The system is complemented by an ideology which binds the separate actors to one another. This is a set of ideas and beliefs commonly held by the actors that helps to bind or integrate the system as an entity.

Each of the actors have its own ideology, but if no form of consensus exists between them, there cannot be a stable system or industrial relations.

Dunlop did not *design this framework* for international industrial relations. According to Dunlop, this model is to describe national system of industrial relations. In this, the sources of power and rules are situated within national framework whereas in multinational enterprise decision-making is no longer tied to borders of national system.

(C) A MODIFIED VERSION OF THE INDUSTRIAL RELATIONS SYSTEM MODEL

A number of authors have recommended changes to Dunlop's initial framework. Craig (1967) took the model out of structural terms and represented it in a more conventional systems approach with the use of an input-output framework. Research within each of the perspectives discussed has also suggested modifications or helped to identify key linkages between different components of the model. John C. Anderson, Morley Gunduson and Allen Ponak in their book, Union Management Relations in Canada, Addison Wesby Publishers have modified the industrial relations system approach on the basis of continuing developments in the study and practice of industrial relations. After discussing these modifications, the authors present the relationship between their approach and the various perspectives on industrial relations.

Figure 2 presents author's modified and updated version of the industrial relations systems framework. It has a number of advantages over Dunlop's original version. First, it *recognizes a wide range of inputs* to industrial relations beyond the market, technological, and power contexts of the system. Industrial relations is not viewed as an isolated sub-system; rather, the identification of inputs stresses the direct importance of the economic, legal, political, and socio-cultural systems in shaping the actors, their interactions, and the outputs of the system.

FIGURE 2

A Modified Version of the Industrial Relations System

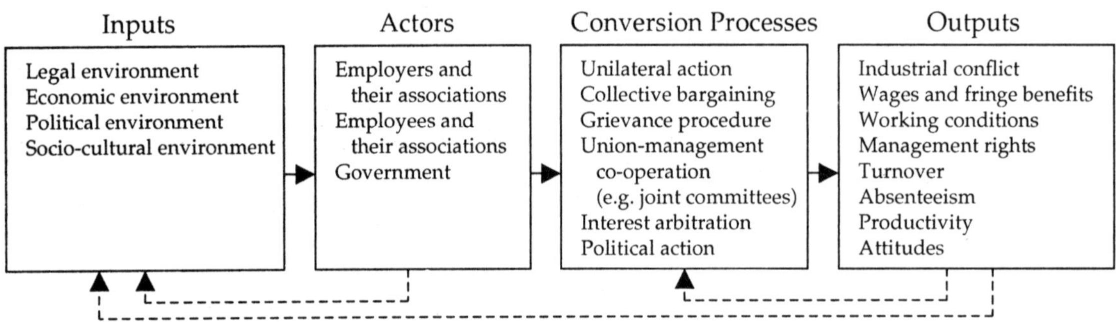

Second, the modified framework also recognizes that the *determination of the outputs of the system*, including the web of rules, may result from unilateral action on the part of any of the actors, or from bilateral action (as in bargaining, grievance processing, labour-management co-operative mechanisms, day-to-day decisions at the workplace, interest arbitration, or political action by management or the union), or from tripartite involvement on some issues. As a result, it is vital to conceptualize the industrial relations system as operating on several levels of society with the web of rules being shaped at the firm, industry, sector, and societal level. Moreover, outputs produced at one level inevitably influence those produced at another.

Third, by distinguishing more clearly between *procedural rules (conversion mechanisms)* and *substantive rules (outputs)*, the framework demands a recognition that the web of rules includes not only wages, benefits, and working conditions, but also all the other outputs of the conversion mechanisms. Such outputs may include changes in legislation, productivity, industrial conflict, industrial accidents, turnover, absenteeism, and employee attitudes.

Finally, the framework reveals that it is important to see the *system as dynamic, rather than static*. That is, outputs at one level (individual, firm, industry, sector or society) or in one time period are likely to become inputs for another level or for another time period. For example, political action that succeeds in effecting a change in collective bargaining legislation (output) will produce a change in the legal environment (an input) from that time forward. Thus, many of the environmental conditions examined as constraints in a static view of the industrial relations system may, in fact, be seen as under the partial control of the actors when a dynamic perspective is adopted.

Although the above conceptual framework addresses some of the criticisms of the industrial relations systems model, it does not solve all of them. Most important, it does not provide directly testable hypotheses. Each of the sets of conceptual variables—*inputs, actors, conversion mechanisms, outputs*—contains a vast number of dimensions that can be identified, measured, and related to variables within the same conceptual set or with variables in other sets.

The conceptual framework indicates a series of sequential relationships, starting with *inputs* and moving through *actors* and *conversion processes* to *outputs*. In reality, however, theory and empirical research exist to indicate that the characteristics of the inputs and actors may have direct effects on the conversion mechanisms and outputs of the system as well as the indirect ones included in the framework (as indicated by the dotted lines in Figure 23.1). Therefore, in thinking about the industrial relations system, it is important to consider the way in which its components interact to shape the outputs.

(D) PERSPECTIVES IN INDUSTRIAL RELATIONS

Industrial relations is associated with regulating of activity of employment. Two terms industrial relations (IR) and employee relations are interchangeably used. While industrial relations is traditional term reflects *unionised* manual workers within manufacturing sector. The other term employee relations is used for *less unionised* white collar employment in service and commercial sectors. The term employee relations is used mostly by the American literature and industrial relations is in United Kingdom and India.

Three different perspectives into industrial relations are:

(i) Unitary perspectives

It legitimises the interests of management and employees as being same and emphasises *management's role of governing in the best interests of the organisations,* as a whole.

(ii) Pluralistic perspective

It refers to separation of ownership and workers and acceptance of conflict in both spheres. It considers role of trade unions is legitimate and resolution of conflict is through compromise and agreement.

(iii) Radical Marxist perspective

This highlights *class conflict* without which society will stagnate. It is between those who own capital and those who supply their labour. There is imbalance and inequities in economy. Conflicts can be resolved by changing society, so trade unions should develop political awareness and activity.

(E) INDUSTRIAL RELATIONS STRATEGY

Industrial relations strategy refer to that industrial relations activities should contribute to overall *industrial goals* such as *productivity, labour peace* and *industrial democracy. Some areas of focus in industrial strategy are as under:*

(i) Optimising the interests of the employer and those of employees in fields such as:
- Wage and salary administration, retirement and medical benefits, workers' compensation issues.
- Career prospects, training and development.
- Discipline and redress of grievances and counselling.

(ii) *Labour management relations* to be based on trade union recognition, collective agreements and settling industrial disputes. Such disputes to be regulated through legal structure. It highlights managing by collaborative problem-solving approach.

(iii) In global business, industrial relations strategy should *maintain high productivity* for survival of organisation. Some areas to be focused are: upgrading technology and production methods, re-training and re-deployment of surplus labour.

(iv) To introduce industrial democracy in the organisation, i.e. worker's involvement in decision-making may be encouraged.

(v) New collective bargaining (CB) approach is to reach a *win-win solution*. Both parties should collaborate to find a solution acceptable to each of them. The goal is to change negotiation from a zero-sum game to a positive-sum game.

(F) CONTEXTUAL AND CONSTITUTIONAL FRAMEWORK OF IR IN INDIA

Personnel industrial relations in each nation are embedded in societal rules, norms, values and culture as well as historical background.

(i) Contextual factors

In India, we inherited industrial relations from colonial masters and their culture. Our leaders (both political and trade union) had to fulfil promises and pledges made to workers during freedom struggle for better industrial relations after attaining independence. Further, most of the leaders were influenced by Socialist and Communist ideas.

(ii) Constitutional factors

Following ideas of leaders have influenced in framing Constitution of India contained in trinity of approaches:

(a) The preamble of the Constitution, (b) Fundamental rights, and (c) Directive principles of state policies. These three trinity approaches guide the spirit of industrial relations.

(b) These three approaches were further put in practice in various Five Year Plans. Each of the successive Five Year Plans emphasised for well-being of working class, cooperation between workers and employers, maintaining harmonious industrial relations, worker's participation, welfare state, etc.

(c) The Industrial Policy Resolution, 1956 facilitated the growth of Public Sector Undertakings (PSUs) to be role-model of IR.

(d) In 1958, Voluntary Code of Discipline and Code of Conduct were introduced in tripartite industrial relations meetings.

(e) Further, over a period, two National Labour Commissions (1969 and 2001) have made significant recommendations for improving IR and labour laws in India.

(f) Indian judiciary has displayed judicial activism by giving pro-labour judgements in 1970's and 1980's.

(g) Various labour laws have been enacted after independence, which have considerably improved the working environment and living standards of industrial workers.

References

Willem de Nijs, Article on International Human Resource Management and Industrial Relations: A Framework for Analysis, in book International Human Resource Management edited by Anne Wil Harzing and Joris Van Ruyss Eveldt.

S.K. Bhatia and Nirmal Singh, Industrial Relations and Collective Bargaining, Deep & Deep Publications Pvt. Ltd., New Delhi.

Part Two

LABOUR LAWS

Labour Laws: Perspectives

With a view to stimulating economic growth and development, raising levels of living, a country has to promote productive employment. Employer's have to provide their workers safe, healthy living, employment, job security and working conditions. When employer's fail to honour this obligation, then government attempts to safeguard the interest of workers by enacting laws.

Thus, labour laws refer to body of laws which are enacted to protect and promote the interest of working class. Objective of labour laws is to ensure:

(a) Good working and living conditions for workers;
(b) To protect the workers from being exploited and giving a fair deal;
(c) To maintain industrial peace and cordial relations between employers and workers, to curb unfair labour practices on the part of both employers and workers;
(d) To increase productivity and development of the country; and
(e) To provide adequate compensation, welfare and social security measures.

Labour laws mostly deal with:

(i) Employment;
(ii) Wages;
(iii) Working conditions;
(iv) Industrial relations;
(v) Social security; and
(vi) Labour welfare.

Principles of labour legislation are:

(a) Social justice;
(b) Social equality;

(c) International uniformity (ILO); and
(d) Development of national economy.

EMERGENCE OF LABOUR LAWS

(a) In India, labour legislation has history extending over 150 years. In 1850, Apprentices Act was enacted with the object of enabling destitute children, brought up by public charity, find employment when they come up of age. This was followed by Fatal Accidents Act, 1855, Mines Act and series of laws relating to plantation labour, etc. The pace of labour legislation increased after independence due to economic and social conditions and meet the aspirations of the working class.

(b) Constitutional Framework of Labour Legislation

The Constitution of India has guaranteed some fundamental rights to the citizens and also laid down certain Directive Principles of State Policy for the achievement of a social order based on justice, liberty, equality and fraternity:

(i) Fundamental Rights in the Constitution of India Guarantees:

(a) equality before law or equal protection of laws,
(b) right to form associations or unions,
(c) freedom of speech and assembly,
(d) no discrimination on grounds of caste, sex, religion,
(e) protection against exploitation,
(f) no child below 14 years shall be employed in factory/mine or in hazardous employment, and
(g) prohibition of traffic in human beings and forced labour.

These are enforceable in courts and are constitutionally binding.

(ii) Directive Principles of State Policy in Part IV of the Constitution (Article 43)

These are not enforceable by any court but are fundamental in the governance of the country. It is the duty of the State to apply these principles in making laws. Some principles relevant are:

(a) Equal pay for equal work for men and women.
(b) Children are protected against exploitation.
(c) To secure the participation of workers in the management of establishments.
(d) Just and humane conditions of work and maternity relief.
(e) Living wage.

(iii) Labour is a concurrent subject under the constitution. Article 246(4) of the Constitution of India empowers both the Union and the States to legislate on labour matters. The Central Government enacts labour laws ensuring uniformity throughout the country. The State Governments are empowered to either accept a central law, as it is, or after making suitable changes considering the typical conditions of labour in their states. In case of any

repugnancy between the union and the State legislation, the legislation of the union shall prevail. Besides, the State Governments are the administering authority having powers to make rules and appoint authorities for implementation of labour laws.

However, regulation of labour in railways, mines, oil fields, defence industries and industries of national importance in naval, military and air forces, is controlled by the Central Government exclusively.

We have over 140 labour laws and cannot even name them. These laws are not only restrictive, but also protective and beneficial. At present, most of the practices and procedures relating to labour matters such as: employment and working conditions, obligations and rights of employers and workers and their day-to-day relations, are regulated by various labour laws. Denial of benefits and privileges provided by labour laws becomes a source of industrial conflicts and disputes.

(c) Role of International Labour Organisation (ILO)

India has been one of the founder-members of the ILO. The three main functions of the ILO are:

(i) to establish international labour standards;
(ii) to collect and disseminate information on labour and industrial conditions; and
(iii) to provide technical assistance for carrying out programmes of social and economic development.

ILO's international standards are in the form of conventions and recommendations. India has ratified various conventions and incorporated in the existing legislation. Conventions, which are not ratified have indirectly guided and shaped the Indian Labour Legislation.

(d) Role of Concept of Social Justice

A.M. Sarma has observed that "The philosophy of social justice has now become an integral part of industrial jurisprudence. The concept of social justice is a very important variable in the function of industrial relations. In a welfare state it is necessary to apply the general principles of social and economic justice to remove the imbalances in the political, economic and social life of the people."

"The *concept of social justice* is founded on the basic *ideal of socio-economic equality* and its aim is to assist the removal of socio-economic disparities and inequalities in dealing with industrial matters. It, therefore, endeavours to resolve the competing claims of employers and employees by finding a solution which is just and fair to both parties with the object of establishing harmony between capital and labour and good relationship." (*J.K. Cotton Spinning and Weaving Mills Co. Ltd.* v. *Labour Appellate Tribunal*, 1963-11 LLJ 436).

CLASSIFICATION OF LABOUR LAWS

The labour laws can broadly be classified in five groups as under:

(i) Laws on Compensation

(a) The Payment of Wages Act, 1936;
(b) The Minimum Wages Act, 1948;

(c) The Payment of Bonus Act, 1965; and
(d) The Equal Remuneration Act, 1976.

(ii) Laws on Working Conditions

(a) The Factories Act, 1948;
(b) The Shops and Establishment Act;
(c) The Mines Act, 1952;
(d) The Plantations Labour Act, 1951;
(e) The Contract Labour (Regulation and Abolition) Act, 1970; and
(f) The Motor Transport Worker's Act, 1961.

(iii) Laws on Industrial Relations

(a) The Industrial Disputes Act, 1947;
(b) The Trade Unions Act, 1926; and
(c) The Industrial Employment (Standing Orders) Act, 1946.

(iv) Laws on Social Security

(a) The Workmen's Compensation Act, 1923;
(b) The Employees' State Insurance Act, 1948;
(c) The Employee's Provident Funds and Miscellaneous Provisions Act, 1952;
(d) The Employees' Pension Scheme, 1995;
(e) The Payment of Gratuity Act, 1972; and
(f) The Maternity Benefit Act, 1961.

(v) Miscellaneous Legislation

(a) The Apprentices Act, 1961; and
(b) The Collection of Statistics Act, 1953.

THE NEED TO CHANGE THE LABOUR LAWS DUE TO CHANGE IN NEW ECONOMIC POLICY

Many labour laws have become out dated in the context of changes in the economy.

An attempt was made to introduce a Comprehensive Trade Unions and Industrial Disputes (Amendment) Bill in 1988. But bill could not go through due to lack of consensus.

In free market economy, workers are becoming surplus. But due to prohibition on lay-off and retrenchment in The Industrial Disputes Act, employer's have to continue with large number of workforce as the governments do not permit these, in order to maintain employment in industry.

(i) One way is there that in the changed circumstances government may change its policy and grant permission liberally for lay-off and retrenchment on merits of each case, even though a blanket permission is not given to industry.
(ii) Section 9-A of The Industrial Disputes Act requires an industry, before introducing modernisation or rationalisation, to give a notice of change to workers, if the industries undertake to tackle problem of surplus labour by redeployment, re-training, expansion and establishing new units, there should be no obligation on the employers to give notice of change, etc.

(iii) When the industries found that the government was not willing to give permission to retrench the workers or closure of loss-making units, some successfully did by introducing voluntary retirement schemes.

Now that National Commission on Labour (2002) has given its recommendations, labour laws may undergo amendments.

There has been an agreement on the need for reform due to changes in economic policies and global competitive environment. It will be appropriate to conclude with observations of A.M. Sarma as under:

> "There are basically two schools of thought concerning the role of the law in industrial relations. On the one hand, there are those who believe that the law should fulfil an abstentionist role; that is that the substantive matters of industrial relations should be regulated by the parties themselves free from legal constraint or obligation. On the other hand, there is the view that the law should be a main instrument of directing and controlling the system. If the system is acknowledged to be in need of reform, then the law should be the instrument of that reform. This view implies an extensive system of regulatory legislation directing the parties in their activities and forcing changes wherever necessary.
>
> The distinction between these two views does not lie in the presence or absence of the law. All systems of industrial relations have a legal framework if they operate within a legal system. The legal framework may take the form of recognizing the development of certain institutions and remove any impediments to their existence. The role of law in an industrial relations system may be perceived by the extent to which it attempts to regulate relationships, the extent to which it is obligatory rather than optional and the attitudes of the parties to the legal system."

This volume contains all the important labour laws to promote a critical understanding of substantive and procedural aspects. These labour laws have been presented in concise and summary form for easy understanding and to avoid legal complications. Contents of laws will help in appreciating the approaches, interpretations and working implications for managements, trade unions and workmen alike.

References

A.M. Sarma, "Industrial Relations", Himalaya Publishing House, Mumbai.

Constitution of India.

Nirmal Singh and S.K. Bhatia, "Industrial Relations and Collective Bargaining", Deep & Deep Publications Pvt. Ltd., New Delhi.

25

The Trade Union Act, 1926

OBJECTIVES

The Trade Unions Act, 1926 provides for registration of trade unions with a view to render lawful organisation of labour to enable collective bargaining. The Act also confers on a registered trade union certain protection and privileges.

SCOPE AND COVERAGE

The Act extends to the whole of India and it applies to all kinds of unions of workers and associations of employers which aim at regularizing the Labour-Management relations.

ADMINISTRATIVE AUTHORITY

The Act is administered by and large, by the State Governments. Trade Unions whose objectives are not restricted to one State, are the subject of the Central Government. The State Government shall appoint a Registrar of Trade Unions assisted by Additional or Deputy Registrar, for each State.

MEANING OF TRADE UNION

In common parlance, a trade union connotes an association of workers in a particular trade or industry. As per section 2(u), a trade union means any combination, whether temporary or permanent, formed primarily to regulate the relations between workmen and employers, or workmen and workmen, or employers and employers and for imposing any restrictive conditions on the conduct of any trade or business. Further, any federation of 2 or more trade unions shall also be a trade union.

SALIENT PROVISIONS

(i) Registration of Trade Unions.
(ii) Who can be a Member.
(iii) Appointment of Office-bearers.
(iv) Legal Status of a Registered Trade Union.
(v) Cancellation of Registration.
(vi) Change of Name.
(vii) Change of Registered Office.
(viii) Dissolution of Trade Union.
(ix) Amalgamation of Trade Unions.
(x) Obligations of Registered Trade Unions.
(xi) Rights of Registered Trade Unions.
(xii) Offences and Penalties.

(i) Registration of Trade Unions

Registration of a trade union is not compulsory but is desirable since a registered trade union enjoys certain rights and privileges under the Act.

Minimum seven workers of an establishment (or seven employers) can form a trade union and apply to the Registrar for its registration. The application for registration should be in the prescribed form and accompanied by the prescribed fee, a copy of the rules of the union signed by atleast 7 members, and a statement containing—(a) the names, addresses and occupations of the members making the application, (b) the same of the trade union and the address of its head office, and (c) the titles, names, ages, addresses and occupations of its office-bearers. If the union has been in existence for more than a year, then a statement of its assets and liabilities in the prescribed form, should also be submitted along with the application.

The executive committee/office-bearers of the union should be constituted in accordance with the provisions of the Act.

The rules of the trade union should clearly mention its name and objects, the purposes for which its funds can be used, provision for maintenance of a list of members, procedure for admission of ordinary, honorary or temporary members, rate of subscription (being not less than Re. 0.25 p.m. per member), procedure for amending or rescinding rules, manner of appointing executive committee and other office-bearers, safe custody of funds, audit and inspection of account books, procedure for dissolution of the union and changing its union.

The Registrar may call for further information for satisfying himself that the application is complete and is in accordance with the provision of sections 5 and 6, and that the proposed name of the union does not resemble with the name of any other existing trade union.

On being satisfied with all the requirements, the Registrar shall register the trade union and issue a certificate of registration, which shall be a conclusive evidence of its registration.

(ii) Who can be a Member?

Any person who has attained the age of 15 years, is eligible to be a member of a registered trade union, subject to the rules of the union.

(iii) Appointment of Office-bearers

At least 50% of the office-bearers of a union should be actually engaged or employed in the industry with which the trade union is concerned, and the remaining 50% (or less) can be outsiders such as lawyers, politicians, social workers, etc. For being appointed as an office-bearer or executive of a registered trade union, a person must have:

(a) attained the age of 18 years, and

(b) not been convicted of any offence involving moral turpitude and sentenced to imprisonment, or a period of atleast 5 years has elapsed since his release.

(iv) Legal Status of a Registered Trade Union

(i) A registered trade union is a body corporate with perpetual succession and a common seal.

(ii) It can acquire, hold, sell or transfer any movable or immovable property and can be a party to contracts.

(iii) A registered trade union can sue and be sued, in its own name.

(iv) No civil suit or other legal proceeding can be initiated against a registered trade union in respect of any act done in furtherance of a trade dispute under certain conditions.

(v) No agreement between the members of a registered trade union shall be void or voidable merely on the ground that any of its objects is in restraint of trade.

(v) Cancellation of Registration

The Registrar can withdraw or cancel registration of a trade union on an application being made for its cancellation or by giving atleast 2 months' notice under any of the following circumstances:

(a) if registration has been obtained by fraud or mistake,

(b) if the union has ceased to exist,

(c) if it has willfully contravened any of the provisions of the Act, or

(d) if any rule which is required under Section 6, has been deleted.

(vi) Change of Name

A registered trade union may change its name, with the consent of atleast 2/3rd of the total number of its members. Notice of change of name in writing and signed by the secretary and 7 members of the union, should be sent to the Registrar. The Registrar shall register the change in name if it is satisfied that the proposed name is not identical with the name of any other existing union and the requirements in respect of change of name have been complied with.

The change of name shall not affect any rights or obligations of the trade union or render any legal proceeding by or against the trade union, as defective.

(vii) Change of Registered Office

All notice and correspondence to a registered trade union are addressed to its registered office. Notice of any change in registered office address should be given to the Registrar in writing, within 14 days of such change.

(viii) Dissolution of Trade Union

A registered trade union can be dissolved in accordance with the rules of the union. A notice of dissolution signed by any seven members and the Secretary of the Union should be sent to the Registrar within 14 days of the dissolution. On being satisfied, the Registrar shall register the notice and the union shall stand dissolved from the date. The funds of the union shall be divided by the Registrar amongst its members in the manner prescribed under the rules of the union or as laid down by the government.

(ix) Amalgamation of Trade Unions

Any registered trade union may amalgamate with any other union(s), provided that atleast 50% of the members of each such union records their votes and atleast 60% of votes so recorded are in favour of amalgamation. A notice of amalgamation signed by the Secretary and atleast 7 members of each amalgamating union, should be sent to the Registrar, and the amalgamation shall be in operation after the Registrar registers the notice.

(x) Obligations of Registered Trade Unions

(1) The general funds of a registered trade union should be spent only for the objects specified under section 15, such as—payment of salaries, allowances and expenses of its office-bearers, its administrative and audit expenses, prosecution or defence of any legal proceedings for securing or protecting its rights, conduct of trade disputes, compensation for loss arising out of trade disputes, provision of educational, social or religious benefits and allowances on account of death, old-age, sickness, accident or unemployment to its members, publication of labour journals, etc. The trade union may set-up a separate political fund for furtherance of civic and political interests of members, contribution to this fund shall not be compulsory

(2) The account books and membership register of the trade union should be kept open for inspection by any of its members or office-bearers

(3) A copy of every alteration made in the rules of the union should be sent to the Registrar within 15 days of making the alteration.

(4) An annual statement of receipts and expenditures and assets and liabilities of the union for the year ending on 31st December, prepared in the prescribed forms and duly audited should be sent to the Registrar within the prescribed time. This statement should be accompanied by a statement showing changes in office-bearers during the year and a copy of the rules as amended up to date.

(xi) Rights of Registered Trade Unions

A trade union has a right to demonstrate. A trade union has a right to appeal against an order of the Registrar either refusing or cancelling registration, to the Civil Court/High Court, within the prescribed time.

(xii) Offences and Penalties

Sl. No.	*Offence*	*Penalty*
(1)	If the registered trade union/its office-bearers or members fail to give any notice or send any statement as required under the Act.	Fine upto Rs. 5 plus additional fine upto Rs. 5 per week in case of continuing offence. (Maximum fine imposable Rs. 50)
(2)	If any person wilfully makes any false entry in the annual statement of the union or its rules.	Fine upto Rs. 500
(3)	If any person, with intent to deceive, gives an incorrect copy of rules of the union to any member or a prospective member.	Fine upto Rs. 200

26

The Industrial Disputes Act, 1947

OBJECTIVES

The Industrial Disputes Act, 1947, was enacted to secure industrial peace and harmony by providing machinery and procedure for the investigation and settlement of industrial disputes by negotiations instead of trial of strength through strikes and lock-outs. The legislation is calculated to ensure social justice to both employers and employees and thereby promote industrial progress.

SCOPE AND COVERAGE

The Act extends to the whole of India and applies to every industrial establishment carrying on any business, trade, manufacture or distribution of goods and services, irrespective of the number of workmen employed therein, i.e. even in case of a single employee the Act shall apply

MEANING OF INDUSTRY

'Industry' means any business, trade, undertaking, manufacture or calling of employers and includes any calling, service, employment, handicraft or industrial occupation or avocation of workmen.

According to the Supreme Court this term would cover professions like those of lawyers, etc., clubs, educational institutions like universities, cooperatives, research institutes, charitable projects. It includes making on a large scale *prasad* or food. It also includes welfare activities or economic adventures or projects undertaken by the Government or statutory bodies, which are "Industries" and which are substantially severable units. Thus, the State Insurance and Provident Fund Departments of the Government, godowns of Food Corporation of India have been held to be an industry

However, as per the proposed definition, industry shall not include purely mainly agricultural activities, hospitals, dispensaries, educational, scientific, research or training institutions, charitable, social or philanthropic institutions. Khadi or village industries, sovereign functions of the Government dealing with defence, research, atomic energy and space, domestic services, professional activities of a cooperative society, club or other such body, if the number of persons employed by these is less than ten.

EMPLOYEES COVERED

Every person employed in an establishment for hire or reward, (including contract labour, apprentices) and part-time employees to do any manual, clerical, skilled, unskilled, technical, operational or supervisory work, is covered by the Act. However, the Act does not apply to:

(a) persons employed mainly in a managerial or administrative capacity,
(b) persons employed in a supervisory capacity and drawing wages exceeding Rs. 1600 p.m. or exercising functions mainly of managerial nature, and
(c) persons subject to Army Act, Air Force Act, Navy Act or those employed in the police service or as an officer or employee of a prison.

The designation of an employee is not the criterion to determine the status of an employee as to whether he is a workman or not. The test is the nature of duties of an employee. Daily rated and piece rated workers and temporary employees, who have not been in continuous service for one year under an employer, are not entitled to the benefit of the Act.

Though educational institution is an industry, teachers employee by such institutions cannot be called 'workmen', irrespective of the fact whether such institutions are imparting primary, secondary, graduate or post-graduate education. In order to be a workman an employee should be employed to do any skilled or unskilled, manual, supervisory, technical or clerical work, imparting of education which is the main function of the teacher, does not fall under any of the categories of work stated above. Similarly, the functions of a research fellow are purely academic in nature, and he cannot be regarded as a workman.

ADMINISTRATIVE AUTHORITIES

Industrial disputes in relation to any industry owned or controlled by the Central Government, railways, any controlled industry, statutory corporations, (air transport service), banking and insurance companies, mines, oil fields, major ports, cantonment boards, etc. are dealt with by the Central Government, whereas all other industrial disputes are the concern of the State Governments.

The Government appoints following authorities for the purpose of this Act:

(a) Conciliation Officers and Boards of Conciliation

These are responsible for mediating in and promoting settlement of industrial disputes.

(b) Courts of Inquiry

For inquiring into any matter connected with an industrial dispute.

(c) Labour Courts, Industrial Tribunals and National Tribunals

For adjudication of industrial disputes relating to matters specified in Schedule II or Schedule III or questions of national importance. The National Tribunal shall adjudicate upon industrial disputes, involving questions of national importance or in which industrial establishments situated in more than one State are affected.

WHAT IS AN 'INDUSTRIAL DISPUTE'?

An 'industrial dispute' means any dispute or difference between employers and employers, or between employers and workmen, or between workmen and workmen, which is connected with the terms and conditions of employment of any person.

WHO CAN RAISE A DISPUTE?

A dispute is said to have arisen when some demand is made by workmen and it is rejected by the management or *vice versa* and the demand is relating to the employment. The Act says, that a workman can raise a dispute. However, it is pertinent to note that a dispute between an employer and single workman does not fall within the definition of industrial dispute, but if the workmen as a body or a considerable section of them make a common cause with the individual workman then such a dispute would be an industrial dispute.

However, certain individual disputes relating to dismissal, discharge, retrenchment or termination of services of a workman, are also covered under this Act, since the Act applies even to industrial establishments employing a single workman. But dispute in relation to a person who is not a 'workman' within the meaning of the Act is not an industrial dispute under Section 2(k).

SALIENT PROVISIONS

1. Notice of Change in Service Conditions.
2. Machinery for Investigating and Settlement of Disputes:
   - (a) Works Committee
   - (b) Grievance Settlement Authority
   - (c) Conciliation Officers
   - (d) Boards of Conciliation
   - (e) Courts of Inquiry
   - (f) Voluntary Arbitration
   - (g) Reference of Disputes for Adjudication:
     - ❑ Labour Courts, Industrial and National Tribunals
     - ❑ Procedure and Powers of Labour Court and Tribunal
     - ❑ Payment of Wages to Workmen Pending Proceedings in Higher Courts
     - ❑ Prohibition of Strikes and Lock-outs in Public Utility Services
     - ❑ Protection of Workmen during Pendency of Proceedings
3. Prohibition Strikes and Lock-out:
   - ❑ Prohibitions
   - ❑ Restrictions
   - ❑ Illegal Strikes and Lock-outs

4. Lay-off:
   - Notice of Lay-off
   - Lay-off Compensation
5. Retrenchment:
   - Conditions for Retrenchment
   - Retrenchment Compensation
   - Re-employment of Retrenched Workmen
6. Closure of an Undertaking:
   - Approval of the Government
   - Notice/Notice Pay and Compensation
   - Illegal Closure
7. Unfair Labour Practices
8. Obligations of Employers under the Act
9. Obligations of Employees
10. Offences and Penalties

1. Notice of Change in Service Conditions

The employer should not make any change in the conditions of service specified in the Fourth Schedule of the Act (such as payment and amount of wages and allowances, contribution to pension and provident fund, hours of work, rest intervals, leaves, holidays, timings of shifts, classification or trades, etc.) without giving atleast 21 days' notice in Form E to the workmen likely to be affected by such change.

However, the employer need not give such notice if the change is effected by virtue of any settlement or award, or in case of employees governed by Government rules and regulations, or where the establishment has been exempted from this requirement.

2. Machinery for Investigating and Settlement of Disputes

(a) Works Committee

Any industrial establishment wherein 100 or more workmen are employed or were employed on any day during the preceding 12 months, may be required by the Government to constitute a Works Committee comprising of equal number of representatives of labour and management. The representatives of workmen on the Works Committee shall be chosen in the prescribed manner from amongst the workmen engaged in the establishment and in consultation with their registered trade union, if any. The main functions of the Works Committee are to preserve amity and establish cordial relations between workers and employers and to resolve differences of opinion in matters of common interest, through negotiations.

(b) Grievance Settlement Authority

The employer in relation to an industrial establishment wherein 50 or more workmen are employed or were employed on any day during the preceding 12 months, shall set-up a Grievance Settlement Authority for settlement of individual disputes of the workmen employed in that establishment.

Any workman or any trade union of which such workman is a member, may refer a dispute to the Grievance Settlement Authority.

No dispute shall be referred for adjudication by the Conciliation Board, Labour Court or

Tribunal, unless it has been referred to the Grievance Settlement Authority and the decision of the Authority is not acceptable to any of the parties to the dispute.

(c) Conciliation Proceedings

If the employer and the workmen fail to arrive at a settlement through negotiations, the Conciliation Officer may intervene as a mediator, endeavour to reconcile the differences of opinion and help the labour and management in achieving a successful settlement. However, Conciliation Officer is not competent to decide the various points of issue between the opposing parties. Intervention by the Conciliation Officer is mandatory in case of industrial dispute has arisen in a public utility service and a notice of strike or lockout (u/s 22) has been served.

The Conciliation Officer shall send a report of proceedings to the Government, as to whether a settlement has been achieved or not, within 14 days of the commencement of the conciliation proceedings or within such extended time as may be allowed and in the prescribed manner, if a settlement is arrived at as a result of conciliation proceedings, a memorandum of settlement is worked out and becomes binding on all parties concerned for a period agreed upon.

A settlement arrived at in the course of conciliation proceedings with a recognised majority union will be binding on the workmen of the establishment, even to those who belong to the minority union which had objected to the settlement.

If no settlement is arrived at, the conciliation officer shall as soon as practicable after the close of the investigation, send a full report to the appropriate Government setting forth the steps taken by him to ascertaining the facts and circumstances relating to the dispute, and for bringing about a settlement thereof, and the reasons on account of which a settlement could not be reached. On consideration of the report, the appropriate Government may, if it feels necessary refer the dispute to the Conciliation Board, Labour Court, Tribunal or National Tribunal. If no such reference is made, the appropriate government shall record and communicate to the parties concerned the reasons therefor.

(d) Boards of Conciliation

Where a dispute is referred to the Conciliation Board, the Board shall endeavour to bring about a settlement of the same after investigating into the dispute. If a settlement has been arrived at, the Board shall send a report thereof together with a memorandum of settlement signed by the parties to the dispute, to the appropriate Government, within two months of the reference or within such extended time as may be allowed.

If no settlement is arrived at, the Board shall also send a similar detailed report as required above from the Conciliation Officer.

The Settlement

A settlement arrived at, in the course of conciliation proceeding comes into operation:

(a) on such date as is agreed upon by the parties to the dispute, and
(b) where no such date is agreed upon, on the date on which the memorandum of settlement is signed by the parties to the dispute.

The settlement shall be binding:

(a) for the period agreed upon by the parties, and
(b) where no such period is agreed upon, for a period of six months from the date on which the memorandum of settlement is signed.

The settlement shall remain binding for a further period until the expiry of two months from the date on which a notice in writing for termination of the settlement is given by any one party to the other party or parties.

(e) The Courts of Inquiry

A Court of Inquiry is required to inquire into any matter connected with, or relevant to, an industrial dispute, which may be referred to it by the appropriate Government. The Court shall ordinarily submit its report within six months from the commencement of its inquiry.

(f) Voluntary Arbitration

Before an industrial dispute is referred to a Labour Court or Tribunal or National Tribunal, the employer and the workmen may refer the dispute to arbitration of any person or persons of their choice, by means of a written arbitration agreement A copy of the arbitration agreement, signed by representatives of both the parties representing majority of each party should be forwarded to the Government and the conciliation officer. The arbitrator or arbitrators shall investigate into the dispute and submit the arbitration award to the government, who shall within one month of the receipt thereof, publish the same in the Official Gazette.

(g) Reference of Disputes for Adjudication

If a dispute is not settled by negotiations or conciliation, and the parties do not agree to refer the dispute to arbitration, the government may, on its own discretion, or on an application by the parties to the dispute representing the majority, separately or jointly, refer the dispute to the Labour Court or Industrial Tribunal for adjudication. If a dispute involves a question of national importance or is likely to affect the interests of industrial establishments situated in more than one State, the Central Government shall refer the dispute to the National Tribunal. The Government should exercise the discretion of reference to the Labour Court or Industrial Tribunal after applying its mind.

An order of reference shall specify the period within which the award is to be submitted to the Government.

Payment of Wages to Workman Pending Proceedings in Higher Courts

If a labour court or tribunal by its award directs reinstatement of a worker and the employer appeals against such award in a High Court or the Supreme Court, the employer shall, during the period of pendency of such appeal proceedings, either employ the workman provisionally or pay to him full wages last drawn by him including any maintenance allowance allowable under any rule, if the workman had not been employed in any establishment during such period and an affidavit to that effect has been filed in the Court by such workman.

The words "full wages last drawn" would take into their fold the wages drawn on the date of termination of services plus the yearly increment and the dearness allowance to be worked out till the date of the award.

Prohibition of Strikes and Lock-outs in Public Utility Services

The Government may also prohibit continuance of any strike or lock-out in connection with a dispute which has been referred for adjudication to a Labour Court or Tribunal or National Tribunal or has been referred to a Board of Arbitration.

Protection of Workmen during Pendency of Proceedings

During pendency of any conciliation, adjudication and arbitration proceedings before a conciliation officer, Board of Conciliation, Arbitrator, Labour Court and Tribunal, in respect of any dispute, no employer can alter the conditions of service to the prejudice of the workmen concerned with the dispute or dismiss or punish any such workman without obtaining written permission of the authority concerned.

(3) Strikes and Lock-out

Strike means suspension or cessation of work by a group of employees employed in any industry, acting in combination. Partial stoppage of work, hunger strike accompanied with cessation of work and sitting in strike are also held to be strike. A pen-down strike also falls within the definition of 'strike'. Lockouts is temporary shutting down or closing the place of business by the employer. It differs from closure of the undertaking. While in the case of 'closure' the employer does not merely close down the place of business but finally closes the business itself, in the case of 'lock-out' the employer closes the place of business only

Strike and lock-out are two coercive measures resorted to by the employees and the employers, respectively for compelling the employers or employees to accept their demands or conditions of service.

Sections 22 to 25 of the Act aim at restricting the right to strike or lock-out, which is to be exercised under certain conditions only and after all peaceful measures to avert the same have been exhausted.

Prohibitions

A strike or lock-out is prohibited in any industrial establishment, in the following cases:

(a) during the pendency of conciliation proceedings before a Board and 7 days after the conclusion of such proceedings,
(b) during the pendency of arbitration proceedings or proceedings before a Labour Court, Tribunal or National Tribunal, and two months after the conclusion of such proceedings, and
(c) during the period in which a settlement or award is in operation, in respect of any of the matters covered by the settlement or award.

Restrictions

Besides, some more restrictions have been laid down in regard to strikes or lock-outs in public utility services, viz.,

(i) *Notice*: The employees or the employers shall give a notice of strike or lock-out respectively to the other party. The strike or lock-out shall commence from the date specified in the notice, which shall in no case, be earlier than 14 days and later than six weeks.

A strike or lock-out which has commenced before the expiry of 14 days notice period, shall be illegal only for unexpired period of notice and thereafter it shall be legal.

The employer shall intimate to the Government, in the prescribed manner, within five days of receiving any notice of strike or giving any notice of lock-out.

(ii) The employees or the employers shall not go on a strike or declare a lock-out, during the pendency of any proceedings before a Conciliation Officer and seven days after the conclusion of such proceedings.

Illegal Strikes and Lock-outs

Any strike or lock-out commenced or declared or continued, in contravention of any of the above restrictions or any prohibitory order of the government under Section 10 or 10-A, shall be illegal. No person should knowingly finance any illegal strike or lock-out.

A strike or lock-out in pursuance of an industrial dispute, which has already commenced before the reference of such dispute to arbitration (u/s 10A) or for adjudication (u/s 10), shall not become illegal merely by its continuance after such reference, unless the strike or lock-out was illegal at its commencement.

Further, a lock-out declared in consequence of an illegal strike or a strike declared in consequence of an illegal lock-out shall not be deemed to be illegal.

If the strike is illegal, workmen are not only liable to lose wages but are also liable to punishment by way of discharge or dismissal. Workers are, however, entitled to wages for the period of lock-out which is illegal and unjustified.

The employer cannot demand a written undertaking from the striking workman not to repeat such an act after the strike is called-off.

In a recent judgment the full bench of the Supreme Court has authoritatively laid down the law relating to wages during the strike period and held that workmen would not be entitled to wages for the strike period unless the strike was illegal and also justified.

4. Lay-off

An employee is said to have been laid-off on any day, if the employer fails, refuses or is unable to provide him employment on that day within two hours of his presenting himself for work at the normal appointed time, on account of shortage of coal, power or raw materials, or accumulation of stocks or break-down or machinery or natural calamity or for any such other reason. The expression "any other reason" should be construed to mean reason similar or analogous to the preceding reasons.

A lay-off must be distinguished from a lock-out. Lay-off generally occurs in the continuing business, whereas a lock-out is the closure of the business itself. In the case of a lay-off, owing to the reasons stated above, the employer is unable to give employment to one or more workmen. In the case of a lock-out the employer closes the business and lock-out the whole body of workmen for reasons other than those stated above.

Notice of Lay-off

The employer is required to give a notice of lay-off to workers in Form O-1 within 7 days of such lay-off. Notice of withdrawal of lay-off is also to be given in Form O-2, within 7 days of such withdrawal.

In case of factories, mines and plantation establishments employing 100 or more workers, on an average per working day in the preceding 12 months (excluding seasonal establishment), the employer cannot lay-off any workman without obtaining prior approval of the Government, except when such lay-off is due to shortage of power of natural calamity and in case of mines due to fire, flood, excess of inflammable gas or explosion.

Lay-off Compensation

The employer of any factory, mine or plantation establishment (excluding seasonal establishment), employing atleast 50 but less than 100 workmen on an average per working day is required to pay compensation to the workmen being laid-off. The compensation shall be payable at the rate of 50% of basic wages and dearness allowance, for all days of lay-off except weekly holidays.

Conditions for Entitlement to Compensation

A worker (other than casual or *badli* worker) who is on the muster rolls of the establishment and who has been in continuous service under an employer for atleast one year, shall be entitled to compensation on being laid-off.

5. Retrenchment

Retrenchment means termination by the employer, of the service of a workman for any reason whatsoever, but excludes:

(a) dismissal inflected by way of disciplinary action,
(b) voluntary retirement of the workman,
(c) retirement on reaching the age of superannuation,
(d) termination as a result of non-renewal of contract of employment, and
(e) termination due to continued ill-health of the workman.

Termination due to reduction in volume of work, or on the ground that the worker did not pass the test which would have enabled him to be confirmed, or which is not in accordance with the standing orders, shall amount to retrenchment.

Conditions for Retrenchment

No workman who has been in continuous service for at least one year, shall be retrenched until the unless the following conditions are fulfilled:

(a) In case of a factory, mine or plantation establishment (other than seasonal establishment) wherein at least 100 workmen were employed on an average per working day for the preceding 12 months:
   (i) *Notice/Notice Pay:* The employer is required to serve three months' notice of his intention to retrench the workman with reasons for the same, in the prescribed form, to every workman who is being so retrenched.
   Alternatively, the employer may pay wages for the period of the notice, in lieu thereof.
   (ii) *Approval of the Government:* The employer is required to obtain prior approval of the appropriate Government. Permission can be obtained by submitting an application in Form P-A within 60 days before the proposed retrenchment. The

application should clearly state the reasons for the intended retrenchment.

A copy of the application should be served simultaneously on the workman concerned.

Where no order is communicated to the employer within 60 days from the date of the application, the approval shall be deemed to have been allowed.

(iii) *Retrenchment Compensation:* Where the approval of the Government has been granted or is deemed to have been granted, the workman being retrenchment shall be entitled to receive retrenchment compensation.

(b) In case of a factory, mine or plantation establishment (other than seasonal establishment) wherein at least 50 but less than 100 workmen have been employed on an average per day during the preceding calendar month.

(i) *Notice/Notice Pay:* The employer is required to serve one month's notice of his intention to retrench the workman with reasons for the same in the prescribed form to every workman who is being so retrenched.

Alternatively, the employer may pay wages for the period of the notice in lieu thereof.

(ii) *Notice to the Government:* The employer is also required to give a notice of his intention to retrench; to the appropriate Government in the prescribed manner.

(iii) *Retrenchment Compensation:* The employer is required to pay retrenchment compensation to every workman being retrenched, at the time of retrenchment.

Note:—A daily wage worker who has worked for more than 240 days within one year immediately preceding the termination of his service, cannot be terminated from service unless the procedure stated above is followed. However, where a daily wage worker was appointed with a condition that his service would be liable to termination without any notice, his service could be terminated on the basis of this condition, without following the aforesaid procedure.

Retrenchment Compensation

The employer is liable to pay compensation to each workman who is being retrenched which shall be equal to 15 days' average pay for every completed year of continuous service or any part thereof in excess of six months. Offer of an alternative appointment by the employer to a retrenched workman would not disentitle him from retrenchment compensation.

Non-payment of compensation will render the termination inoperative.

Last Come First Go

The employer shall ordinarily retrench the person last employed in that category, unless there is an agreement to the contrary or for reasons to be recorded by the employer. For this purpose the employer shall prepare a seniority list of all workmen, in each particular category from which workmen are to be retrenched.

Failure to comply with the principle of 'last come first go' for effecting retrenchment will render it invalid. The rule is however, not inflexible and can be departed from, on grounds of inefficiency, unreliability or habitual irregularity, but the employer must prove existence of such valid reasons.

Re-employment of Retrenched Workmen

Where any workmen are retrenched, and the employer proposes to employ any person, the retrenched workmen who are citizens of India, shall be given preference for re-employment (at their option) over the other persons.

6. Closure

Intimation to/Approval of the Government

An employer who intends to close down an undertaking, wherein 50 or more workmen are employed or were employed during the preceding 12 months, has to serve a notice in Form Q on the government, atleast 60 days before the date of the intended closure, stating reasons for the same.

An employer who intends to close down an undertaking, employing 100 or more workers on an average in the preceding 12 months, has to obtain prior approval of the government, at least 89 days before the date of the intended closure, stating in the application in Form Q-A, the reasons for the same. A copy of the application shall be simultaneously served on the representatives of the workmen also.

However, undertakings engaged in the construction of buildings, bridges, roads, canals, dams, etc. are not required to serve the notice or obtain the approval of the Government.

If no order is communicated by the government within 60 days from the date of the application for closure by the employer, the permission shall be deemed to have been granted after the said period of 60 days.

Notice/Notice Pay and Compensation

In case of closure of an undertaking wherein atleast 50 workmen are employed, or were employed on an average per working day in the preceding 12 months, every employee who has been in continuous service for atleast one year, shall be—

(a) served by the employer, atleast one month's notice of intended closure or paid wages for the notice-period; and
(b) paid compensation equal to 15 days' average pay for every completed year of continuous service or any part thereof in excess of 6 months (as provided for in case of 'retrenchment').

However, an undertaking engaged in the construction of buildings, bridges, roads, canals, dams, etc. which is closed down on account of the completion of the work within two years from the date on which it was set-up, shall not be required to pay any compensation on such closure. But if the construction work is not so completed within two years, the workmen employed in the undertaking shall be entitled to notice and compensation for every completed year of continuous service or any part thereof in excess of six months.

Illegal Closure

Where no application for permission u/s 25-O(1) is made within the specified period or where the permission for closure has been refused, the closure of the undertaking shall be deemed to be illegal from the date of closure and the workmen shall be entitled to all the benefits available under law as if the undertaking had not been closed down.

7. Unfair Labour Practices

No employer, workman or a trade union should indulge in any unfair labour practice as mentioned in Fifth Schedule of the Act.

8. Obligations of Employers

The obligations of employers, as per the foregoing discussion, are summarised below:

(1) Not to make any change in the service conditions of the workmen, without giving a notice as prescribed under section 9A.
(2) To constitute Works Committee and to ensure that it functions properly.
(3) To assist the conciliation officer/board and the arbitrator in resolving any dispute.
(4) To implement all agreements, settlements and awards.
(5) To maintain a muster-roll of the workmen employed in the establishment, even at the time when workmen have been laid-off, and to ensure that the names of the workmen who present themselves for work at the appointed hours, are entered therein.
(6) Not to declare, support or finance an illegal lock-out, in the establishment.
(7) Not to lay-off or retrench any workman or close down an undertaking, without obtaining prior approval of the government if so required.
(8) To pay lay-off, retrenchment and closure compensation, compensation to workmen for illegal lock-out, as prescribed under the provisions of the Act.
(9) Not to indulge in unfair labour practices.

9. Obligations of Employees

The workmen of an establishment are obliged:

(1) To assist and co-operate with the conciliation officer/board, arbitrator and other authorities, in resolving any industrial dispute.
(2) Not to participate in, support or finance an illegal strike.
(3) To abide by all agreements, settlements and awards.
(4) Not to indulge in unfair labour practices.

10. Offences *Penalties*

Sl. No.	*Offences*	*Penalties*
(1)	Any employer who lays-off or retrenches workman without obtaining prior permission from the government.	Imprisonment upto one month or fine upto Rs. 1000 or both.
(2)	Closure of an undertaking without obtaining prior approval of the government.	Imprisonment upto six months or fine upto Rs. 5000 or both.
(3)	Closure of an undertaking in contravention of an order refusing to	Imprisonment upto one year or fine upto Rs. 5000 or both. In case of a continuing

grant permission for closure, or non-compliance of an order to reopen a closed undertaking.	offence a further fine upto Rs. 2000 per day.
(4) Closure of an undertaking without giving a notice to the workmen under Section 25-FFA.	Imprisonment upto six months or fine upto Rs. 5000 or both.
(5) Any workman who participates or acts in furtherance of an illegal strike.	Imprisonment upto one month or fine upto Rs. 50 or both.
(6) An employer who declares an illegal lock-outs or acts in furtherance of the same.	Imprisonment upto one month or fine upto Rs. 1000 or both.
(7) Any person, who instigates or incites another person to take part in, or finances any illegal strike or lock-out, or commits any unfair labour practice.	Imprisonment upto six months or fine upto Rs. 1000 or both.
(8) Any person who commits a breach of any settlement or award binding on him.	Imprisonment upto six months or fine or both. In case of a continuing breach an additional fine upto Rs. 200 per day.
(9) Any person who wilfully discloses an information which is declared to be confidential u/s 21.	Imprisonment upto six months or fine upto Rs. 1000 or both.
(10) Contravention of any other provision of the Act or the rules made thereunder.	Fine upto Rs. 100.

Note: In case of an offence by a company, body corporate or other association, its director, manager, secretary, agent or other officer concerned with its management, shall be deemed to be guilty of that offence unless he proves that the offence was committed without his knowledge or consent.

THE INDUSTRIAL DISPUTES ACT, 1947—A REVIEW

Industrial Disputes Act is restrictive as well as a beneficial and protective legislation.

1. It is restrictive as it abridges the rights of employer to:

(1) Lock-out, retrenchment, dismiss and discharge his workers, change employment and service conditions without giving any notice to employees.

(2) Transfer and close his undertaking except as regulated in the Act.

(3) The payment of full wages to workmen if employee goes in appeal to High Court or Supreme Court against award of reinstatement of Labour Court/Tribunal. If it is proved in High Court that workmen has been employed during such period. The court shall order no wages be payable for such period employed.

(4) The act also restricts the right of workmen to strike by making it same illegal under certain circumstances.

(5) But all these restrictions are beneficial and intended to promote industrial harmony.
(6) Other beneficial provision of Act are payment on lay-off and retrenchment compensation. These are described as social security measures, as it protects workmen against risk of unemployment.

2. Some Preventive Measures

These are:

(i) Works committees,
(ii) Maintenance of *status quo* during pendency of proceedings for settlement,
(iii) Prior notice for making any change in service conditions, and
(iv) Payment of lay-off and retrenchment compensation.

3. Criticism of the Act

Act lays too much stress on compulsory conciliation and adjudication of disputes and thus preventing mutual settlement of disputes by collective bargaining does not provide for recognition of unions as bargaining agent.

THE FIRST SCHEDULE

[See Section 2n(vi)]

Industries which may be Declared to be Public Utility Services under sub-clause (vi) or Clause (n) of Section 2

1. Transport (other than railways) for the carriage of passengers of goods by land or water
2. Banking
3. Cement
4. Coal
5. Cotton textiles
6. Foodstuffs
7. Iron and steel
8. Defence establishments
9. Service in hospitals and dispensaries
10. Fire brigade service
11. Indian Government mints
12. Indian Security Press
13. Copper mining
14. Lead mining
15. Zinc mining
16. Iron ore mining
17. Service in any oil fields
18. Any service in, or in connection with the working of any major port or dock
19. Service in the uranium industry.

THE SECOND SCHEDULE

(See Section 7)

Matters within the Jurisdiction of Labour Courts

1. The propriety or legality of an order passed by an employer under the standing orders;
2. The application and interpretation of standing orders;
3. Discharge or dismissal of workmen including reinstatement of, or grant of relief to workmen wrongfully dismissed;
4. Withdrawal of any customary concession or privilege;
5. Illegality or otherwise of a strike or lockout; and
6. All matters other than those specified in the Third Schedule.

THE THIRD SCHEDULE

(See Section 7A)

Matters within the jurisdiction of Industrial Tribunals

1. Wages, including the period and mode of payment;
2. Compensatory and other allowances;
3. Hour of work and rest intervals;
4. Leave with wages and holidays;
5. Bonus, profit-sharing, provident fund and gratuity;
6. Shift working otherwise than in accordance with standing orders;
7. Classifications by grades;
8. Rules of discipline;
9. Rationalisation;
10. Retrenchment of workmen and closure of establishment; and
11. Any other matter that may be prescribed.

THE FOURTH SCHEDULE

(See Section 9A)

Conditions of Service for Change of which Notice is to be given

1. Wages, including the period and mode of payment;
2. Contribution paid, or payable, by the employer to any provident fund or pension fund or for the benefit of the workmen under any law for the time being in force;
3. Compensatory and other allowances;
4. Hours of work and rest intervals;
5. Leave with wages and holidays;
6. Starting, alteration or discontinuance of shift working otherwise than in accordance with standing orders;

7. Classification by grades;
8. Withdrawal of any customary concession or privilege or change in usage;
9. Introduction of new rules of discipline, or alteration of existing rules, except in so far as they are provided in standing orders; and
10. Rationalisation, standardisation or improvement of plant or technique which is likely to lead to retrenchment of workmen; and
11. Any increase of reduction (other than causal) in the number of persons employed or to be employed in any occupation or process or department or shift, not occasioned by circumstances over which the employer has no control.

THE FIFTH SCHEDULE

(Unfair Labour Practices)

On the part of Employers

(i) To interfere with, restrain from, or coerce, workmen in the exercise of their right to organise, form, join or assist a trade union or to engage in concerted activities for the purposes of collective bargaining or other mutual aid or protection, that is to say,
   (a) threatening workmen with discharge or dismissal, if they join a trade union:
   (b) threatening a lock-out or closure, if a trade union is organised;
   (c) granting wage increase to workmen at crucial periods of trade union organisation with a view to undermine its efforts.

(ii) To dominate, interfere with or contribute support, financial or otherwise, to any trade union, that is to say—,
   (a) an employer taking an active interest in organising a trade union of his workmen; and
   (b) an employer showing partiality or granting favour to one or several trade unions attempting to organise his workmen, or to its members where such a trade union is not a recognised trade union.

(iii) To establish employer-sponsored unions of workmen.

(iv) To encourage or discourage membership in any trade union by discriminating against any workman, that is to say:
   (a) discharging or punishing a workman, because he urged other workmen to join or organise a trade union;
   (b) discharging or dismissing a workman for taking part in any strike (not being a strike which is deemed to be illegal under the Act);
   (c) changing seniority rating of workmen because of trade union activities;
   (d) refusing to promote workmen to higher posts on account of their trade union activities;
   (e) giving unmerited promotion to certain workmen with a view of creating discord amongst other workmen, or to undermine the strength of their trade union; and
   (f) discharging office-bearers of active members of the trade union on account of their trade union activities.

(v) To discharge or dismiss workmen:
  (a) by way of victimisation;
  (b) for patently false reasons;
  (c) not in good faith, but in the colourable exercise of the employer's rights;
  (d) by falsely implicating a workman in a criminal case on false or concocted evidence;
  (e) on untrue or trumped up allegations of absence without leave;
  (f) in utter disregard of the principles of natural justice in the conduct of domestic enquiry or with undue haste; and
  (g) for misconduct of a minor or technical character, without having any regard to the nature of the particular misconduct or the past record or service or workman, thereby leading to disproportionate punishment.

(vi) To abolish the work of a regular nature being done by workmen and to give such work to contractors as measure of breaking a strike.

(vii) To transfer a workman *malafide* from one place to another, under the guises of following management policy.

(viii) To insist upon individual workmen who are on a legal strike to sign a good conduct bond, as a precondition to allowing them to resume work.

(ix) To show favoritism or partiality to one set of workers regardless of merit.

(x) To employ workman as "Badlis", casuals, or temporaries, and to continue them as such for years, with the object of depriving them of the status and privileges of permanent workmen.

(xi) To discharge or discriminate against any workman for filing charges or testifying against an employer in an enquiry or proceedings relating to any industrial dispute.

(xii) To recruit workmen during a strike which is not illegal.

(xiii) Failure to implement award, settlement or agreement.

(xiv) To indulge in acts of force or violence.

(xv) To refuse to bargain collectively in good faith with the recognised union.

(xvi) Proposing and continuing a lock-out deemed to be illegal under this Act.

On the Part of Workmen and Trade Unions of Workmen

(i) To advise or actively support or instigate any strike deemed to be illegal under this Act.

(ii) To coerce workmen in the exercise of the right of self-organisation or to join a trade union or refrain from joining a trade union, that is to say:
  (a) for a trade union or its members to picketing in such a manner that non-striking workmen are physically debarred from entering the work place; and
  (b) to indulge in acts of force or violence or to hold out threats of intimidation in connection with a strike against non-striking workmen or against managerial staff.

(iii) For a recognised union to refuse to bargain collectively in good faith with the employer.

(iv) To indulge in coercive activities against certification of a bargaining representative.

(v) To stage, encourage or instigate such forms of coercive actions as wilful go-slow, squatting on the work premises after working hours, or 'Gherao' of any of the member of the managerial or other staff.

(vi) To stage demonstration at the residence of the employers or the managerial staff members.

(vii) To incite or indulge in wilful damage to employer's property connected with industry.

(viii) To indulge in acts of force or violence, or to hold out threats of intimidation against any workman with a view to prevent him from attending work.

27

The Industrial Employment (Standing Orders) Act, 1946

BACKGROUND

Before this law, terms and conditions of employment were vague and unknown to employees. These were changed frequently.

Hiring and firing without following any procedure of giving any opportunity to explain and arbitrary dismissals were there.

These were source of constant friction between workers and managements and disputes in courts and lead to bad industrial relations.

OBJECTIVE

Purpose of this Act is to improve industrial relations. The Act requires employer's to define and standardise conditions of employment and make it known to workmen.

COVERAGE

It is applicable to industrial establishments employing 50 or more workmen. Some states, i.e. U.P., W.B. have reduced the number. Some states, e.g. M.P. and Bombay have their own standing orders acts.

PROVISIONS

1. Every employer is required to submit draft standing orders with required information to the certifying officer for certification.

2. Draft standing orders should conform to model standing orders prepared by government and should cover all the matters.
3. Procedure for certification is laid to be followed by the certifying officer:
   - ❑ Should supply copy of draft standing orders to workmen/unions,
   - ❑ Workmen to be given opportunity to be heard,
   - ❑ After discussion of draft standing orders by the union, management, the certifying officer certifies and gives copies to all concerned; and
   - ❑ Appeal can be made by any party.
5. Certified Standing Orders come into operation after 30 days.
6. Modification can be made after only 6 months except when there is agreement between employer and workmen. But it has to be approved by certifying officer.
7. Penalty can be imposed upto Rs. 5000 for non-submission of draft standing orders.

This Act forms the basis of day-to-day labour-management relations, harmonious working conditions and discipline, etc.

MODEL STANDING ORDERS

Main provisions in the model standing orders are on following matters. A copy of model standing orders is at Appendix I.

- ❑ Classification of workmen, such as permanent, probationers, casual, apprentices, etc.,
- ❑ Publication of working time and shift working,
- ❑ Notice of change in shift working,
- ❑ Attendance and late coming,
- ❑ Leave and absence,
- ❑ Payment of wages—procedures,
- ❑ Stoppage of work,
- ❑ Termination and disciplinary action for misconduct, to pay notice pay, except disciplinary action termination,
- ❑ Procedure to be laid for complaints by workers,
- ❑ Suspension:
  - Subsistence allowance to be paid @ ½ of wages + DA upto 90 days.
  - Subsistence allowance to be paid @ ¾ of wages + DA exceeding 90 days. (*Note:* If disciplinary action is prolonged for reasons directly attributable to workman ¼th of wages).
  - Treatment of suspension period is as under:

Not guilty	*For dismissal*	*Fine/stoppage of increment/reduction to lower grade*
❑ On duty ❑ Full wages minus subsistence allowance	❑ Nil wages ❑ Only subsistence allowance already paid	❑ On duty ❑ Wages minus subsistence allowance already paid

APPENDIX I

MODEL STANDING ORDERS

Classification of Workers

Model Standing Orders classify workers into six categories, namely, permanent, probationers, *badlis,* temporary, casual and apprentices.

A *permanent worker* has been defined one who has been engaged on a permanent basis and as any person who has satisfactorily completed a probationary period of three months in the same or another occupation in the industrial establishment, including breaks due to sickness, accident, leave, lock-out, strike (other than illegal strike) or voluntary closure of the establishment.

A *probationer* is a worker who is provisionally employed to fill a permanent vacancy in a post and has not completed three months service therein.

A *badli* is a worker who is appointed in the post of a permanent worker or probationer who is temporarily absent.

A *temporary worker* is one who has been engaged for work of an essentially temporary nature likely to be finished within a limited period.

A *casual worker* is one whose employment is of a casual nature.

An *apprentice* is a learner who is paid an allowance during the period of his training.

Tickets, Under the Model Standing Orders, every worker should be given a permanent ticket, unless he is a probationer, *badli* or temporary worker, or an apprentice; and every permanent worker should be provided with a departmental ticket showing his number which shall be subject to inspection by an authorised person.

Every *badli* worker should be provided with a *badli card* and the number of days he has worked should be recorded on it. The card shall be surrendered if the *badli* worker obtains permanent employment.

Every temporary worker should be provided with a temporary ticket which shall be surrendered on his discharge. Every casual worker should be provided with a casual card on which the number of days he has worked in the establishment shall be recorded and every apprentice should be furnished with an apprentice card, which he shall surrender on obtaining permanent employment.

Publication of Work Time, Holidays, Pay Days and Wage Rates

The periods and hours of work for all classes of workers in each shift should exhibited in English and in the principal languages of workers on the notice boards maintained at or near the main entrance of the establishment and at the time-keepers' office, if any. Notice specifying the dates of holidays, the pay days and the rates of wages payable to and for all cases of workers and work should be displayed on the notice boards meant for the purpose.

Shift Working

The Model Standing Orders provide that more than one shift may be worked in the departments/sections of the establishment at the discretion of the employer and that in such case workers shall be liable to be transferred from one shift to another. No shift work should be discontinued without two months' prior written notice to workers. However, no such notice is required if the shift is discontinued under an agreement with the affected workers. The Model

Standing Orders lay down that if any worker is retrenched as a result of the discontinuance of a shift, such retrenchment should be effected under the provisions of the Industrial Disputes Act, 1947, and the rules framed thereunder. If the shift is re-started, the workers shall be given notice and re-employed in accordance with the provisions of the said Act and rules.

Attendance and Late Coming

All workers should be present at the establishment at the appointed time. In case of late attendance, the concerned worker shall be liable to deductions under the Payment of Wages Act, 1936.

Leave and Holidays

The Model Standing Orders lay down that holidays with pay should be allowed to workers as provided for in the Factories Act, 1948, and other holidays in accordance with law, contract, custom and usage.

If a worker desires to obtain leave, he should apply to the manager and the manager should issue orders on the leave application within a week of its submission or two days prior to the commencement of the leave, whichever is earlier. If the required leave is to commence on the date of application or within three days thereof, the order should be given on the same day. If leave is granted, a leave pass should be issued to the worker. If leave is refused, the fact of such a refusal or postponement and the reasons thereof should be recorded in the register maintained for this purpose. A copy of such entry may also be supplied to the worker. The manager is required to send a written reply granting or refusing leave to the worker if his address is available and if such reply is likely to reach him before expiry of the leave originally granted to the worker. The worker shall lose his lien on his appointment if he remains absent beyond the period of the leave originally granted or extended, unless he returns within eight days of the expiry of the leave and explains his inability to return in time to the satisfaction of the manager. If the worker loses his lien, he shall be entitled to be on the *badli* list.

Causal Leave

A worker may granted 10 days' causal leave in a calender year to meet unforeseen circumstances, but not exceeding three days at a time, except in cases of sickness. Generally, prior permission of the head of the department in the establishment should be obtained before availing of this leave; if this is not possible, he should be informed in writing of the absence and the duration of such absence.

Payment of Wages

The Model Standing Orders provide that wages should be paid to all workers on a working day but before the expiry of the seventh or tenth day of the last day of the concerned wage period depending on whether the number of workers employed in the establishment does not exceed or exceeds one thousand. Any unclaimed wages shall be paid by the employer on an unclaimed wage pay day in each week after notice to this effect has been displayed on the notice board.

Stoppage of Work

In the event of fire, catastrophe, breakdown of machinery or stoppage of power supply, epidemic, civil commotion or other causes beyond one's control, the employer may stop the working of any section of the establishment, wholly or partially, for any period of time without notice at any time. In the event of such stoppage during working hours, the affected workers should be notified, as soon as possible, as to whether they are to remain or to leave the place of work. Ordinarily, workers should not be required to remain for more than two hours after the commencement of the stoppage. If they are detained for more than an hour, they shall be entitled to receive wages for the whole time detained on account of stoppage but to no other compensation. In case of piece-rated workers, the average daily earning in the previous months is to be taken as the daily wage. Reasonable notice for resumption of duty shall be given to workers, wherever possible. If they are laid-off for short periods on account of failure of plant or a temporary curtailment of production, the period of unemployment shall be treated as compulsory leave, either with or without pay. However, in case of an indefinite or long period of lay-off, the workers may be retrenched after giving them due notice or pay in lieu thereof.

In the event of a strike affecting, wholly or partially, any section or department of the establishment, the employer may close down, wholly or partially, that section/department or any other section or department affected by such closure. Such closure shall be duly notified to workers, as also the date when the work shall be resumed.

Termination of Employment

In order to terminate the employment of a permanent worker, one month's notice in writing if he is monthly rated, and two weeks' notice in other cases, should be given to him or pay in lieu thereof by the employer. However, no temporary, probationer or *badli* worker shall be entitled to any notice or pay in lieu thereof, but the services of a temporary worker shall not be terminated as a punishment unless he has been given an opportunity of explaining the charges of misconduct alleged against him. In case of termination of employment, the worker's earned wages and other dues shall be paid to him before the expiry of the second working day from the day on which his employment is terminated.

Disciplinary Action for Misconduct

The Model Standing Orders provide that a worker may be fined upto two per cent of his wages in a month for any acts or omissions specified therein. They may also be suspended for a period not exceeding four days at a time of dismissed without notice or pay in lieu thereof, if he is found guilty of misconduct. The acts and omissions, which are to be treated as misconduct according to the Model Standing Orders, are: wilful in subordination or disobedience; theft, fraud of dishonesty in connection with the employer's business or property; wilful damage or loss of employer's property; taking or giving bribes or any illegal gratification; habitual absence without leave for more than 10 days; habitual late attendance; habitual breach of any law applicable to the establishment; riotous or disorderly behaviour during working hours or any act subversive of discipline; habitual negligence or neglect of work; frequent repetition of any act or omission for which a fine may be imposed to a maximum of two per cent of the wages in a month; and striking work or inciting others to strike work in contravention of law.

However, no dismissal shall be made unless the concerned worker is informed in writing and is given an opportunity to explain the alleged charges. But in every case the approval of the manager or the employer (where there is no manager) is to be obtained in case of dismissal; and if warranted, the manager/employer may institute independent enquiries before dealing with the charges against him. If he is covered by Article 311 of Clause 2 of the Constitution of India, the provisions of that Article shall be complied with.

Suspension

In case of suspension, the order of suspension shall be in writing and may take effect immediately on delivery to the worker. Such order should set out in detail the alleged misconduct and the worker should be given an opportunity to explain the allegations. If on enquiry the order is confirmed, the worker shall be deemed to have been absent from duty for the period of his suspension and shall not be entitled to any remuneration. If, however, the order is rescinded, then he shall be deemed to have been on duty during the suspension period and paid full wages.

The Model Standing Orders provide that, in awarding punishment, the manager shall take into account the gravity of the misconduct, the previous record of the worker and any extenuating or aggravating circumstances that may exist, he forward a copy of his order to the concerned worker.

Complaints

All complaints arising out of employment, including those related to unfair treatment or wrongful exactions on the part of the employer or his agent, shall be submitted to the manager or other authorised person, with the right of appeal to the employer.

Every permanent worker shall be entitled to a service certificate at the time of his dismissal, discharge or retirement from service.

The manager of the establishment shall personally be held responsible for a proper and faithful compliance with the Standing Orders.

The Model Orders provide that a copy of the orders in English and in the principal languages of the workers shall be pasted near the manager's office and on the notice board maintain at or near the main entrance of the establishment, and shall be kept in legible condition.

The Factories Act, 1948

The Factories Act, 1948 is inforce with amendments made during last five decades.

OBJECTIVES

Main objectives are:

(i) To regulate working conditions for workers in factories,

(ii) To ensure that basic minimum requirements for safety, health and welfare of workers are provided, and

(iii) To regulate the working hours, leave, holidays, overtime, employment of children, women and young persons.

DEFINITIONS

Factory [Sec 2(m)] includes:

- any premises,
- where manufacturing process is carried on,
- wherein 10 or more workers are working with aid of power, or
- wherein 20 or more workers are working without the aid of power, and
- but does not include any mine, mobile unit of army, railway running shed, hotel, restaurant or eating place, or computer unit, as no manufacturing process is carried on.

MANUFACTURING PROCESS

Manufacturing process [Sec. 2(k)] means:

(i) making, altering, repairing, finishing, packing, washing, breaking-up, any articles with a view to its use, sale, transport, or
(ii) pumping oil, water, sewage or any other substance,
(iii) generating, transforming or transmitting power, or
(iv) composing types for printing, printing, book binding,
(v) constructing, repairing, fitting or breaking up ships or vessels, and
(vi) reserving or storing any article in cold storage.

Note: Extraction of salt from sea and *bidi*-making are held to be manufacturing process.
- EDP unit not a factory as no manufacturing process.
- Railway running shed or hotel or restaurant are factories.

WORKER

Worker [Sec. 2(l)] means:

- ❑ a person employed directly or through an agency (contractor),
- ❑ with or without the knowledge of principal employer,
- ❑ whether for remuneration or not, and
- ❑ in any manufacturing process,

(but does not include any member of armed forces).

OCCUPIER

Occupier [Sec. 2(n)] of factory means the person who has ultimate control over the affairs of the factory—

- ❑ In case of firm or association of individuals—one of the individual partner,
- ❑ In case of company, one of the director,
- ❑ In case of government (state/central) person appointed to manage affairs of the factory, and
- ❑ Owner or his agent or master of the ship.

Obligations of Employers

1. The occupier of factory to *obtain compulsory* approval of State Government for the site on which factory is to be constructed,

   If no reply is received of the Government within 3 months, approval shall be deemed to have been granted.

2. The occupier to *obtain licence* for operating and get the factory registered. Licensee to be renew every year by the occupier by paying prescribed fee, at least 30 days before its expiry.
3. *Change of manager* to be informed to chief inspector of factories within seven days of takeover of charge.
4. Occupier to provide for *health measures* as under:
   (a) On cleanliness,
   (b) Disposal of wastes and affluents,
   (c) Proper ventilation and temperatures,
   (d) Protection against dust and fumes,
   (e) Avoidance of over-crowding,
   (f) Protection from glare. Provision of sufficient natural light and artificial lights, drinking cool water at suitable points, and
   (g) Separate latrines and urinals for male and female workers to be provided in sufficient number and kept clean.
5. Undertake *safety measures*:
   (i) Dangerous parts of machinery to be securely fenced,
   (ii) Keep floors and stairs free from obstruction,
   (iii) Prohibition of young persons and women at certain places,
   (iv) Periodical examination of hoists, lifts, cranes and chains, etc.,
   (v) Provision of safety appliances, e.g. goggles, gloves, hats and equipment for fire fighting, and
   (vi) Appoint safety officer if 1000 or more workers in the factory.
6. Provide *welfare measures*:
   (i) Washing facilities, storing of clothes not work during working hours,
   (ii) First aid boxes at least 1 for 150 employees under the charge of one person,
   (iii) A canteen when—250 or more workers in the factory and lunch room—if 150 workers or more are there,
   (iv) Creches, when 30 women and more workers are employed,
   (v) Ambulance room when 500 or more workers are employed in the factory,
   (vi) Working hours, and
   (vii) Welfare officer for 500 or more workers are in the factory.
7. *Working hours/holidays and over time*:
   (a) Restrictions on employment of women, children and adolescents—
      - Women not to be employed between 7 p.m. and 6 a.m.
      - No child below age of 14 years to be employed.
      - No dual employment if he has worked in any other factory.

(b) Working hours:

- Working hours of an adult worker not to exceed 48 hours in a week and 9 hours a day.

  Rest interval of ½ hour before 5 hours at a stretch.

  Spread over not more than 10½ hours in a day.

(c) No overlapping of shifts in the factory.

(d) Weekly holiday to worker in a week. Compensatory holiday is given if worker is required to work on a weekly holiday within the same month or within two months.

(e) Overtime:

- A worker working more than 9 hours on any day, or for more than 48 hours in any week shall be entitled to overtime wages, in respect of such overtime work at twice "The Ordinary Rate of Wages".
- Total working hours in a week including overtime hours should not exceed 60, and the total overtime hours in a quarter should not exceed 50.

(f) Notice of periods of work:

- The manager is required to display on notice board periods of work.
- Periods of work can be changed only after obtaining approval of the inspector.

(g) Manager to maintain registers of workers giving particulars, such as:

- Name, Nature of work, shift.
- No worker to be allowed to work unless his name appears in the register/master roll.

Exemptions: (i) The above provisions from item 'b' to 'f' not to apply to persons holding position of supervision or management.

(ii) The State Government may grant exemptions for urgent repairs, printing of newspapers, loading and unloading of railway wagons or any other work which is of national importance.

8. *Provide leave with wages*:

Earned Leave: Worker who has worked for a period of 240 days or more during a calendar year shall be entitled to earned leave during next calendar year:

(i) One day for every 20 days worked for adult.

(ii) One day for every 15 days worked for a child.

This is the minimum limit.

Notes: I. Leave shall be exclusive of all holidays whether occurring during or at either end of period of leave.

II. Leave can be accumulated upto 30 days. However, if leave refused, leave can be carried forward to next 6 years without any limit.

III. Application for leave to be given 15 days in advance except in case of illness.

IV. Wages in lieu of leave in credit to be paid on leaving or on death of worker.

V. The manager is required to maintain leave register of employees.

9. The manager has to *display notices, maintain registers* and submit returns as required.
10. The manager has to *send notices of fatal and other accidents* causing disablement for a period of 48 hours, dangerous occurrences and contracting of any occupational disease to worker within such time as laid by State Government.

    State Government may direct an enquiry into the causes of accident and diseases.
11. *Employer's obligations regarding hazardous processes/substances.* These provisions have been made after the Bhopal Tragedy and are salutary. The manager of a factory wherein a hazardous process is carried on, or any hazardous substance is manufactured, stored, handled or transported is required to take following measures for ensuring safety of life and health of workers and the public in the vicinity of the factory:
    (a) At the time of registration of factory occupier to lay health and safety policy. Give details of hazardous process.
    (b) The occupier to inform hazardous process before commencement.
    (c) The occupier to inform workers, the chief inspector and general public about dangers, health hazards and measures taken to overcome these and safety measures.
    (d) The occupier to draw up:
        (i) an on-site emergency plan,
        (ii) measures for handling, and
        (iii) storage of hazardous substances inside and disposal outside the factory.
    (e) The occupier to appoint qualified persons and experienced in handling hazardous substances. Also to keep up-to-date medical records of workers' health who are exposed to harmful substances.
    (f) The occupier to constitute a safety committee of equal number of representatives of workers and management to ensure safety and health measures and review periodically.
    (g) The workers to bring to notice of the occupier, in case of any danger and who will take remedial action and report the matter to the inspector.

OBLIGATIONS OF WORKERS

1. A worker should not wilfully misuse any appliances provided for securing health of workers.
2. A worker should not wilfully endanger himself and others.
3. A worker should not neglect to make use of safety appliances.

OFFENCES AND PENALTIES

Sl. No.	*Offences*	*Penalties*
(1)	If occupier and manager contravenes any of provisions of act or rules shall be guilty of offence.	Imprisonment to each upto 2 years or fine upto Rs. 1 lakh or both.
(2)	Failure to comply with any safety measures or precuations against dangerous operations which result in an accident causing: (a) Death Rs. 25,000. (b) Serious body injury Rs. 5,000.	
(3)	Failure to comply with precautions against hazardous processes and substances.	Imprisonment upto 7 years and fine upto Rs. 2 lakh.
(4)	Any person who wilfully obstructs and inspector or fails to produce any records/ documents.	Imprisonment upto 6 months or fine upto Rs. 10,000 or both.
(5)	Any medical practitioner, who attends on a worker who is found suffering from an occupational disease, fails to report to chief inspector.	Fine upto Rs. 1,000.
(6)	Any worker who contravenes any provisions of act or rules.	Fine upto Rs. 500.

29

The Shops and Establishment Act, 1954

The Shop and Establishment Act is a state legislation and every state/union territory government has enacted such legislation and has also framed the rules for its enforcement. It is administered by the State Governments in their respective territories.

Note: After considering the response received from the State Governments, the proposal for a central law for shops and establishments was dropped in 1950, because practically all the State Governments, including some Union Territories, had already enacted such a legislation with practically the same provisions as contained in the proposed central bill. The Delhi Shop and Establishment Act, 1954 passed by Delhi Legislative Assembly received the assent of the President of India in June, 1954 after it repealed the Punjab Trade Employees' Act, 1940, then inforce in Delhi.

OBJECTIVES

(i) Is to regulate the working and employment conditions of workers in so called unorganised sector, i.e. shops and establishments (including commercial establishments which are not covered by the Factories Act or Mines Act.

(ii) The Act provides for the working hours, rest intervals, overtime, holidays, leave, termination of service and other rights and obligations of the employers and employees.

SCOPE AND COVERAGE

The Act extends to the whole of the State and covers all establishments irrespective of their size, turnover and persons employed. The Act applies to following types of establishments:

(a) A shop carrying retail, or wholesale trade or service,

(b) Offices of all types,

(c) A store room, godown, etc.,
(d) Banks, stock exchanges, share brokers, commission agents,
(e) Printing establishment with less than 10 employees,
(f) Educational institutions run for private gain, and
(g) Hotels and restaurants, clubs, canteens, theatres, cinemas and other places of public entertainment or amusement.

Act not applicable to:

(i) Offices of Central or State Governments or local authorities,
(ii) Establishments employing members of employer's family,
(iii) Establishments for care of infirm or mentally unfit,
(iv) Fairs for charitable work,
(v) Libraries where lending of books is not for profit, and
(vi) Persons occupying positions of management and persons whose work is inherently intermittent.

EMPLOYEES COVERED

The Act applies to all persons, whether directly or through an agency or contractor, and whether for wages or not, including apprentices, in business of an establishment.

OBLIGATIONS OF EMPLOYERS

Important obligations of employers under this Act are:

1. *Compulsory registration* of shop or an establishment by the chief inspector, for specified period and should be displayed at establishment.
2. *Health and safety*:
   - ❑ Shop and establishment to be kept clean, free from any drain,
   - ❑ To be painted at regular intervals,
   - ❑ Have sufficient light and ventilation,
   - ❑ Taking necessary precautions against fire, and
   - ❑ Supply of drinking water to employees.
3. *Employer to observe*:
   - ❑ Daily and weekly hours of work for employees is for 9 hours in a day and 48 hours in any week.
   - ❑ Spread-over not more than 12 hours inclusive or rest interval. Some states have different spread-over between 10.30 to 14 hours.
   - ❑ Rest interval of atleast ½ hour so that worker has not to work for more than 5 hours.
   - ❑ Opening and closing hours to be fixed by the State Government for different areas and seasons. Generally upto ½ hour allowed after closing time to serve the customers already inside the shop.
   - ❑ Closed day or weekly off to be notified by the employer and not to change. Alteration is to be communicated to the inspector and notice displayed in the

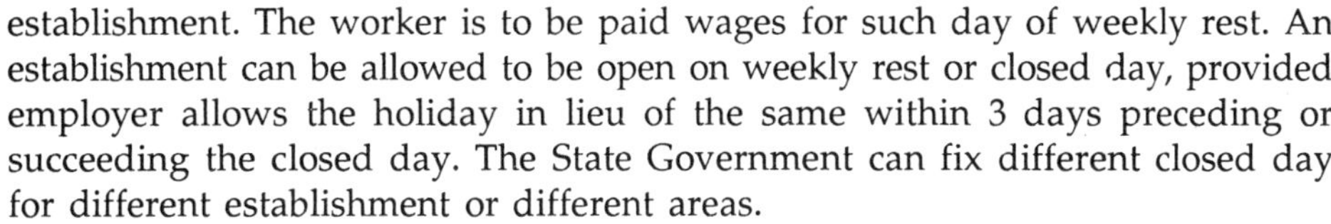

establishment. The worker is to be paid wages for such day of weekly rest. An establishment can be allowed to be open on weekly rest or closed day, provided employer allows the holiday in lieu of the same within 3 days preceding or succeeding the closed day. The State Government can fix different closed day for different establishment or different areas.

- ❑ National and religious holidays:
  Three of the national holidays each year as Government may specify.
- ❑ Overtime working not to exceed one hour per day or 50 hours in 3 months.
- ❑ Employment of children, young persons and women:
  Restrictions imposed under this Act are:
  (i) No child below 12 years of age can be employed,
  (ii) No woman and young person to be employed between 7 p.m. and 8 a.m.
  (iii) A young person below 18 years can not be employed for more than 6 hours in a day. He has to be given rest interval of half an hour after working for three to four hours.
- ❑ Annual leave with wages:
  5 days leave on completion of 4 months of continuous employment (15 days for 12 months) carried forward upto 30 days.

Explanation: (i) The leave admissible is to be exclusive of all holidays occurring during or at either end of the periods of leave.

(ii) Employer has to pay full wages for the period of leave due to him on discharge or he quits.

(iii) Leave cannot be taken for more than 3 times in a year, and application for leave should be made 15 days before date of availing.

(iv) If workers in any establishment have better leave privileges, they may be exempted by the State Government from this Act.

- ❑ Maternity leave with wages for 6 weeks before and 6 weeks after the delivery. This leave is also granted in case of miscarriage—
  - No dismissal within 6 months before delivery of child can deprive of the maternity benefit.
  - No removal of women during maternity leave.
  - She is to be allowed to breaks of ½ hour in addition to regular rest interval, for nursing the child.
- ❑ Sickness and casual leave: In Delhi, combined sickness and casual leave of 12 days is allowed in a year with wages.

4. *Workmen's Compensation Act, 1923* and Payment of Wages Act, 1936 are applicable.
5. *Letter of appointment has to be given* by employer in Delhi containing hours of work and date of appointment.
   - ❑ Notice of termination of service of 1 month or pay in lieu has to be given by employer if put in 3 months service by employee. Similarly, employee has to give notice while leaving or pay in lieu of such notice.

   No notice for termination of service is required for proved misconduct as per standing orders of the company.
6. *Employer to maintain registers* and records in the premises and submit returns as required by the Government.

7. For enforcement and inspection, State Government to appoint inspectors or entrust to local authority. Inspectors are public servants within the meaning of Indian Penal Code and can enter the premise and inspect registers. Employer to cooperate with inspector and produce registers to ensure compliance.

Penalties of fines from Rs. 10 to Rs. 500 for contravention of provisions and for subsequent offence upto Rs. 1,000. In Delhi for false entries and returns punishable with imprisonment for 3-6 months and fine upto Rs. 1,000 or with both.

GENERAL OBSERVATIONS

(a) The legislation is largely to *improve the working and employment conditions* of white collar employees working in shops and establishments.

(b) Practically all states have enacted such acts.

(c) The Act also *provides job, social security and protection of earned wages* by requiring employers to issue letter of appointment and not terminate their service without giving them notice and by applying provisions of the Workmen Compensation Act, Maternity Benefit Act, Payment of Wages Act. It is comprehensive legislation like Factories and Mines Act.

(d) *Main complaint is its inadequate implementation.* The position is made worse by entrusting the administration of this Act to local authorities.

(e) National Commission on labour recommended:

 (i) Limiting the coverage to establishments with stipulated minimum number of employees, and

 (ii) To be administered by Labour Commissioner so that right type of persons are inspectors. This will be more beneficial for workers.

30

The Contract Labour (Regulation and Abolition) Act, 1970

1. OBJECTIVE

Employing contract labour is age-old practice. Malpractices of exploiting labour are attributed to contract labour.

One objective of this Act was to *regulate employment of contract* labour so as to place it at par with labour employed directly, with regard to working conditions and certain other benefits available under labour laws.

The Act also empowers the appropriate Government *to prohibit employment of contract labour* in any process, operation or other work in any establishment.

2. SCOPE AND COVERAGE

The Act covers:

(a) Every establishment where 20 or more workmen are or were employed on any of preceding 12 months, and

(b) Every contractor who employs 20 or more workmen.

Note: The Act does not apply to establishment where work is of casual (irregular or occasional) or intermittent (interrupted or non-continuous) nature.

Work performed in an establishment shall not be intermittent nature if:

(i) It was performed for more than 120 days in 12 months, or

(ii) It is of a seasonal character and is performed for more than 60 days in a year.

3. DEFINITIONS

Establishment means any industry, trade business, manufacture of occupation is carried on or any office of the Government or local authority.

Contractor (including sub-contractor) means a person who undertakes to produce a given result for an establishment through contract labour or who supplies contract labour for any work in an establishment.

- Persons who merely supply goods to or manufacture articles for an establishment are not contractors.
- Contractor is employed to produce the given result for the benefit of the principal employer.

4. CONTRACT LABOUR

Workmen who are hired for work by or through contractors, with or without the knowledge of the principal employer. But excludes:

(i) Persons employed in managerial or administrative capacity,
(ii) Persons employed as supervisors and receiving wages exceeding Rs. 1,600 p.m., and
(iii) 'Out-workers' to whom materials are given for manufacturing or processing at his own premises.

5. ADMINISTRATIVE AUTHORITY

The Act is administered by the Central-State Governments in their respective jurisdictions. They set-up *advisory boards* consisting of representatives of industry, contractor, workers and Government nominees.

6. PROHIBITION OF CONTRACT LABOUR

Both Central and State Governments can prohibit employment of contract labour in any process, operation or other work after consulting their advisory boards.

Prohibition can be in the following circumstances:

(a) The work is of *perineal nature,*
(b) It is *incidental* to and necessary for the industry, trade, business in the establishment, and
(c) It is ordinarily done through regular workmen.

Some of the processes where contract labour may be permitted to be employed:

(i) Loading and unloading,
(ii) Stacking and unstacking, and
(iii) Construction works, renovation of machinery, etc.

7. OBLIGATIONS OF EMPLOYERS/CONTRACTORS

1. Registration of establishment by the *principal employee* and obtain registration certificate from registration officer. An establishment cannot employ contract labour if it does not hold a certificate of registration.
2. The contractor to obtain licence from licensing officer failure to do so entails penal provisions.
3. Contractor to provide welfare and health amenities for contract labour:
   (i) Provide canteen if number of contract workers employed is 100 or more.
   (ii) Supply of drinking water and provision of latrines, urinals and washing facilities.
   (iii) First aid boxes: If contractor fails to provide these amenities, the principal employer shall be liable to provide the same and recover the expenses from contractor.
4. Contractor to pay wages to contract labour regularly and timely, in presence of representative of the principal employer. If contractor fails to pay wages, the principal employer should make the payment and recover the same from the contractor.

   However, gratuity and bonus will not be payable by the principal employer, since these do not come within the definition of wages.
5. Principal employer and contractor should maintain such registers, records, send prescribed returns and exhibit notices containing hours of work, etc.
6. Coverage of contractor's employees under EPF Act and ESI Act by contractor if establishment covered under ESI.
7. Applicability of other labour laws to contract labour, e.g. Factories Act, Payment of Wages Act, ID Act, Workmen's Compensation Act as applicable to regular workers.
8. Persons who get displaced, on expiry of contract, do not get statutory right for absorption in regular service of the employer.

8. OFFENCES AND PENALTIES

(a) Fine upto Rs. 500/Rs. 1,000 or/and imprisonment upto 3 months.
(b) Director, partner or principal officer is responsible for the conduct of affairs and liable to be punished.

9. GENERAL REMARKS

Objective

Regulation: One of the objective was to regulate the employment of contract labour so as to place at par with labour employed directly, with regard to working conditions and certain other benefits available under laws.

Abolition: The Act also empowers the appropriate Government to prohibit employment of contract labour in any process, operation and other work in any establishment. Thus, proper implementation of the regulatory provision of the Act can ensure such working and employment conditions to contract labour that it may cease to be cheap and exploited labour.

Actual Working

But it has happened, that it has become a stumbling block of employing flexible labour in the changed economic environment.

State Governments are on a spree of abolishing contract labour system anywhere, which has infact, changed the purpose of the Act viz. from the regulation of contract labour to total abolition of contract labour.

Further, rulings of High and Supreme Courts have encouraged the State Governments to further issue notifications for abolition of contract labour system and also absorption of the contract worker in the employment of the principal employer. This is case of judicial activism.

Thus, out-sourcing and venderisation is restricted.

This law has become a major source of problem for organisations to compete in global environment where our prices are not competitive. Organisations are concerned and are demanding overall review of labour laws as these are also discouraging MNCs to open new factories.

New Supreme Court decision (2001) modifying its earlier judgement has given relief to organisations.

31

The Minimum Wages Act, 1948

1. OBJECTIVES

- To ensure *minimum statutory* wages for *scheduled employments* and to avoid the chances of exploitation by paying very low wages.
- The Act also provides for maximum daily *working hours, weekly rest day* and *overtime.*
- Minimum wages fixed by the State Governments under the Act prevail over the rates if fixed lower under award/agreement. Thus, minimum wages set the floor.

2. DEFINITION AND MEANING OF WAGES

Wages means all remuneration *expressible* in money terms including HRA but excluding value of any—house accommodation, supply of light, water, medical attendance, contribution to provident fund, travelling allowance, gratuity, etc.

3. FIXATION OF MINIMUM RATE OF WAGES

State Governments are empowered under the Act to *fix minimum rates* of wages for different classes of employees—skilled, unskilled, clerical, supervisory, etc. employed in scheduled employments and to revise the same, *fixation of working hours.* The Government may:

(a) Fix the number of working hours for a working day.

(b) Provide for rest day with wages in every period of seven days.

(c) Provide for payment for work on a rest day at a rate not less than the over time rate.

(d) *Overtime wage* is to be paid in excess of normal working hours for every hour or for part of an hour under this Act or under any other law, whichever is higher. As per

The Factories Act, 1947, over time wages are to be paid at twice the normal rate of wages. Employer is required to maintain prescribed registers for this purpose.

(e) Undistributed amount shall be deposited by employer with prescribed authority.

(f) Also to fix cost of living allowance, considering the change in price index from time to time.

4. PENALTIES FOR OFFENCES

Payment of wages at less than the minimum wages fixed under the Act entails imprisonment upto six months or fine upto Rs. 500 or both.

32

The Payment of Wages Act, 1936

1. OBJECTIVES

- To eliminate malpractices of short payment and irregular payments and maintain good labour relations, which were main sources of grievances. The Act ensures payment of wages at regular intervals without unauthorised deductions by:
  - (a) laying down *wage periods;*
  - (b) time for making payments;
  - (c) no unauthorised *deductions* from wages; and
  - (d) regulating imposition of fines.
- The Act is administered by State Government except for railways, mines, oil fields, central air transports which is enforced by Central Government.

2. OBLIGATIONS OF EMPLOYEES

- The Act is applicable to the employees receiving wages below Rs. 1600 per month.
- Employer is to fix wage period which is not to exceed one month.
- To pay wages on *working day,* before expiry of seventh day (upto 1000 workers)/ tenth day for above 1000 workers.
- Employer to make no deductions except as authorised, i.e. adjustment of advances, income tax, provident fund, ESI, etc. Deduction for loss can be made after giving opportunity to show cause for deductions.
- Fines can be imposed after proper opportunity to employee to explain and fine not to exceed 3% of wages in instalments. Fine amount to be used for benefit of workmen.
- Total amount of deductions in any wage period should not exceed 50% of the wages.

- *Registers* to be maintained by the employer for wages paid.
- Employer can deduct, if employees go on strike without notice, wages upto 8 days.
- After obtaining written authorisation of employee, employer may pay wages either by *cheque* or credit in his bank account.
- Discharged worker is to be paid wages within 2 days when employment is terminated.
- If wages of an employee who has expired, cannot be paid to person nominated by him, the amount is to be deposited with the prescribed authority.
- For deduction of wages government appoints courts for appeal, where employee can go for even non-payment of wages.

3. PENALTIES

- Penalties range from Rs. 500 to Rs. 1000, if registers are not maintained or refusal to give information, or failure to fix wage period, or non-payment of wages or making any unauthorised deduction, etc.

33

The Equal Remuneration Act, 1978

OBJECTIVES

This act:

(i) provides for payment of equal remuneration to men and women workers, for same work or work of a similar nature,

(ii) for prevention of discrimination, on grounds of sex, against women in the matter of employment, and

(iii) the appropriate government (central or state) to constitute advisory committee to recommend employment for increasing employment opportunities for women.

OBLIGATION OF EMPLOYERS

(i) Equal wages for equal work: The employer shall pay equal wages to men and women employees for performing same work or work of similar nature.

(ii) There shall not be discrimination against women while doing recruitment of employees for same work or work of a similar nature, or in respect of their promotion, training or transfer, etc.

OFFENCES AND PENALTIES

Offence

Discrimination against women in recruitment, etc. or payment of unequal wages to men and women.

Penalty

Fine upto Rs. 20,000 (minimum Rs. 10,000) or imprisonment upto one year (minimum 3 months) or both by the Central and State governments in their respective spheres.

34

The Payment of Bonus Act, 1965

1. OBJECTIVES

(i) The Act aims at providing for payment of bonus (*linked with profits or productivity*) to the employees;

(ii) To define principles for payment of bonus according to prescribed formula;

(iii) Payment of minimum and maximum bonus and link the scheme of "set-off and set-on"; and

(iv) To provide *machinery for enforcement* of liability for payment of bonus, with a view to *minimising the disputes* on this account.

2. COVERAGE

- Applicable to every factory (without power) and every establishment where 20 or more workmen are employed (part-time employees are also included). Factory with power where 10 or more persons (government may extend to more than 10 employees also).
- Employees of different establishments functioning in the same premises, shall not be clubbed together.
- Where for any accounting year a separate *balance sheet* and profit and loss account are prepared for any department or branch of establishment, then such shall be treated as separate establishment for computation of bonus for that year.

3. EMPLOYEES ENTITLED

- Every employee receiving wages upto Rs. 3500 per month and has worked for at least 30 days in that year,

- A probationer is eligible for bonus,
- Bonus also payable to daily wage earners,
- Apprentice is *not eligible,* and
- Government employees not entitled to bonus under this Act.

4. SALARY OR WAGES INCLUDED

Basic pay plus dearness allowance.

Wage does not include

- Not other allowances,
- Value of accommodation, light, water, medical attendance, tiffen,
- Travelling concession,
- Contribution to provident fund by the employer,
- Incentive, e.g. production, attendance,
- Leave salary encashment, and
- Retrenchment compensation.

5. MINIMUM BONUS UNDER THE ACT

(a) 8.33% of wages during the accounting year; or
(b) Rs. 100 whichever is higher.

- If employee has not worked for all the working days in an accounting year, the minimum bonus shall be proportionately reduced.
- In case of new establishment, in the first five accounting years following the year in which the employer begins to *sell his goods,* bonus is payable only, in respect of that accounting year, in which the employer *draws profits.*

6. MAXIMUM BONUS

- Not to exceed 20% of wages earned during the accounting year.
- *Time limit for payment of bonus* is 8 months from the close of the accounting year.
- Bonus is payable only annually (not half-yearly basis).

7. CALCULATION OF BONUS

The method for calculation of annual bonus is as follows:

(i) *Calculate the gross profit* (as mentioned in second schedule).
(ii) *Calculate the available surplus:*
Available surplus = A + B
A = (gross profit – depreciation under I.T. Act and development rebate investment allowance)
B = Direct taxes for accounting year

(iii) *Calculate allocable surplus*
= 60% of available surplus (67% in case of foreign companies)

(iv) Make adjustment for 'set-on' and 'set-off' from previous years to allocable surplus.

(v) This allocable surplus is distributed in proportion of wages received in accounting year.
Note: In case of employees receiving wages between Rs. 2500 and Rs. 3500, the bonus payable is calculated as if their wages were Rs. 2500 per month.

8. SET-ON AND SET-OFF

- If in an accounting year, the allocable *surplus exceeds* the amount of maximum bonus payable, then such *excess shall be carried forward* for being *'set-on'* in the succeeding four accounting years. Whereafter the amount of set-on remaining unutilised shall lapse. The amount to be *carried forward* should not exceed 20% of wages for that accounting year.
- If there is no allocable surplus or if the allocable surplus falls short of the minimum bonus payable, then such deficiency be met out of the amount brought forward for being *set-on* from the previous accounting year, if any.
- If there is still any deficiency, then such amount be carried forward for being *set-off* in the succeeding four accounting years, whereafter the amount of *set-off* remaining unadjusted shall lapse.
- While calculating bonus for succeeding accounting years, the amount of *'set-on'* or *'set-off'* carried forward from the earliest accounting year shall first be taken into account.

9. RIGHTS OF EMPLOYER

- Employer has right to forfeit bonus of an employee, who has been dismissed from service for fraud, riotous or violent behaviour or theft, misappropriation or sabotage of any property of the establishment.
- Right makes permissible deductions from bonus payable such as interim bonus or loss caused by misconduct of the employee.

10. OFFENCES AND PENALITIES

- Contravention of the provisions of the Act or Rules: imprisonment upto 6 months or fine upto Rs. 1000 or both.

11. RECOMMENDATIONS OF THE NATIONAL COMMISSION ON LABOUR, 2002 ON BONUS

Both wage ceilings for reckoning to be enhanced.

	For Entitlement	*Calculation of Bonus*
Existing	Rs. 3500	Rs. 2500
Proposal	Rs. 7500	Rs. 3500

35

The Workmen's Compensation Act, 1923

1. OBJECTIVES

- This is first social security measure for workers in India.
- The Act confers on workmen and/or their dependents a legal right to claim compensation for disablement or death by employment injury or an occupational disease.
- Neither Government nor workman contributes but relief provided by employer.

2. SCOPE AND COVERAGE

- Applicable to all establishments specified, except which are covered by the employees State Insurance Act.

3. OBLIGATIONS OF EMPLOYERS

Some important obligations of employers under this Act and Workmen's Compensation (Amendment) Act, 1995:

(i) Employer to pay compensation for employment injury/death as required as soon as it falls due, or deposit with the Commissioner for Workmen's Compensation within one month:
  - Compensation to be payable when employment injury is caused by *accident arising out of* and *in the course of his employment*.
  - Which disables him for more than three days.
  - Covers injury/death due to occupational disease as employment injury.

(ii) Act distinguishes into three types of injuries (in Schedule I):
   (a) *Permanent total disablement:* loss of total earning capacity (100%).
   (b) *Permanent partial disablement*: when it reduces for all times earning capacity in the present job.
   (c) *Temporary (period) disablement*: less than three days.

(iii) *Amount of compensation payable by the employer* (Sec. 4A):
   (a) *Where death of workman from injury*: An Amount equal to 50 per cent of monthly wages of deceased × relevant factor or Rs. 80,000 whichever is more and Rs. 2,500 for funeral expenses. (*Note*: Relevant factor specified in Schedule IV of this Act).
   (b) *Where total disablement results*: An amount equal to 60 per cent of the monthly wages × relevant factor or an amount of Rs. 90,000 whichever is more depending on the wage and age of the workman at the time of disablement.
   (c) The total compensation payable may be about Rs. 2.28 lakh in case of death and Rs. 2.74 lakh in case of permanent disability.
   (d) *Where temporary disablement results from injury*: Half-monthly payment equivalent to 25 per cent of his monthly wages for the period of disablement or 5 years, whichever is shorter.
   (e) No deduction from compensation any amount which is paid by employer for medical treatment (Sec. 6).
   (f) Employer to get registered with the Commissioner, any agreement made with the worker or his dependents settling the amount of lumpsum payable as compensation (Sec. 28).
   (g) Any workman relinquishing his right for personal injury not permissible (Sec. 17).
   (h) When the monthly wages are more than Rs. 4000 per month, it will be deemed Rs. 4000.

(iv) *Compensation when not payable by the employer*:
   (i) When injury does not cause disablement for more than 3 days.
   (ii) When injury, not resulting in death, is directly attributable to employee's wilful disobedience of safety rules or disregard of safety devices or employee under the influence of drink or drug.
   (iii) When employee has contracted a disease which is not directly attributable to a specific injury caused by accident or to that occupation.
   (iv) When the employee has filed a suit for damages in a civil court.
   (v) The *employer to notify* to the Commissioner or any other authority specified, any accident which results in death or serious bodily injury within 7 days of occurrence. Penalty if he fails to do so.
   (vi) The employer to maintain a notice book in the prescribed form for recording the accident.
   (vii) The employer to submit annual return to the Government.
   (viii) The employer to get workman examined by a qualified medical practitioner within 3 days from receiving the notice of accident the employee must present for such examination, otherwise he shall loose his right to the compensation.
   (ix) No compensation payable can be attached or passed on to any person other than the workman, nor can it be set-off against any other claim.

4. OFFENCES AND PENALTIES

Sl. No.	Offences	Penalties
(1)	Unjustified delay in payment of compensation beyond one month.	Upto 50% of the amount of compensation besides interest.
(2)	(i) Failure to maintain a notice book.	Fine upto Rs. 5,000.
	(ii) Failure to submit a statement of fatal accident.	As above.
	(iii) Failure to submit an accident report.	As above.
	(iv) Failure to file annual return of compensation.	As above.

5. GENERAL

1. Whether Workman or not under the Act

The relation between employer and the person claiming compensation can be determined on the basis of following principles:

(a) Whether the person is having contract of service; or
(b) Whether the master can order what is to be done;
(c) Whether it is obligatory on the part of the person to obey his orders; and
(d) Whether a person is having any agreement to serve the employer only or employed for his trade or business.

In nutshell, any person engaged in such premises who is contributing for the intended manufacturing process would be deemed to be workman for the purpose of the Act.

Case: A contractor entered into construction contract and agreed to work himself and also employ his labour. The contractor died while working himself, it was held that dependents of the deceased were entitled to compensation.

2. Accident Arising out of and in the Course of Employment

Three tests for determining whether an accident arose out of employment are:

(i) At the time of injury workman must have been engaged in the business of the employer and must not be doing some thing for his personal benefit,
(ii) The accident occurred at the place where he was performing his duties, and
(iii) Injury must have resulted from some risk incidental to the duties of the service, or inherent in the nature or condition of employment.

The general principles that are evolved are:

(i) There must be a casual connection between the injury and the accident and the work done in the course of employment,

(ii) The onus is upon the applicant to show that it was the work and the resulting strain which aggravated the injury,
(iii) It is not necessary that workman must be actually working at the time of death, and
(iv) Evidence shows that work contributed to the causing of the personal injury, it would be enough for the workman to succeed.

There are some cases when a workman is not performing actual duties and dies, the employer was liable for compensation:

- A workman had gone to canteen to take tea, where he died. Held accident injury arose in course of employment and the period of recess did not disrupt the continuity of employment.
- A factory worker suffering from a heart disease, while coming out of the factory, died inside premises. Held stress and strain of work were accelerating factors to the death.
- In another case, a workman complained chest pain while at work and died in hospital next morning. Held death should not be only in factory. Workman may be suffering gradually due to working in his employment and it is commulative effect that lead to death in hospital.

3. Doctrine of notional extension of the employer's premises so as to include an area which workman passes in going to and in leaving the actual place of work. Some examples of notional extension of employer's premises are:

- An accident sustained by transport staff while travelling between depot and residence, or *vice versa*, has to be treated as arising in the course of employment.
- Where a workman was standing in queue waiting for the bus provided by the employer for reaching the place of work and workman was run over by the bus by which he was to travel. It was held workman died as a result of employment injury.
- It has also been held in another case, that employer to pay compensation if workman meets with an accident while proceeding to his work place on a bicycle.
- Yet in another case, a mill worker has stabbed in a communal riot, while he was returning home after night shift and died just at a short distance from the mill. It was held that the case fell within the definition of employment injury.

36

The Employee's State Insurance Act, 1948

1 OBJECTIVE

A land mark of contributory system—social security measure. To provide worker's medical benefit, sickness cash benefits, maternity benefits, compensation for injuries and occupational diseases, in an integrated form on a contributory basis.

2 COVERAGE

(a) *Factories*: Using power 10 or more persons. Non-power 20 or more persons.
(b) Shops, hotels, cinemas, newspaper establishments employing 20 or more persons.
(c) Beedi manufacturing—10 or more persons.
(d) The Act covers all employees whose wages do not exceed Rs. 7500 p.m.

3. CONTRIBUTIONS

- It is contributory scheme. 1.75% of wages of employees is the contribution.
- And 4.75% of wages is contributed by employers.
- Employer is responsible for both contributions and also in respect of contract labour.
- Deemed wages include basic pay, DA, HRA, CCA, production incentive, night shift allowance.
- Contribution periods are:
  1st April to 30th September
  1st October to 31st March
- Employer has to register his factory and get code number from Regional office.

4. BENEFITS TO EMPLOYEES

1. *Medical benefit* as out patient at hospital. Retired persons and disabled persons can also get this treatment on payment Rs. 120 per annum.
2. *Sickness benefit.*
   - Payment to employee @ 50% to 55% wages for period upto 91 days excluding waiting period of 2 days. In special diseases, more leave is admissible. Sickness benefit to commence after 9 months from date of joining
   - Extended sickness benefit in certain specified disease (ESB) is given for 2 years. The rate of ESB is 14% of sickness benefit rate.
3. *Maternity benefit* is payable for 12 weeks in case of confinement at the double the standard benefit rate (almost full wages). And for 6 weeks in case of miscarriage or on medical termination.
4. *Disablement benefit* for employment injury or occupational disease if incapacity exceeds 3 days, 7% of wages.
   - 4.1 Temporary disablement benefit: @ 14% of standard sickness benefit rate.
   - 4.2 Permanent disablement benefit: @ based on rate recommended by Medical Board.
5. *Dependent's benefit* if employee dies of employment injury, then payment is made as under:
   - (a) Widow @ 2/5th of disable benefit.
   - (b) Child @ 2/5th of disable benefit upto 18 years of age as pension.
6. *Funeral expenses.* Actual upto Rs. 2500.
7. *Rehabilitation allowance.* For the period employee is admitted in artificial limb centre and free of cost artifical limbs.

Free supply of spectacles if impairment of eye sight is due to employment injury/disease. Similarly, denture and hearing aids are provided.

Provision for exemption of factory/establishment from ESI Act for a period of year at a time, if employees are in receipt of benefits similar or superior to provided under the Act (S. 90), subject to the conditions, e.g. inspection, meet proportionate maintenance cost of ESI establishment and services in areas.

5. PUNITIVE ACTION

- Where employer deducts contributions but does not pay to ESI which is criminal breach under IPC.
- Failure to fulfil obligations under Act to any person.
- If payment is delayed by the employer then rate of damage is upto 2 months—5%; 2-4 months—10%; 4-6 months—15%; above 6 months—25%.
- Different punishment have been provided for different offences ranging from six months to 2 years imprisonment and fine Rs. 5000.

6. COMPARISON OF ESI ACT, 1948 AND WORKMEN'S COMPENSATION ACT, 1923

This is given below in tabular form:

ESI Act, 1948	*Workmen's Compensation Act, 1923*
• A compulsory and contributory health insurance scheme for industrial workers. • Administered by ESI Corpn. from its own ESI fund. • Employer's contribution 4.75% • Employee's contribution 1.75% • State Govt. contributes 12.5 of expenditure on medical care. • Scheme applicable to employees upto remuneration Rs. 7,500	Compensation to be paid by employer in case of industrial *accidents* & certain *occupation* diseases, resulting in *death* or disablement. • Applicable upto wage of Rs. 3,500. • Employees in administrative or clerical capacity are not covered.
Benefits	**Benefits**
1. **Sickness Benefit**—Cash payment for 91 days during sickness & unable to attend (1/2 of wages). 2. **Medical Benefit**—In ESI dispensary or hospital for whole 3. **Maternity Benefit** 4. **Disablement Benefit** * Temporary Disablement—full pay * Permanent Disablement—cash benefit for life 5. **Dependent's Benefit**—of deceased insured worker Widow Pension—for life or upto remarriage—@ 3/5 of disablement • Two children upto 18 years @ 2/5 of disablement 6. Funeral Benefit for employee upto Rs. 2,500 7. Rehabilitation allowance when admitted in artificial limb centre 8. Old age medical care	1. Permanent total disablement (60,000 to 2.74 lakhs) 2. Death (50,000 to 2.98 lakhs)

Box 1

ESIC Scheme comes a Croper

The scheme aimed to provide social security to unemployed workers which was launched with a lot of fanfare last year by the Employee's State Insurance Corporation (ESIC) under the Rajiv Gandhi Shramik Kalyan Yojna, has flopped miserably.

ESIC has been able to use only Rs. 15 crore of the total Rs. 300 crore sanctioned for the scheme in the last one and half years though it was supposed to use all the money by March 31, 2006. The scheme was launched in April 2005. Senior labour ministry and ESIC officers are of the view that the main cause of failure of the scheme was "lack of awareness among the people." In a bid to bolster the ESIC health and insurance scheme which covers over 3.5 crore workers and their families, the social security wing of International Labour Organisation (ILO), called International Social Security Association (ISSA), will now assist ESIC.

37

The Employee's Provident Funds, Miscellaneous Provisions Act, 1952 and The Employee's Pension Scheme, 1955

The Employee's Provident Funds and Miscellaneous Provisions Act, 1952 is one of the social security laws. It had three schemes framed under the Act, namely:

(i) The *Employee's Provident Fund Scheme*, 1952 (EPF)

(ii) The *Employee's Family Pension Scheme*, 1995 (Formerly The *Employee's Family Pension Scheme*, 1971 (EFPS)

(iv) The *Employees Deposit Linked Insurance Scheme*, 1976. It is to provide *additional benefit* equal to average balance in EPF account of *the deceased* subject to a maximum of Rs. 60,000.

Note: However, the need to provide a *monthly pension* scheme in the event of retirement, permanent and total disablement, death, etc. was also felt. Therefore, *The Employee's Pension Scheme, 1995 was introduced w.e.f. 16.11.1996* and the Employee's Family Pension Scheme, 1971 ceased.

I. EMPLOYEE'S PROVIDENT FUND ACT, 1952

(a) Objective

EPF is a compulsory contributory fund for the future of the employee after his retirement or for his dependents in case of his early death.

(b) Coverage

It is applicable to:

(a) Every *factory* in which 20 or more workmen are employed.
(b) To every other *commercial establishment* employing 20 or more persons.
(c) In case of cinema/theatre employing 5 employees.

Note:

- *Contract labour* is to be included but casual labour is excluded for counting strength of employees.
- Once *this Act applies* to any establishment, it shall continue to be governed by the Act, even if number falls below 20.
- The Act applies to *educational* institutions.
- All departments and branches shall be treated as part of same establishment.
- Construction industry is excluded.
- Cooperative society employing less than 50 persons are excluded.
- The employer and majority of employees of an establishment may agree for voluntary application of this Act.

(c) Employees Entitled

- Every employee (including through contractor but excluding apprentice or casual labour) whose wages are upto Rs. 5000 per month.
- Employees are eligible for joining the EPF *from date of joining service* (w.e.f. 1.11.1990).

(d) Employer's and Employee's Contribution

(i) In all establishments employing 20 or more persons 12 per cent of the wages plus dearness allowance of each employee.
(ii) Establishments with less than 20 persons or sick industrial companies (BIFR) or jute, *beedi*, brick, coir industry—10 per cent of wages plus dearness allowance of each employee.

Notes: (a) Where pay of employees exceeds Rs. 5,000 per month, the contribution payable to pension fund is limited to the amount payable on his pay of Rs. 5,000 only.

(b) Employer to deduct *employee's contribution* at the rates given in items: (i) & (ii) above deposit into provident fund account of the employee along with his own contribution.

(c) *A part of employer's contribution* is remitted to pension fund as under:

EPFs	= 3.67%
Employee's Pension Scheme	= 8.33%
Employee's Deposit Linked Insurance Scheme	= 0.5%

(d) *The Central Government contribution* to the pension fund is 1.16% of pay of members.

(e) The employer to pay *administrative charges* to EPFs and deposit linked insurance fund at the rate of 1-10% and 0-01% respectively.

(f) The employer to deposit the total amount within 15 days of the close of every month to the Provident Fund Commissioner. If there is default in payment by the employer, he shall be liable to the damages at the rate of per cent interest.

	Rate of demands (% p.a.)
Less than 2 months	17%
2 months but less than 4 months	22%
4 months but less than 6 months	27%
6 months and above	37%

(e) Benefits Admissibility

- Lum-sum payment with interest on retirement or leaving the job, or retrenchment or leaving on VRS.
- Partial withdrawal during job for specified purposes.
- Upon death of member, payment is made to nominee (if made) or if no nomination exists then proceeds shall be payable to legal heirs.

Private provident fund scheme (PtPFS)

Establishments employing 100 or more persons may opt for private provident fund scheme after getting approval from the commissioner (u/s 16A).

Transfer of accounts

Where an employee covered by the Act leaves and obtains employment in another establishment where the Act applies, the accumulations shall be transferred.

Obligations of employees

(a) To furnish nomination in prescribed form at the time of employment.

(b) Allow employer to deduct EPF every month.

Obligations of employers

(a) To regularly deposit employer and employees contributions and also administrative charges.

(b) To furnish returns to the P.F. Commissioner.

(c) To allot P.F. account number to a member-employees.

(d) To maintain registers:

- Contribution cards for each employee,
- Eligibility register,
- Inspection book.

(e) To allow employees to avail temporary/permanent withdrawals and other benefits.

2. EMPLOYEE'S PENSION SCHEME, 1995

Contribution to EPF

- Rate of contribution of employer towards EPF is @ 8.33% of pay with dearness allowance. The contribution is to be diverted from employer's share of PF.
- The Central Government will also contribute @ 1.16% of the pay of members.

Pensionable Salary

To be determined as average pay for last 12 months contributing service.

Pensionable Service

Total service rendered by member for which contributions made under EFPS, 1971 and EPS, 1995.

Types of Pension

Monthly Member's pension	On retirement
Monthly Widow's pension	After death in service or death after retirement of member
Monthly Children's pension	After death of member to 2 children along with widow/dower
Monthly Orphan's pension	After death of member and widow/widower
Disablement pension	On permanent and total disablement during employment
Return of capital	After opting for reduced pension

Formula or Method for Calculation of Pension

$$\text{Monthly Member's Pension} = \frac{\text{Pensionable salary} \times \text{Pensionable service}}{70}$$

CONDITIONS FOR BENEFITS

1. Pension is applicable to member after putting *10 years of eligible service.* Minimum service is not applicable in case of widow's pension, disablement pension, children's pension, orphan's pension.
2. Widow's pension, children's pension and orphan's pension is payable on *only 30 days* of actual contribution.
3. A member *can opt* for reduced pension before the age of 58 but not earlier than 50 years.
4. Provision of a nomination in the absence of the member's family is made.
5. On completing 33 years of service, the pension entitlement is 50% of pay at the time of retirement.

6. Pension entitlement is 60% of pay on completion of 40 years of service.
7. Family pension covers for widow/widower for life or until her/his remarriage, and for two children upto 25 years of age on the death of member (be it in service, out of service or after receiving the pension on retirement).
8. *Mode of Payment*: Pension disbursement is made through post office, bank or treasury.

3. THE EMPLOYEE'S DEPOSIT LINKED INSURANCE SCHEME (EDLI SCHEME), 1976

Contributions

- Employer 0.5% of basic wage of employee
- Employee None
- Benefit the scheme provides for payment of assurance benefit, upon death of the member while in service; linked to the average balance in the provident fund account of the deceased member.
- Provides lump-sum benefit upon death, equal to average balance in the EPF account during the preceding 12 months of death, if average PF balance is less than Rs. 35,000.
- In case average balance exceeds Rs. 35,000, amount paid will be Rs. 35,000 plus 25% of average balance in excess of Rs. 35,000 upto Rs. 60,000.

Protection of Provident Fund

Amount at credit of the member cannot be assigned or attached by a court for any debt liability.

The Payment of Gratuity Act, 1972

1. OBJECTIVES

- A social security measure to provide against risk of old-age.
- Acceptance of gratuity as a compulsory statutory retiral benefit for long service to the employer.

2. COVERAGE

The Act is applicable to:

- Every factory, mine, oil field, plantation, port, railways or every shop and commercial establishment, or educational institutions, clubs, motor transport, local bodies, chambers of commerce and industry.
- In which 10 or more persons are employed.

3. EMPLOYEES ENTITLED

- Every employee irrespective of wages after he has rendered continuous service for 5 years or more.
- Every employee to submit his nomination within 30 days of completion of one year. Employee can change his nominee at any time.

When Gratuity is Payable

(i) On superannuation, or
(ii) On resignation,

(iii) On retrenchment, termination, and

(iv) On death or disablement (the condition of 5 years service is not necessary). Payable to legal nominee in case of deceased.

4. CALCULATION OF GRATUITY

- Gratuity Payable = 15 days wages × No. of completed years of service (part of a year in excess of six months is counted as one year)
- Maximum Gratuity amount should not exceed Rs. 3.5 lakhs.
- Gratuity Amount = $\frac{\text{Monthly wages} \times 15 \times \text{years of service}}{26}$
- Protection of Gratuity, Deductions from Gratuity amount cannot be made or attached in execution of decree orders of the court.
- Employer can withhold Gratuity, if service is terminated due to disorderly conduct or moral turpitude.
- Forefeiture of gratuity can also be wholly or partially for wilfully causing loss, destruction of property, etc. after affording opportunity.
- Payment of Gratuity to be made within 30 days it becomes payable.
  Gratuity cannot be withheld for not vacating the employer—company's quarter.

5. PENALTIES

- Imprisonment for 6 months or fine upto Rs. 10,000 for avoiding to make payment by making false statement.

39

The Maternity Benefit Act, 1948

1. OBJECTIVES

(i) This Act aims at regulation of employment of women employees for certain periods before and after child birth; and
(ii) Provision of maternity and certain other benefits.

2. SCOPE AND COVERAGE

The act is applicable to every factory, mine or plantation (including those belonging to government) and to every shop or establishment wherein 10 or more persons are employed.

State Government may extend this Act to any other establishment, industrial, commercial, agricultural, etc.

However, the Act does not apply to any such factory/establishment to which provisions of ESI Act are applicable for the time being. Where the woman is not eligible for maternity benefit under ESI Act, as her wages exceed Rs. 3000 per month, then such woman is entitled to claim maternity benefit under this Act.

3. EMPLOYEE ENTITLED

Every woman employee, whether employed directly or through contractor, who has worked for a period of at least 80 days during 12 months immediately preceding the date of her expected delivery, is entitled to receive maternity benefit.

There is neither a wage ceiling for coverage under the Act nor there is any restriction as regards the type of work a woman is engaged in.

4. ADMINISTRATIVE AUTHORITY

It is looked after by State Governments except for mines. State/Central inspectors are appointed and enforce the Act.

5. OBLIGATIONS OF THE EMPLOYER

1. Restriction on employment of pregnant women. *Not to engage* pregnant woman during the period of 6 weeks immediately following the day of her delivery, or miscarriage, or medical termination of pregnancy. Besides, no woman should work in any establishment during said period of 6 weeks. Further, the employer should *not require a pregnant woman to do any arduous work* involving long hours of standing or any work which is likely to interfere with her pregnancy, during the period one month preceding the period of 6 weeks before date of her expected delivery.
2. *Not to discharge or dismiss* a pregnant woman employee during the period of maternity leave or to vary to her disadvantage any of the conditions of her service. Discharge or dismissal is to be void and shall not disentitle her to maternity benefit or medical bonus under the Act.
3. *To pay maternity benefit and/or medical bonus, etc.*
   - After the amendment of 1989, now in case a woman employee does not avail six weeks' leave preceding the date of her delivery, she can avail that leave following her delivery provided the total leave period, i.e. preceding and following the day of her delivery, does not exceed 12 weeks.
   - Amount of benefit is payable at the average daily wages for the period of actual absence, during benefit period. Wages includes—basic wage, DA, HRA, incentive bonus.
   - Women employees may give notice to employer of pregnancy, and employer shall permit the woman to absent herself.
   - Employer to pay maternity benefit for the period preceding the date of expected delivery in advance on production of the proof of pregnancy. Balance of amount for the subsequent period should be paid within 48 hours of production of proof of delivery.
   - In case of death of woman employee entitled to maternity benefit, the employer shall pay the amount to her nominee or legal representative.
   - Employer to pay medical bonus of Rs. 250 if no pre-natal confinement and post-natal care is provided by the employer free of charge.
   - Leave for illness arising out of pregnancy, etc. upto one month with wages at maternity benefit are allowable.
   - Leave for miscarriage or medical termination of pregnancy shall of entitled to woman for leave with wages at the rate of maternity benefit, for a period of 6 weeks following the day of her miscarriage, etc.
   - Leave for tubectomy operation shall be given with wages for a period of two weeks following the day of operation.
   - Two nursing breaks of 15 minutes each for nursing the child on daily work to be provided until the child attains the age of 15 months.

- ❑ No deduction from normal wages of woman to be made for lighter work or nursing breaks.

4. To *maintain prescribed records* and submit the prescribed returns.
5. *Exhibit provisions of the Act* in the local language.

6. OFFENCES AND PENALTIES

Offence	*Penalty*
(1) (a) Failure to pay maternity benefit as provided for under the Act (b) Dismissal or discharge of a woman employee in contravention of the Act.	Imprisonment upto one year and fine upto Rs. 5000. (Minimum 3 months and Rs. 2000 respectively)
(2) Failure to produce any register or document before the Inspector or obstructing the Inspector.	Imprisonment upto one year and fine upto Rs. 5000 or both.
(3) Contravention of any other provision of the Act or the rules.	As above

The Apprentices Act, 1961

OBJECTIVES

- To supplement the programme of institutional training by on-the-job training and increase availability of trained technical personnel for the industry.
- Regulate and control the training of apprentices in designated trades.
- It also covers graduate engineers and diploma holders for giving them practical training under factory conditions for improving their employment potential as per amendment of the Act in 1973.

SCOPE AND ADMINISTRATION

- The Act applies to industries specified by the government.
- The Act is administered by the Central and State Governments.
- The State and Central Governments have to appoint the following authorities for administering the Act.
  - (a) The National State Councils for training in vocational trades;
  - (b) Apprenticeship Councils;
  - (c) All India and State Councils of Technical Education;
  - (d) Regional Boards of Apprenticeship Training at Chennai, Mumbai, Kolkata and Kanpur; and
  - (e) The Central and State Apprenticeship Advisors.

OBLIGATIONS OF EMPLOYERS

1. Engagement of Apprentices

A person can undergo apprenticeship training in any designated trade only if,

(a) he is not less than 14 years of age,
(b) he satisfies the prescribed standard of education and physical fitness, and
(c) has entered into a contract of apprenticeship with the employer.

2. Registration of Contract of Apprenticeship

The employer to submit the contract of apprenticeship within three months to the apprenticeship advisor for its registration.

3. Make Arrangements for Practical Training

- The employer should make arrangements for imparting practical training for the period specified in the contract of apprenticeship. The duration of training varies from six months to 4 years depending on the requirements of the trades.
- The employer who has more than 500 workers has to bear the cost of basic and practical training and payment of stipends to the apprentices.
- In case of graduates and technical apprentices the cost of stipends may be equally shared the Government upto prescribed limit.
- In case of establishments employing less than 500 workers, basic training is to be imparted in industrial training institutes set-up by the Government.
- Syllabus and other facilities for practical and basic training are approved by the Government.

4. Working Hours, Leave and Holidays

- The employer should not require the apprentice to work overtime, in excess of the weekly hours prescribed under the rules and on any day between 10 p.m. to 6 a.m.
- The apprentices should be allowed casual leave, medical leave and extra-ordinary leave, as prescribed under the rules. Holidays will be as are observed in the establishment.

5. Payment of Compensation in Accident Injury

In case of personal injury, an apprentice is entitled to compensation payable under the Workmen's Compensation Act and the Schedule Appended to this Act.

6. Status of Apprentice

An apprentice is only to be trainee and not a worker, and provision of any labour law are not applicable to him.

7. Record of Progress and Submission of Returns

- Employer has to maintain records of progress of training of each apprentice in the prescribed form. He is to furnish returns to authorities.
- On completion of training and passing the test conducted by the National Council, the apprentices are granted a proficiency certificate in the trade by the council.

8. Employment of Apprentices after Training

There is no obligation to provide a job to the apprentice. Similarly, an apprentice is not bound to accept the employment under an employer. If there is any such condition in the contract of apprenticeship, the employer will have to offer a suitable employment to the apprentice after completion of training. However, there is a practice of giving reference to apprentices for regular appointment.

9. Compensation for Termination of Apprenticeship

- The contract of apprenticeship terminates on the completion of training.
- It can, however, be terminated earlier by the apprentice or employer, on payment of prescribed compensation, i.e. three months' stipend.

OFFENCES AND PENALTIES

Any employer who:

(a) fails his obligations under the contract;
(b) does no engage the required number of apprentices;
(c) refuses to furnish any information or return;
(d) obstructs any inspection, examination or inquiry; and
(e) requires an apprentice to work overtime or to do any work not connected with his training;

shall be punishable with imprisonment upto 6 months or with fine or with both.

Part Three

FUTURISTIC ISSUES IN INDUSTRIAL RELATIONS

Redesigning Industrial Relations:
An Approach

INTRODUCTION

The goal of industrial relations has been on "disputes management" and attempting 'industrial peace' with the assumption peace would lead to higher productivity, which has now been proved otherwise.

Indian industry is presently facing changes brought by new economic policy and other global changes. The crisis has made us to realise that there is great need for industrial relations system, which would avoid the pitfalls of old system and give new direction to Indian economy. In this process, trade unions, managements and government has to rejuvenate itself. We have to look to some good practices abroad on industrial relations.

New industrial relations system to have following features:

1. There has to be continued emphasis on "developing healthy relations" between management and employees.
2. The "work place governance" has to promote productivity, quality and competitiveness.
3. A continued attention to trade unions and management conflicts and "disputes resolution forms."

Thus to rectify and redefine industrial relations, the responsibilities lies on the following: stakeholders of industrial relations: (i) Government, (ii) employer, (iii) trade unions, and (iv) professionals.

1. The Government

The government has always used negative indicators to measure health of industrial relations, i.e. mandays lost, incidence of strikes and lock-outs, number of disputes, incidence of closures, retrenchments and lay-offs are standard tools.

(a) However government responsibility lies in creating more *positive parameters for measuring* industrial relations and in playing a more proactive role in making changes in labour relations in the country.
(b) The government should also maintain a stance of less intervention and should allow *bipartism to flourish,* since it is the employer and trade unions, who have to necessarily interact all the time. Infact, they are the ones who are actually affected by any change in an industrial relations system.
(c) The procedures for *solving industrial disputes* to be simplified for speedy resolution at local level itself.

2. The Employers

(a) The main concern of employers seems to *develop a working relationship with unions* on one hand and to handle problems of employee indiscipline through legal means. Though this attitude has worked in the past but will not work with challenges brought about by liberalisation of economy.
(b) Employers and managements have to be define role so as to look *unions as partners* in creating healthy industrial relations and more proactive role.
(c) To broaden industrial relations system as *joint concern* of line management, industrial relations, personnel management, HRD departments. They should not be working as separate compartments.
(d) *Encourage enterprise* level collective bargaining.
(e) *Encourage enterprise* level joint consultation.

3. The Trade Unions

They have performed important role to protect the interest of working class. But today trade unions are, as elsewhere at cross-roads. There are glaring organisational weaknesses in trade unions and have failed to build-up vibrant industrial relations system to meet changing demands of restructuring the economy. They have worked with narrow vision and confined to economic issues. They have to play and redefine role in the social process (societal interest). In America, Europe, Eastern Europe, there is decline in unions' membership since 1989. Trade unions have to shed adversarial attitudes and learn to *cooperate with management*. Unions have not taken any serious concern for enterprise or industry. They have not evoked constructive response to issues like linking wages with productivity or upgradation of technology, etc.

In the changing economic environment, trade unions need to adjust in environment. Their reaction can be proactive. Trade unions to develop an attitude of cooperation with the organisation and customers.

Trade union to help in evolving appropriate labour policy which is integral part of national policy/community interest and not to look to sectional interest only.

4. Professionals/Academicians

If we want to redefine industrial relations, then it is essential that industrial relations professionals being trained at management institutes should be trained not just in union negotiations, labour laws and collective bargaining but also in motivation, morale, job satisfaction, leadership and collaborative efforts and work towards *developing relationships* in the organisation.

Industrial relations, the world over, are shifting from collective bargaining to individual bargaining. This indicates importance given to the individual in the organisation and not trade unions alone. We should give identity to worker and not just concentrate on trade unions.

Job Flexibility

MEANING

When labour flexibility is introduced, it provides more freedom to employer in the deployment of employees. Kanawaty argues that flexibility in labour can be viewed differently, viz.,

(a) ability to *reduce or increase employment,* or wage levels with ease;
(b) ability to *increase mobility* in the deployment of employees;
(c) ability to use more *elastic use of skills* for greater occupational flexibility; and
(d) ability to introduce *non-conventional working arrangements* such as part-time work, temporary work, sub-contacting, self-employment, etc.

NEED FOR ADJUSTMENT TO CHANGE

Restructuring of enterprise involves many aspects:

(a) The change in products, processes and competitive pressure of markets, technology;
(b) The changes in management and organisation, plant relocation;
(c) The modernisation, mergers and acquisitions, buyouts, recapitalisation, downsizing, privatisation; and
(d) The changes in specialisation, retraining, reduction in hierarchy, multi-skilling, linking rewards to skills and performance.

Restructuring is inevitable and imperative if organisation is to remain viable, efficient and competitive. It has to adopt spiralling cost reduction strategies:

(a) *The employer's* want to retrench employees and want change in labour laws (The Indutrialised Disputes Act) concerning prior notice for lay-offs, closures, retrenchments, etc.

(b) *Trade unions,* in turn, want guarantees against change, i.e. employment security and stability. They want safeguards against retrenchment and also maintenance of the existing strength.

Reconciling sharp differences in view points of unions and managements is not easy. There is need for positive thinking and search for creative alternatives by both parties with mutuality of interests and survival of the organisation.

MANAGEMENT STRATEGIES FOR FLEXIBILITY

To facilitate flexibility, managements have to ensure:

(i) To *build trust* through communication and educational campaign so to promote understanding about changes due to market economy.

(ii) To ensure that technological modernisation does not lead to obsolescence. *Training and retraining of employees* should receive priority and in this trade unions to be involved.

(iii) To *involve unions and employees* in issue concerning security of employment and explain rationale and benefits of change. Trade unions also to accord priority to firm's survival.

(iv) Management to ensure that *work force reduction* should be the *last resort.*

(v) The management to impose restrictions in hiring new employees and resort to internal transfers, training and retraining, voluntary retirement scheme with income protection, restriction on over time, reduction of normal hours of work, impart out-placement conselling to employees so as to encourage entrepreneurship and alternative livelihood opportunities, e.g. small business development, awarding contracts for clearing and forwarding of materials cleaning, catering, maintenance, job works, dealerships, training, material and machine help, encourage and assist setting up employee cooperatives.

(vi) To *promote employee participation* to build mutual trust and cooperation, consensus and commitment.

(vii) Provide opportunities to employees to *change their occupation* two or three times during working life and to meet their rising expectations. Such steps will help to achieve adaptability and mobility to withstand pressures of changing market.

(viii) The management should focus more on *horizonal promotions* (than vertical patterns) that are relevant for flat organisation structure.

(ix) The management should attempt to move away from occupational groupings to *skill groupings* (combine a variety of related job/skills into one) and encouraging employees to learn one more skill, e.g. crane operator to operate rigs and repair electrical work, etc.

In sum, the right flexibility mould should comprise of industrial growth with concern for human competence and welfare.

43

Employee Engagement is Crucial for Business Success

Having the right employees with the right set of skills is a critical success factor in any business today. With the changing environment, both the nature of employment and nature of the employer-employee relationship are evolving. Most organizations have realized that in times like today providing higher remunerations and excellent amenities is not sufficient to retain the employee, who is the most valuable resource of an organization. The order of the day *calls for engaged and loyal employees who are committed with the organization's mission, goals, and values has become an important factor in today's business.*

In this chapter following aspects of "employee engagement crucial for employer-employee relations and business success are discussed:

1. Definition of employee engagement.
2. Elements of employee engagement.
3. Benefits of employee engagement.
4. Measuring employee engagement.
5. Employee engagement measuring challenges.
6. Role of HR.
7. Conclusion.

1. DEFINITION OF EMPLOYEE ENGAGEMENT

Engagement is the extent to which people value, enjoy, and believe in what they do. There is no consistency in definition of employee engagement. Organization's view and define 'employee engagement' in different ways. For some, it is job satisfaction while for others it is the employee's emotional commitment to their organization and often organization use employee engagement and retention interchangeably. But there is a significant difference between engagement, commitment, and satisfaction (Figure 1).

FIGURE 1

Employee Engagement, Commitment and Satisfaction

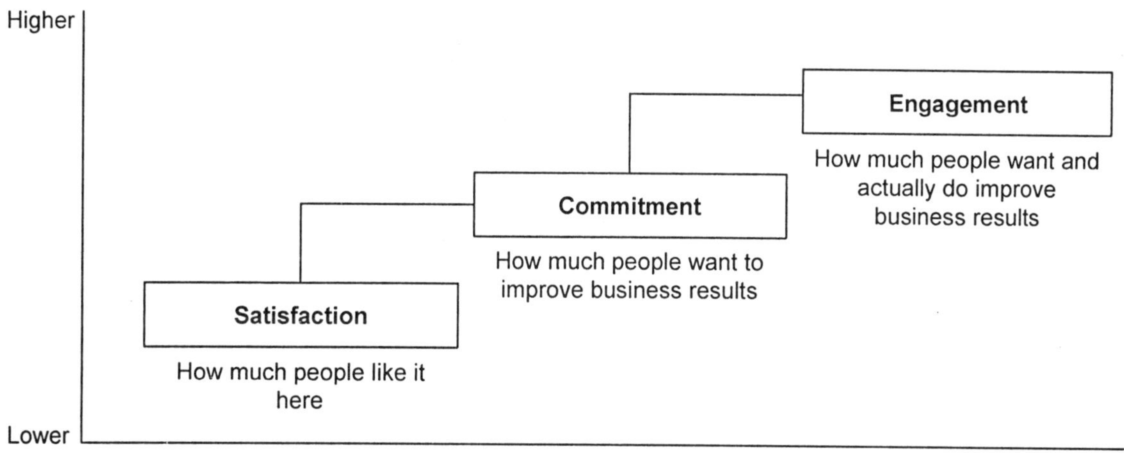

Employees who are engaged to the organization are not just planning to stick to their organization, they are not just happy or proud to be associated with the organization, but they are in fact enthused and geared to use their skills and talent to make a difference and help achieve the employer's pursuit for sustainable business success. *Engagement is the energy, passion or fire that the employees have toward their work and the employer.*

Employment engagement can be defined as *a positive attitude* held by the employee towards the organization and its value. An engaged employee is aware of the business context, and *works with colleagues to improve performance* within the job *for the benefit of the organization* (Figure 2).

FIGURE 2

Defining engagement

- Desire to be a member of an organization and stay.
- Speak positively about the organization.
- Strive to go beyond what is minimally required.

2. ELEMENTS OF ENGAGEMENT

Engagement comprises of three important elements. They are individual values, focused work, and inter-personal support.

(i) Doing meaningful work

Employees feel engaged when they do meaningful work at the organization and experience empowerment. Meaningful work is defined as the work that makes a difference or an impact to the organization.

(ii) Focused work

Apart from contribution, employees *need clear direction and feedback from the top management* on their performance to keep them in track and be accountable for their performance and an efficient work environment.

(iii) Having positive working relationships

Employees feel more engaged when there is inter-personal harmony among the employees. Employees value positive working relationships and are excited about the thought of working with these kinds of colleagues.

3. BENEFITS OF EMPLOYEE ENGAGEMENT

Some benefits include as under:

(i) Employee engagement is all about *motivating the employees* to give their best to the organization. Engaging employees with the organization's mission, goals and values has become an important factor in today's business success.

(ii) Employee engagement gauges the *relationship of an employee* with the employer and it offers practical solutions to issues and concerns between them, if any. For example, when organizations go global or diversely their operations into their business, employees feel separated and alienated in such a dispersed workforce. In such scenario, employee engagement helps make the employees feel that they are important in the company and *provide them with an organizational identity.*

(iii) Employee engagement *invokes passion for their work* among the employees and drivers them to meet and even exceed their expectations. Employees want to be engaged—a research conducted by the Harvard Business Review (HBR) found that employees rank "feeling of accomplishment that one gets from work" higher than pay as a prime motivator.

(iv) Engaged employees are more *committed and more loyal to the organization*. More the number of loyal employees, lesser will be the cost of recruiting, hiring, training and developing not to mention the higher levels of performance and productivity than those who are not engaged.

(v) Engaged employees *put in extra efforts whenever organizations need it*. These employees having spent considerable amount of time with the company and tend to function as one family and exhibit less internal rivalries. Engaged employees work hard and create more satisfied customers. Highly engaged employees speak *positively about the organization* to the new recruits and co-workers: drives them to perform better and help them assimilate with the work culture seamlessly.

(vi) Engaged employees are more likely to *stay longer in their organization*, advocate its products and services and contribute to the overall success of an organization. (Box 1).

Box I

Toyota Motors in USA have higher level of employee engagement

Toyota Motors largest manufacturing plant located at Georgetown, US has employee engagement levels about 10% higher than the US average. According to Pete Gritton, Vice-President, Administration, Toyota Motors, the *corporate culture that supports* both individual creativity and team work at the plant is the reason for such high levels of engagement. It is the responsibility of the management to support the employees and be committed to the overall success of both the employee and the company itself. In addition, the management must develop employee's trust on a daily basis otherwise it can disappear immediately through one's careless act.

4. MEASURING EMPLOYEE ENGAGEMENT

Companies have recognized the importance of measuring employee engagement, identifying the factors which drive it, and aligning their HR policies accordingly. Employee engagement can be measured in several ways, including *increase in productivity* of the employees, *growth in business*, annual surveys, tracking *attrition rates*, and *increase in the number of employee referrals*. In many organization, employee satisfaction survey is the most popular method for measuring how happy the employees are in the organization. However, off late these methods are replaced by *surveys that can measure employee engagement effectively*. Here the employee engagement is measured in three stages. In the first stage, the employee engagement is measured under five areas of focus at the individual levels and in the second stage, the overall engagement levels of employees are linked to the financial performance of the organization. At third stage, when employees are asked feedback, it is essential to communicate the action taken on them. The employee engagement levels are continuously measured, analysed, acted upon and refined.

5. ROLE OF HR

The HR plays a significant role in creating an appropriate engagement programme for the employees of the organization. Another important function of HR is to link the individual engagement levels and organizational performance and develop reward programmes for the employees. Finally, they measure the effectiveness of the engagement programme, provide the results to the top management and present suggestions to top management in view of the findings. These lead to the virtuous cycle of engagement and performance.

6. CONCLUSION

Jack Welch, Former Chairman and CEO of General Electric once said, "The best companies now know without a doubt, where productivity—real and limitless productivity—comes from. It comes from challenged, empowered, excited, and rewarded teams of people. It comes from *engaging every single mind in the organization*, making everyone part of the action, and allowing everyone to have a voice i.e.—a role—in the success of the enterprise. Doing so raises productivity not incrementally, but by multiples." In any organization, the talented employee is both the biggest asset and liability and so it becomes paramount to measure how well the human capital is adding value. Since engagement levels correlate to business performance, engagement becomes an important human capital metric and measuring it tells us how well the company is doing in the competition for talent."

REFERENCES

1. M.S. Balaji and M.B. Supriya, 'Blue Print for Measuring Employee Engagement', The ICFAI, University Press, Hyderabad. Gratefully acknowledged.
2. S.K. Bhatia, HRM—'A Competitive Advantage', Deep and Deep Publications, New Delhi.

Business Process Outsourcing

1. INTRODUCTION

Outsourcing is not new. It is widely prevalent in the manufacturing sector. However, the rapid development of IT (Information Technology) in the country has lead to increased cross-border trade of ITES (Information-Technology Enabled Services), thereby widening the scope of outsourcing. All the same, out sourcing has undergone a sea change. Developing countries like India, Brazil, Philippine, China, etc. have become the fertile ground for providing BPO (Business Process Outsourcing) services for the developed countries. Cheaper labour cost, higher efficiency and better quality are the main driving forces of these BPO providers.

Whatever the motive, BPO has come to stay. It has not only changed the way business is conducted but has also changed the very fabric of life in the globe as a whole. This paper presents the implications of BPO in the Indian society and also the challenges faced by the HR professionals engaged in the BPO sector in this regard.

In the global era, with the optimal utilization of the Information and Communication Technologies (IC), economics of labour and other factors, international borders are becoming more transient and virtual. Offshore outsourcing in the ITES sector is the 'in-thing' and this sector means a lot to the business of developing countries as it boosts the economy.

2. MEANING OF BPO

Business process outsourcing is the practice of turning over the operation of an internal business process, like customer care or transaction processing, to a service provider mostly, a third party. Service providers leverage their process-expertise, resources and ability to scale. The client company ("client") manages and compensates the service provider by defining measurable performance metrics and then evaluating the service provider's performance using those metrics. BPO is the 'in-thing' and has come to stay. The underlying premise that promotes IT/ITES outsourcing is that IT skills, knowledge and services can be competitively extracted, reconstructed and delivered across borders, time zones and business entities.

3. OPPORTUNITIES FOR BUSINESS

According to a recent Associate Press article, India controls 44 percent of the global offshore outsourcing market of software and back-office services. The article indicates that as many as 400 of the Fortune 500 companies either have their own centres in India or are currently outsourcing work to Indian technology companies. The report, albeit optimistic, projected a 51% market share increase by India by March 2008. (Outsourcing times.com).

"The worldwide BPO market is likely to grow at an annual 9% rate, to touch $ One trillion by 2008 from $ 773 billion in 2002, according to IDC. . . . The EPO industry in India would grow at 54% annually for 2002-06. The EPO services are expected to grow from $ 2 billion in 2002 to $ 12 billion in 2006." (http://www.itfacts.biz/index.php?idP728). According to Ma Foi Employment Survey, 2005, in India, IT and BPO sectors were the biggest job providers during January-March 2005. (The Hindu, 21 March, 2005).

4. COVERAGE

This chapter gives an overview of the phenomenon of IT offshore outsourcing, and explores some It offshore outsourcing impacts. Attempts are made to present the implications of "offshore outsourcing" in the Indian scenario.

5. RATIONALE FOR OUTSOURCING

"Outsourcing involves transferring certain value contributing activities, processes and/or services to the premises of one's own or an agent primarily to save costs and/or for the principal to increasingly focus on its areas of key competence."(Ramachandran K. and Voleti).

"Saving money is a prime motivator, of course, but advocates claim that strategy also enters into the equation. . . . Outsourcing has become a management tool, freeing companies to build upon their core competencies by leaving the non-core stuff to specialized providers." (http://www.cfo.com/article.cfm/3001 269?f=related). From the vendor point of view, non-core activities, or those activities that could be done more effectively by others are often outsourced. The activities often outsourced include (i) Data entry, (ii) Rules set processing, (iii) Decision-making, (iv) Direct customer interface, and (v) Expert knowledge services. For example, in the insurance sector, activities like claims processing, voice support may be outsourced to a EPO. The key IT functions generally outsourced over the years 2002 and 2004 are portrayed in Figure 1.

6. BENEFITS OF BPO

(i) The outsourcing of business processes means lower overhead costs without sacrificing quality and productivity,

(ii) Further, it enables the Vendor Company to concentrate on its core competencies, (iii)BPO providers have a process expensive and enjoy significant economies of scale and scope by offering the same services to different clients. According to NASSCOM (2004), BPO results in quantum operational improvement on account of cost, time and quality benefits. They include 30-50 per cent reduction in processing cost,

FIGURE I

Key IT Functions Outsourced—Buyer Perspectives

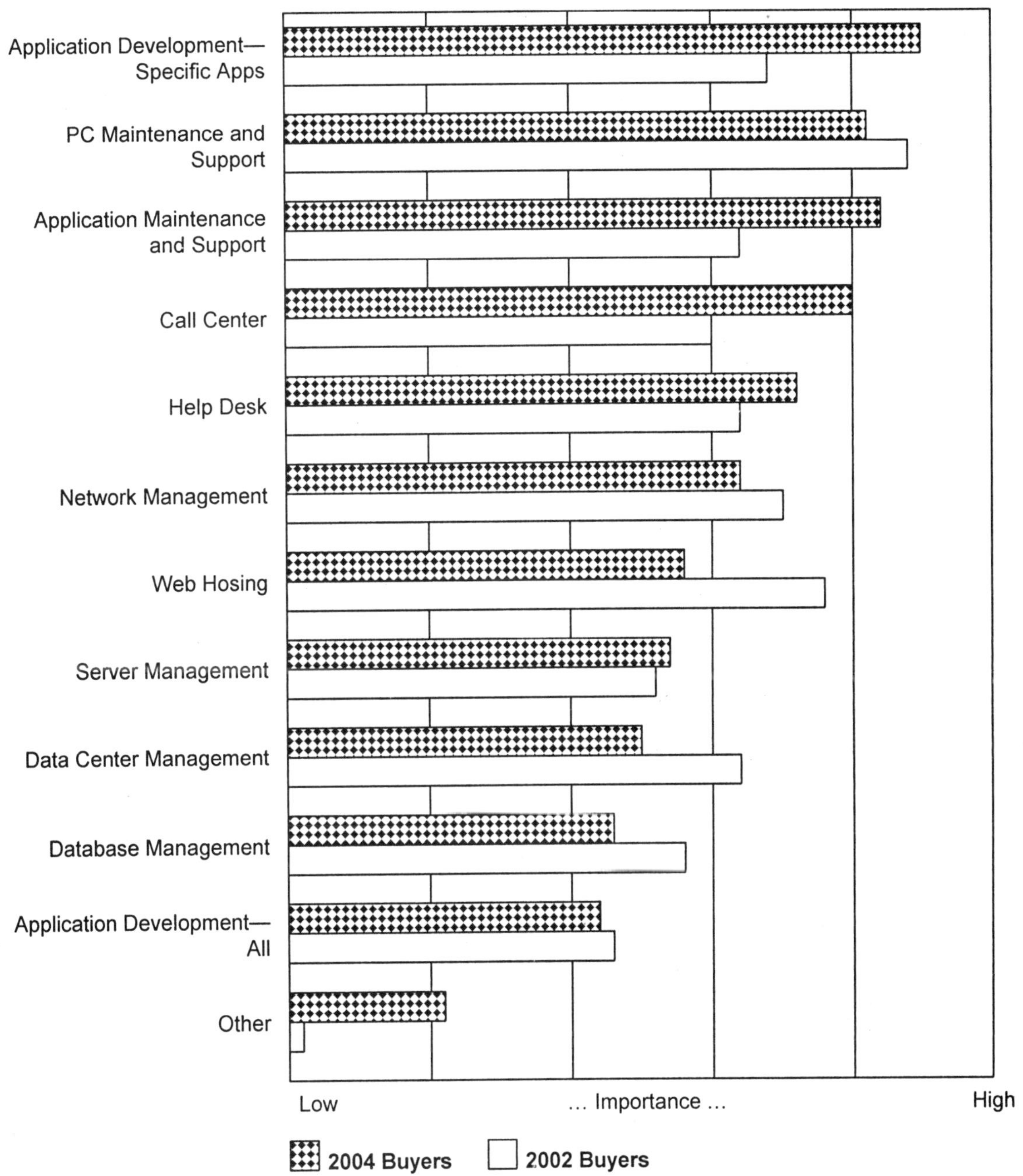

Source: 2002 and 2004 IT Outsourcing Trends by Job Category (Rogers, 2004).

(iv) Additional benefits from process redesign and "pooling" like shared common infrastructure,

(v) 24 × 7 service and reduction in turnaround time by leveraging time zone differences, and

(vi) Specialisation and enhanced ability to set, measure and monitor quality targets.

7. IMPLICATIONS OF BUSINESS PROCESS OUTSOURCING IN THE INDIAN SCENARIO

Outsourcing has not only transformed the way business is carried out, but also has brought in a host of new dimensions to be addressed. Outsourcing has affected not only organizations, but also business, people and the economy as a whole. The implications of outsourcing may be studied from the perspectives of the donor or recipient countries. Further, they may be classified as: (1) Economic implications, (2) Political implications, (3) Cultural and social implications, (4) Implications with respect to entrepreneurship, (5) Educational implications, (6) Career implications, (7) Technological implications, and (8) Other implications.

For the purpose of this chapter, the implications of outsourcing have been presented as economic and non-economic implications with respect to India as a recipient country.

7.1 Economic Implications

(a) Job front

Offshore outsourcing not only means increased employment opportunities for recipient countries, but also means widened job prospects for women. The ITES sector is an Equal opportunity employer. Hence, it has resulted in jobs being available to competent personnel irrespective of the gender.

(b) Investment front

New organisations are set-up every day. This not only means additional capital investment either through FDI or other means. This provides a boost to the economy. Further, developmental inputs in terms of infrastructure and technology are pumped in to keep in line with the demands of the industry. This gives a major fillip to the economic activity. The outcome of the same is increased turnover or revenues that add up the GDP of the Indian economy.

(c) Effective conduct of business

The concept of outsourcing takes advantage of regional labour markets and results in cost-effective, competitive conduct of business.

(d) Boost to the spirit of entrepreneurship

Many Small and Medium Enterprises (SMEs) with a small amount of start-up capital, basic telecommunication and other ICT infrastructure and a pool of (relatively low-wage) employees can provide BPO services. Thus, the concept of outsourcing has given a boost to the spirit of entrepreneurship.

(e) Innovative business models to tap available resources

With the ever-growing need for competent employees, organisations are looking forward to innovative ways of enlarging the talent pool. For example, a popular Chennai-based BPO has resorted to employing the educated folk of a nearby village to do the data-entry work for its operations. This "village model" employs the women of that area but their salary is not on par with the urban folk engaged in similar activities. These practices though innovative are also paving way for questions like fairness of the payments made.

(f) The question of Repatriated savings

The issue of repatriated savings needs to be studied in detail to assess the actual value addition to the Indian economy.

7.2 Non-economic Implications

(i) Political implications

International relations between donor and recipient countries need to be at their best to attract better trade. Diplomacy is required to ensure that contracts are not lost on account of any political misgivings. The row in US regarding outsourcing of State jobs is well known.

(ii) Legislations

The ITES sector is of recent origin. This necessitates the enactment of new National ICT policies and strategies not only to facilitate governance, but also ensure fair trade and streamline operations. For example, the Tamil Nadu Government has recently released a new ITES policy during the event CONNECT 2005. 'Enacting legislations to ensure data security, customer privacy and deal with IT-related violations in general, encouraging establishment of Information Technology Enabled/Services (ITES) parts in tier-2 and tier-3 cities and imparting ITES skills in standards 9 and 10 from the next academic year are among the highlights of the ITES policy." (*The Hindu*, 9-9-2005)

(iii) Increasing impetus on Human Resources Management

BPO is person-intensive venture. Hence, the accent is on Human Resource (HR) Management. HR functions like recruitment, talent management, etc. are becoming daunting tasks on account of high demand for competent personnel. Rising per-hire costs, attrition, problems 'bad hire' and choosing the right hunting ground for recruitment are among the challenges that HR managers of person-intensive BPO companies face today. Further, the focus is on developing better metrics and measurement to ensure quality of services or deliverables, etc.

(iv) Increased role of consortium to boost or supplement BPO activity

Given, the nascent origin of the industry, collective effort among industry players is in the offing. For example, NASSCOM proposes to form a not-for-profit initiative for evaluation of talent in the industry. It intends to evaluate potential candidates based on a test of common skills like English (both spoken and written), office software application and some soft skills like listening and attitude. The objective of the initiative is to develop common standards which could cut the recruitment and training cost for BPO companies. Such and other initiatives will help increase the talent pool. (*The Economic Times*, 25 August, 2005). Similarly, industry leaders have called for "immediate employability" of graduates to improve their suitability to enter the IT and ITES sectors. (*The Hindu*, 12 September, 2005).

(v) Gearing to handle the existing lacunae

Instances of abuse of Intellectual Property Rights, cyber crimes, breach of trust, and lack of confidentiality are possible. Data security, lack of product/domain expertise and inability to deliver results consistently pose major threats to the growth of the Indian BPO (business process outsourcing) sector, said Srikanth Karra, Human Resources Leader, GE Capital, India. The sector should work on these issues immediately to grab a larger pie of the global BPO market, he said. (http://sify.com/finance/fullstory.php?id=1 3575709).

(vi) Ensuring executive accountability

There are considerable compliance risks related to BPO, including privacy and data protection, intellectual property rights and executive accountability. Potential security breaches related to physical property and computer networks systems and data create similar exposures. Hence, organisations need to gear up to handle the compliance risks. The measures currently taken include confidentiality clauses, education and sensitisation of employees, using access security, asking employees to keep mobile phones and bags in lockers outside the work-floor, CCTV, disabling floppy and CD drives of employees' work-stations, monitoring e-mail traffic and phone calls, etc. (*The Economic Times*, 25-8-05, p. 7).

(vii) Career implications

Since most employees in BPOs are fresh graduates, formal higher education as an option is affected. These candidates seek for other modes of education like e-learning, distance education programs and so on. It also affects the social life of the individual's concerned; the high pay package ushers in affluence. However, the career prospects needs to be studied. The demand for skilled talent being very high has placed the employee on the higher plane.

(viii) Health implications

The job profile has its personnel blues like burn-out syndrome and high levels of stress. Job in EPOs catering to US or countries of different time zones affects the health of the employees on account of predominantly night shifts. Similarly, the job hazards of employees in call centres include medical complaints like persistent ear pain, etc. due to continuous call handling.

(ix) Social and cultural implications

The change of name of the employees to suit the needs of the offshore customers, celebrating "foreign" festivals in the name of integration, the "partying" culture are creating a melange in the existing social and cultural dogmas of the Indian society.

(x) Boosts from the government to sustain the growth

The Central and the respective State Governments seek to boost the ITES activity through measures like unique ITES policy, ITES industrial parks, tax benefits, lobbying with international organisations (example, WTO) to put in place a regulation to protect against protectionist backlash on outsourcing in the developed countries.

(xi) Moving up the value chain

The Indian outsourcing industry is changing from BPO to KPO. Hence, such innovations in services are in the anvil.

(xii) Organisation of the employees?

Akin to trade unions in the manufacturing sector, employee organisations in the ITES sector are also plausible.

(xiii) Unethical practices

The increasing thrust on increased performance, instant results, unrealistic SLAs has resulted in some business houses turning out to be sweatshops. Reports of such cases have also been highlighted in the newspapers of late.

8. CHALLENGES FACED BY THE HUMAN RESOURCES PROFESSIONAL IN A BPO

Given the nature of business, job characteristics and the work force profile, the role of the human resource professional becomes critical. He has a vital role to play in service delivery. However, the role of the HR professional easier said than done. There are many challenges attributed to the same. "Rising per-hire costs, attrition, problems of 'bad hire' and choosing the right hunting ground for recruitment are among the challenges that HR managers of person-intensive BPO companies face today. (http://www.thehindubusinessline.com/2004/10/16/stories/20041 0160162 1700.htm). Among others, the key challenges may be traced from three perspectives viz., (i) creating value, (ii) sustaining value, and (iii) delivering value. They are presented as under:

8.1 Key challenges in terms of creating value

1. Sourcing the right candidates

Creating the right mix of the resource pool and managing talent is key to making available the right people resources at the right time.

2. Looking out far innovations in sourcing

Given the demand-supply gap for eligible people resources, the HR professional is on the look out for innovative ways of sourcing potential candidates so that the ratio of applicants to joinees is high. Consequently, 4-innovations in sourcing candidates are the need of the hour. For example, a BPO in Gurgaon looks at hotel management graduates as such incumbents are already groomed in terms of handling clients.

8.2 In terms of sustaining value

3. Keeping the work force happy

Given the nature of the job content, job satisfaction may be boosted by handsome pay packets, healthy work place practices, etc. Burn out and stress are common factors that result in employee turn over. Hence, it is but pertinent for the HR professional to organise various people engagement practices like get-together, employee's birthday celebrations, and other work place facilities, etc. to keep the employees popped up.

4. Managing attrition

Attrition in BPOs is generally high because of the limited availability of competent candidates. Call centers for instance have an attrition rate of 30-35 percent. (NASSCOM News Byte, 2003) The demand for candidates with even as much as 3 months, experience is high. Often, competitors are vying for the resources of the fellow companies. So it is important to ensure that the push and pull factors do not compel the employees to leave. The push factors may be poor supervisory styles, stress while pull factors may be better and prospects. The intra-mural interventions may be in the form of healthy work place practices while the extra-mural interventions may be in the form of entering into anti-poaching agreements with competitors.

5. *Providing for job enrichment and enhancing the career prospects of the employees*

Placement in a BPO need not be construed as a stop gap arrangement; it can be evolved into a career like employment in other organizations. Hence, the HR department will have to devise innovative means of job enrichment and clearly portray the career path to the employees.

8.3 Challenges in terms of delivering value

6. *Training*

To ensure service delivery, the workforce should be adequately and appropriately trained. The training includes language training and technical training. The metrics for each employee should be carefully devised. Imparting the required training and ensuring that the employees stay on in the organization for a reasonable period of time is a challenge in deed.

7. *Performance measurement and management*

Since most of the work is team-based, clear cut metrics on performance measurement need to be devised and managed.

8. *Policy deployment*

Having clear-cut policies to govern the processes and practices is essential to have a happy and satisfied work force.

9. *Concluding remarks*

Outsourcing in the ITES sector has come to stay. It is both a hot and touchy topic. It is hot because it is the in-thing and means a host of opportunities for the Indian economy. On the other hand, it is touchy because it means that many jobs in America have been closed down and outsourced offshore. There is resentment and some extent of animosity among Americans regarding the same. It is also a paradox. This is because globalization has hitherto been more beneficial to the developed nations. However, in the global world, BPO has been pre-dominantly beneficial to developing countries. This has raised many eyebrows especially among the developed countries. Outsourcing as a business phenomenon has a lesson to impart: competition and competitiveness has pushed business to find newer and better ways of doing things. Cost-effective alternatives have come to stay. At present, India is the most sought after destination. But there are still some lacunae that need to be addressed. Unless they are addressed appropriately, these opportunities are liable to be cashed on by new market players much to the loss of the Indian economy. And in this regard, the HR professionals have a key role to play.

REFERENCES

This is contribution by Ms. J.S. Gunavathy from "Personnel Today", July-Sept. 2006. Gratefully acknowledged.

Banham, Russ (October 01, 2001). Everything Must Go: Business Process Outsourcing. CFO Magazine. Retrieved from http://www.cfo.com/aflicle.cfm/3001269?f=related on 31-1-2005.

ITFACTS. Global business process outsourcing market to reach $1 trillion by 2006. Retrieved from http://www.itfacts.biz/index.php?id*728 on 31-1-2005.

Morello, Diane (2004). The Organisational Implications of Outsourcing. Gartner Research.

NASSCOM (2003). Managing Attrition. NASSCOM NewsByte, July 2003 Issue retrieved from http://www.nasscom.org/download/mediaupdate/July.pdf on 31.12-05.

NASSCOM (2004). The advantages of BPO. NASSCOM. Retrieved from www.nasscom.org on 26-8-05.

Outsourcingtimes.com. (2005). India controls 44 percent of global outsourcing market. Retrieved from www.blogsource.Org/outsourcingtimesJune2005.html on 24-8-05.

Ramachandran, K. and Voleti, Sudhir (2004). Business Process Outsourcing (BPO): Emerging Scenario and Strategic Options for IT-enabled Services. *Vikalpa*, Volume 29, No. 1, January-March, 2004.

Rogers, 2004 as cited in Slater, William, F., IT Offshore Outsourcing. 2004. University of Phoenix Online retrieved from http://billslater.com/uop/Course_work/CMGT_585_Example_William_Slater.htm Retrieved on 7-1-05.

Sifycom. (2004). Data security is a major threat to EPOs dated Dec. 27, 2004. Retrieved from http://sify.com/finance/fullstory.php?id=13575709 on 6-1-05.

The Economic Times (25 August, 2005). Hand in glove: Common appraisal for BPOs now. Bennett, Coleman and Co. Ltd. p. 5.

The Economic Times (25 August, 2005). The Confidentiality Conundrum. Bennett, Coleman and Co. Ltd. p. 7.

The Hindu (October 15, 2004). Rising per-hire cost, attrition bugbear of FBPO firms. Retrieved from http://www.thehindubusinessline. com/2004/10/16/stories/2004101601621700.htm on September 6, 2005.

The Hindu (21 March, 2005). IT rules job scene. *The Hindu Education Plus*, p. 1.

The Hindu (9 September, 2005). Policy proposes to declare ITES as an essential service. *The Hindu*, p. 6.

The Hindu (12 September, 2005). Preparing for the next wave. *The Hindu Education Plus*, p. 1.

Aligning Employee Expectations with Change in Strategy

Human resource strategies are plans for changing the way things are done in an organization. They are changes developed and initiated by management in support of business strategies, which in turn are externally driven. Some HR strategies may emerge bottom up through an organization, but most are directional and explicit from top to bottom.

Aligning employee expectations with change in strategy it may involve following steps:

(a) *Shaping employee expectations.* Basic task is to prepare employees for changes necessitated by business strategies. Employee attitudes and perceptions that influence behaviour at work are their anticipations regarding the future Managers and employees must recognize the need for change, understand what is required, evaluate and accept the implications of change and needed actions.

(b) *Process of implementing change is the crux of* aligning employee expectations with strategy. Where there is a strong prevailing culture, people are skeptical of the need for change.

(c) *Management Levers.* Management has three primary levers for aligning employee expectations with strategy. (Figure 1)

FIGURE I

Aligning Expectations with Strategies

Expectations	*Strategies*
(i) Recognition of the need for change	• Communicate strategic direction
(ii) Understanding of required changes	• Translate strategies into Performance objectives
(iii) Evaluation and acceptance	• Reshape the culture
(iv) Action	
(v) Feedback	

(i) Communicating the strategic direction

It is always a logical starting point. It requires ongoing communication of the mission, vision values and effort helps employees recognize the need for change and helps them to understand the changes required.

(ii) Translating strategies into performance objectives

Management gives employees some tangible, specific information they can deal with. Performance planning has a potentially broad effect on employee expectations. When integrated with performance evaluation, it provides feed-back that employees expect and desire.

(iii) Reshape the culture

A wide range of management actions help reshape an organizational culture. By various actions, values, beliefs and norms guiding behaviour are changed. Human resource management (HRM) has great role to influence culture. Management efforts to reshape the culture, therefore, have major influence on the employees understanding of required changes, evaluations and acceptance of change, and action. Culture is a powerful competitive weapon. When people share common values and beliefs, and live by common norms of behaviour, they can achieve outstanding results. Organizations such as Disney, Apple Computer, IBM and others with strong cultures believe that they have a distinct advantage in implementing their strategies. The challenge to management is to shape culture (gradually), to strengthen it, and poring it into line with the necessary strategic direction so as to make it dominant culture. Objective is to develop a single, common shared set of values, beliefs and expectations that guide behaviour. The role of managers as leaders is key to implementing strategic change. A *leader adapts* the organization to changing competitive circumstances.

To conclude, according to James W. Walker none of these means of aligning expectations with strategy are new. And none alone will achieve the desired results. Where companies have succeeded in managing board strategic change, including culture change, managers have *effectively used all the levers available to them*. Picking only one or two, or implementing efforts sequentially, fails to attain the mass impact required to overwhelm the *status quo* and direct the attention and energies of employees to the business agenda.

References

Michael Armstrong, Strategic HRM, Kogan Page, London.

James W. Walker, HR Strategy, McGraw-Hill Series in Management, Boston.

Impact of Technological Change and Industrial Relations

In this chapter we shall eleborate:

(a) Impact of Technological Change and Labour Relations,
(b) Effect of Information Technology on Organisations and its Structure,
(c) Change due to e-Era on Industrial Relations, and
(d) Human Resource Function Meeting the Challenges.

MEANING OF TECHNOLOGY

Technology is the intellectual equipment coupled with necessary physical equipment (where relevant) that is required for being applied in the field of trade, business, manufacturing or other profitable activity.

In other words, technology inputs can be effectively utilised to provide more efficient methods and better utilisation of scarce resources, e.g. like manhours, money, methods, etc.

(A) IMPACT OF TECHNOLOGICAL CHANGE AND LABOUR RELATIONS

Industrial Robot as a form of changing technology has/is significantly affecting the work force. Other automatic devices that integrate production process also affect in several ways. For example, in the USA automated radio manufacturing plant where only two employees produce one thousand radios per day, and earlier two hundred employees were required for one thousand radios per day.

Although it is accepted that technology leads to more jobs, but problem is of existing employees who are displaced by technology. It is true technology improves working conditions by eliminating undesirable feature, leading to lessing of monotony. It also creates certain problems of—isolation of employees on the job, greater mental strain as now mistakes can be costly, deterioration of social groups, less job variety, skill requirement downgrading.

Thus, unions have pushed hard for several devices geared to cushioning the impact of technology change. These are, pension, severance pay on retrenchment, extended vacation periods, early retirement provisions (VRS). These are adjustments to automated change. Some aspects are covered in the agreements with unions. These are:

(i) Advance notice of layoff or shut down of product line. Almost six months has been agreed in collective bargaining agreements.
(ii) Adoption of attrition principle to reduce jobs (by deaths, resignations, retirements, etc.)
(iii) Retraining of displaced employees to retain them in other jobs either in the same plant or another one.
(iv) Restrictions on sub-contracting of work in another company, e.g. where specialised equipment is not available with the company, or skill is not there, etc. However, this is an area of large controversy in the collective bargaining.

(B) EFFECT OF I.T. ON ORGANISATIONS AND ITS STRUCTURE

1. I.T. in the form of E-mail, internet, fax and computerised billing, etc. reduces costs and increases attraction of buying goods and services from outside. Thus, outsourcing reduces employees. In this way, it encourages integrating corporate giants, by breaking up into smaller more efficient firms and loosely connected by networks. It encourages decentralisation.

2. As information can be shared instantly and inexpensively in many locations, the value of centralised decision-making and expensive bureaucracies will decreases. The individuals will manage through electronic links.

3. Middlemen will set-up small businesses and provide information services through internet shops to customers who will choose from home the products through electronic stores.

4. Number of full time jobs will begin to shrink and there will be change in employer-employee relationship. There will be class of nomadic workers.

5. Corporations will hire the best talent anywhere from the world.

6. Key advantage of networked, many companies will be flexibility focussed approach of a small organisation in terms of independence. From corporate control and bureaucracy, to push them to excellence. As it leads to better productivity, companies are now using computer which is fifty times more powerful than it was 10 years ago. In 1977, Maruti did business of Rs. 30 crore in spares, but now over internet which amount to about Rs. 1 crore a day. The benefits are faster, cash in the system, reduces costs of working capital, faster movement of inventory, no piling up of stocks, slashing of STD and fax bills. In the long-run e-commerce will pervade the country.

7. I.T. companies ensure that all their operating systems, people and other resources are perfect so as to meet deadlines of customers.

This direction they like to concentrate and get involved only core areas and do not like to waste time and energy on "non-paying or less paying" headache areas. I.T. organisations are based on this concept. Some strategies adopted by I.T. companies are to out-sourcing on areas where they have no expertise, such as:

(a) out-sourcing of transport to outside agencies,
(b) out-sourcing of cafeteria services,
(c) out-sourcing of maintenance of systems,
(d) out-sourcing of supply of uninterrupted power,
(e) out-sourcing of house keeping,
(f) out-sourcing of bulk mailing,
(g) out-sourcing of security, and
(h) out-sourcing of search human resources and training.

(C) CHANGES DUE TO e-ERA ON INDUSTRIAL RELATIONS

The following have been the changes in the industrial relations front on account of the E-era:

1. Reduction on workforce coupled with a phenomenal increase in workplace productivity,
2. Dismantling or underplaying of unions,
3. Change in the academic profile of blue-collar workers,
4. The lone wolf syndrome,
5. ESOPs that give a semblance of ownership of workmen,
6. Negotiated one to one company-wide settlements,
7. Wage-increase based on bench-marking worker productivity through methods like 360 degree performance appraisal,
8. Attitude of non-interference of the state in any dispute between workmen and the management,
9. Arrival of virtual organizations on the scene, and
10. Widespread resort to out-sourcing and contract manufacturing.

Interestingly, dismantling of unions, rapid increase in workplace productivity, etc. far from hurting labour and undermining industrial relations have actually led to greater say of the workmen in the affairs of their company leading to a more meaningful industrial relations.

The changing academic profile of the workmen for instance, could be singularly responsible for empowering them to seek out and redress their grievances themselves rather than resort to an extraneous agency like a Workers' Union. Also the state's attitude on non-interference is actually making managements to prefer arbitration rather than prolonged court litigation, something that even the workmen favour to an extent.

Wherever people exist there are bound to be confrontations and conflicts. The challenge for a Management and HR professional is how to resolve these conflicts so that the relationships between workmen and management remain cordial and healthy.

(D) HUMAN RESOURCE PROFESSIONALS TO MEET THE CHALLENGES

HR managers could do well by adapting the following, in view of the changed conditions:

1. Bring in a transparent work culture.
2. Communicate effectively and all times.
3. Have a system through intranet or otherwise for constant feedback and interaction with workmen.
4. Go for virtual quality circles that operate at all levels.
5. Bring in a culture of rewarding people instantly and make everyone know about it.
6. Have a clear-cut concept about one to one settlement and never give in tendencies to compensate someone just because he/she is a good negotiator. Acquire negotiating skills yourself.
7. To institute systems not merely for workmen appraisal even for workplace productivity and make sure that the productivity remains paramount in the minds of the people, be it workmen or management.
8. To ensure that employees constantly have right skill themselves, which not only empowers them but also makes them invaluable to the company. Training your employee would be much cheaper than hiring an outsider, who besides high price tag will also spend precious organizational time in understanding its ethos and functioning.
9. Consultation rather than confrontation should be the running theme in exchange of views with the employee.
10. Spell your vision and mission in unambiguous terms and let everyone within and outside know and let everyone also be aware of what role they are to play in fulfilling these goals.

References

John Chambers, CEO, Cisco, USA, His address on 22.1.2001 to Confederation of Indian Industry, New Delhi.

A.T. Raman, New Age Management Writer, in *Management Review*, April-June 2001, New Delhi.

Impact of Globalisation on Industrial Relations

1. INTRODUCTION

The economic liberalisation launched in India since July 1991 have resulted in radical change of the direction and structure of the nation. The direction has tended towards market economy and globalisation from the existing socialistic pattern of Indian economy.

Liberalisations aimed at freeing industry business and trade from the clutches of control, decontrolling macro-economy of the country and its economic institutions and changing the structural infirmities. Liberalisation include liberalising industry, business and trade both domestic and foreign. Economic reforms are broader in scope. They include reforms of fiscal and monetary policies besides liberalisation of industry, business and trade.

Thus, the major result of economic reforms is all-round competition. This situation necessitated for the Total Quality and Productivity Management (TQPM) and minimisation of cost through attracting positive factors and eliminating hindering factors.

Now, the survival and development of industry in India, mostly depends on its ability to compete with other Indian firms, multinationals and in foreign markets. The ability to maintain high quality and maximise productivity determine the competitive ability of Indian firms, which in turn is largely dependent on the quality and commitment of human resources.

We would examine impact of globalisation on various aspects of Industrial Relations and Human Resource Management.

2. IMPACT ON COLLECTIVE BARGAINING

The socialistic pattern of society and dominance of trade unionism have attributed importance to collective bargaining in deciding various issues relating to labour problems and personnel policies. But under market economy most of the problems would be decided on *the basis of individual issue rather than collectively*. As Alan Fox observed, management may seek in some cases unilateral act and search for managing new sources of pluralism and individualism at the work place, bypassing collective bargaining. The other way to respond is to promote labour-management cooperation to introduce technological and other changes for modernising and/or restructuring enterprises to overcome crisis and/or withstand competitive pressures. Most of the private sector organisations have been seeking to promote labour-management *cooperation through consultations* rather than collective bargaining. Hence, the *collective bargaining machineries would not enjoy the same privilege under liberalised economy.*

3. IMPACT ON TRADE UNIONS

Trade unions in India played a phenomenal role in protecting the interests of the workers even by controlling and regulating the management at the cost of the organisation. But trade unions now play an important role by *co-operating with the management* as the survival of the organisation under competitive environment would be at stake. Trade unions' role fighting with the management in order to protect the interests of workers would receive dismal stake as most of the *employment conditions would be determined by the market forces rather than by the political* and/or membership strength of the trade unions. Further, the *government would support managements rather than trade unions unlike in the past*, as presently the government's objective is to attain rapid economic development. Hence, the liberalisation would not guarantee the *same role and importance for the trade unions in India.*

Trade unions in India resisted the implementation of economic liberalisation as they do not generally favour multinationals getting free access into the Indian industrial field, do favour the growth of small scale sector, oppose privatisation of public enterprises and do not want to close the sick industrial units. Though the trade union's voice their argument against new economic policy on various platforms and through different means, have, in fact, not responded adequately to the possible fall out in employment and salaries.

4. IMPACT ON PARTICIPATIVE MANAGEMENT AND QUALITY CIRCLES

The purpose of participative management is to satisfy the social and psychological needs of employees for association, sense of belongingness and satisfaction of involvement in decision-making. Among other things, the outcome of participative management is making use of human resources to the maximum extent through satisfying their social and psychological needs. Further, the innovative and creative abilities of employees will find utility value in the organisation under participative management. Participative management provides added competitive advantage to the industries. Hence, the significance of *participative management would be magnified under liberalised economy.*

Quality improvement, upgradation and maintenance are the central plan of the new economic policy. Quality controls to match international standards would be a tough task of Indian enterprises. Quality circles would play a dominant role in quality improvement. But these programmes are not well received at present. However, these *schemes would receive the attention* in Indian industry for the enhancement of skills, upgradation of knowledge, etc., to match the human resources to the requirements of new technology

5. IMPACT ON EMPLOYMENT

There has been significant decline in the growth of employment in almost all sectors of the economy during 1980s. Consequently, rural areas have not only been exporting their manpower to urban centres but also been exporting their unemployment.

Now the organised industry should be of high quality and productivity-oriented and as such adopt most latest technology. These strategies would normally demand for most skilled people with high degree of dedication and commitment which would normally be a thin proportion of the existing human resources of the present organisations. The rest of the human resources would be deployed or retrenched as the organised sector would no longer afford to retain such employees. The magnitude of this problem was more in public sector which has been referred to as 'employment sinks'. The Government of India introduced the Exit Policy/ Golden handshake to get rid of the unwanted segment of the manpower.

The structural shifts caused by liberalisation would *provide better employment to the qualitative human resources* and throwout the inferior and unwanted human resources into the fold of contract labour and/or unorganised sector, at least in the short-run, if not in the long-run.

With economy moving towards double digit figures and opportunities are multiplying in fast growing sectors such as IT, ITES, hospitality, financial services, consumer marketing, telecom and aviation, etc. even corporates are now facing the brunt of talent crunch. With industry and service sector growing, poaching is at an all-time high and also working hard to keep their flock together.

We have to learn the lessons from the South Korea, Thailand and Malaysia which experienced short sharp recessions followed by rapid GDP growth with productivity growth outstripping real wage growth. The miracle of these countries is partly due to the strategy of continuous deployment of their human resources. The problem of unemployment and underemployment caused due to the liberalisation in short-run can be mitigated by developing the country's human resources mostly by the government through its institutions in addition to the efforts of the industry.

6. IMPACT ON HUMAN RESOURCE DEVELOPMENT

Human Resource Development (HRD) plays significant role in market economies and more so in an economy tending towards market conditions like India. Global competitiveness has created customers diagonally opposite to what we have today. This is the problem, challenge and opportunity. Response to global competitiveness involves 'new customers'. Meeting the requirements and desires of new customers, *demands for competent, developed human resources* with human approach towards customers.

7. IMPACT ON WAGES AND BENEFITS

Wage differentials and the principles of socialistic pattern of society do contradict with each other. Hence, government in the past favoured minimisation of wage inequalities. But wage differentials are highly essential under the market economy to attract the skilled, talented and committed human resources through offering higher salaries and benefits. Thus, globalisation *results in higher salaries and benefits for highly skilled, talented and committed people* and low salaries and benefits for those whose skills and talents are in less demand. The salary hikes in the country have stabilised in the range of 12-15% in 2006. A survey by Hewitt Associates that salary hikes in 2007 will remain same.

8. CONCLUSION

Economic liberalisation and globalisation have their impact on all segments of economic activities including personnel management and industrial relations. They demand high skilled and committed personnel and provide the scope for high quality of worklife. Though, they result in unemployment to less skilled personnel in short-run, continuous development of human resources along with setting up of a number of new industries would provide better employment opportunities. The salary and benefits administration would tend towards the market factors.

The industrial relations system may not take much deviation but the actors of industrial relations may be required to play a more coordinated role in order to strengthen the competitive abilities of the organisation. Government would play the role of a facilitator, trade union plays a balanced role of satisfying the demands of managements too, management fulfils its role tending towards individual needs rather than generalising them. Thus, the emphasis may *shift from industrial relations to human relations.*

The competitive culture of market economy would result in personal problems, health problems like executive stress and tension. These changes would call for *special emphasis on counselling worklife balance and human resource maintenance and development.* However, the perseverance of Indian culture would resist the spreading up of such type of ill-effects. Thus, globalisation would have positive impacts on human resource management in long-run in the country.

Part Four

RECOMMENDATIONS AND GUIDELINES

Important Recommendations of the National Commission on Labour, 2000

Ministry of Labour, Government of India

CHAPTER I—THE TERMS OF REFERENCE

1.20 Competitiveness depends not merely on technology, credit, inputs and managerial skills, but also on the contribution that labour makes. The commitment of the workforce to quality and productivity must be high. This commitment and the new work culture that it calls for, can be created only when workers feel that they are receiving fair wages, a fair share of profits and incentives, and the respect or consideration due to partners.

1.27 It is one thing to hold that the role of the State should be minimal, and quite another to hold that industrial relations should be based only on bilateralism. Bilateralism is an essential ingredient of Industrial relations, and both parties should rely on it as far as possible. But it cannot be denied that there is a role that mediation, arbitration, adjudication or third party intervention can play to ensure industrial peace with justice to both sides and to society.

31.81 Our economic security and the success of our efforts to improve the standard of living of our people will, therefore, depend on our ability to identify the conditions that can ensure cooperation between our workers and employers.

1.82 Attitudes of confrontation must give place to an attitude of genuine partnership. Organisations of workers as well as employers, and the State itself, should identify and create the conditions on which the harmonious relations that we need can be created and maintained.

CHAPTER V—APPROACH TO REVIEW OF LAWS

5.29 We recommended that: the Central Government and all State Governments should have a uniform policy on holidays, only 3 national holidays be gazetted, viz. Independence Day, Republic Day and Gandhi Jayanti Day (October 2), two more days may be added to be determined by each state according to its own tradition and apart from these each person must be allowed to avail of 10 restricted holidays in the year, Government holidays should be delinked from holidays under the Negotiable Instruments Act, in case of the option of a five-day week. If a holiday occurs during the week, Saturday should be a working day, and the movement of quality circles should be encouraged. This will enable workers to take Interest in the work they perform and contribute to the improvement in the overall work culture in the organisation.

5.32 The attitude to hours of work should not be rigid. The total number of hours per day should not be more than nine, and hours of work per week should not be more than 48. But within these limits there may be flexibility, and compensation for overtime.

5..36 There are weighty considerations that should temper the demand for an immediate switchover to the contract system and to unrestricted rights of 'hire and fire.'

CHAPTER VI—REVIEW OF LAWS

6.9 From the commitments of the Government of India, it can be deduced that the following rights of workers have been recognised as inalienable and must, therefore, accrue to every worker under any system of labour laws and labour policy. These are:

(a) Right to work of one's choice,
(b) Right against discrimination,
(c) Prohibition of child labour,
(d) Just and humane conditions of work,
(e) Right to social security,
(f) Protection of Wages including right to guaranteed wages,
(g) Right to redress of grievances,
(h) Right to organise and form trade unions and right to collective bargaining, and
(i) Right to participation in management.

6.10 One cannot overlook the fact that rights are also related to duties.

6.11 Keeping all these in view it would appear that perhaps the safest approach, in the context of coverage under labour laws, would be to define the organized sector as consisting of establishments which have a minimum employment limit.

6.16 Whatever be the employment limit, there are certain provisions like maternity benefit, child care, workmen's compensation, medical benefits and other elements of social security and safety which must be applicable to all workers, irrespective of the employment size of that establishment, or the nature of its activity.

6.17 The Commission has given considerable thought to the number of employees that should be fixed as the threshold point for the organised sector. It does not want workers who are already enjoying the protection of laws forfeit their protection or benefits of provisions for safety and security. Nor does it want to add to the problems of small entrepreneurs' financial burdens that affect the viability of their enterprises or compel them to work under irksome conditions. Balancing both these factors, the Commission feels that a limit of 19 workers should be accepted as the socially defensible mean.

6.19 Relatively better-off section of employees categorised as workmen like Airlines Pilots, etc. do not merely carry out instructions from superior authority but are also required and empowered to take various kinds of on the spot decisions in various situations and particularly in exigencies. Their functions, therefore, cannot merely be categorized as those of ordinary workmen. We, therefore, recommend that Government may lay down a list of such highly paid jobs who are presently deemed as workmen category as being outside the purview of the laws relating to workmen and included in the proposed law for the protection of non-workmen. Another alternative is that the Government fix a cut-off limit of remuneration which is substantially high enough, in the present context, such as Rs. 25,000 p.m. beyond which employees will not be treated as ordinary "workmen".

6.20 It would be logical to keep all the supervisory personnel, irrespective of their wage/salary, outside the rank of worker and keep them out of the purview of the labour laws meant for workers. All such supervisory category of employees should be dubbed along with the category of persons who discharge managerial and administrative functions. The Commission would also recommend that such a modified definition of worker could be adopted in all the labour laws. We expect managements to take care of the interests of supervisory staff as they will now be part of the managerial fraternity.

6.21 Existing set of labour laws should be broadly grouped into four or five groups of laws pertaining to: (i) industrial relations, (ii) wages, (iii) social security, (iv) safety, and (v) welfare and working conditions and so on. The Commission is of the view that the coverage as well as the definition of the term 'worker' should be the same in all groups of laws, subject to the stipulation that social security benefits must be available to all employees including administrative, managerial, supervisory and others excluded from the category of workmen and others not treated as workmen or excluded from the category of workmen.

6.22 The Commission agrees with the Study Group that it is necessary to provide a minimum level of protection to Managerial and other (excluded) employees too, against unfair dismissals or removals. This has to be through adjudication by labour Court or Labour Relations Commission or arbitration.

6.26 Central laws relating to the subject of Labour Relations are currently the Industrial Disputes Act, 1947, the Trade Unions Act, 1926 and the Industrial Employment (Standing Orders) Act, 1946. Mention must also be made of the Sales Promotion Employees (Conditions of Service) Act, 1976 and other specific Acts governing Industrial relations in particular trades or employments. There are state level legislations too on the subject. We recommend that the provisions of all these laws be judiciously consolidated into a single law called the Labour Management

Relations Law or the Law on Labour Management Relations. However, we would carve out a section of those workers who are employed in establishments with an employment size of 19 and below, for a different kind of dispensation. In view of our approach, we recommend the repeal of the Sales Promotion Employees (Conditions of Service) Act, 1976 and other specific Acts governing industrial relations in particular trades or employments and also specific laws governing wage fixation in particular trades or employments, in the light of what we recommend later in respect of the law on wages. The general law on industrial relations and wages will apply to them.

6.28 We would recommend the enactment of a special law for small scale units. We have come to the conclusion that the reasonable threshold limit will be 19 workers. Any establishment with workers above that number cannot be regarded as small. The composite law suggested by us for small enterprises has provisions for registration of establishments, (provisions pertaining to) securing safety, health and welfare of the workers, hours of work, leave, payment of wages, payment of bonus, compensation in case of lay-off, retrenchment and closure, resolution of individual and collective disputes of workers, etc. The law suggested by us also has provisions pertaining to social security. We are of the view that a composite law will not only protect the interests of the workers in these enterprises but will make it easier for the small enterprises to comply with the same.

6.34 Thirdly, we recognise that today the extent of unionisation is low and even this low level is being eroded, and that it is time that this trend was reversed and collective negotiations encouraged. Where agreements and understanding between the two parties is not possible, there, recourse to the assistance of a third party should as far as possible be through arbitration or where adjudication is the preferred mode, through labour courts and labour relations commissions of the type we propose later in this regard, and not Governmental intervention. A settlement entered into with a recognised negotiating agent must be binding on all workers.

6.35 Fourthly, we consider that provisions must be made in the law for determining negotiating agents, particularly on behalf of workers.

6.40 It is desirable to define two terms, 'wages' and 'remuneration'; the former to include only basic wages and dearness allowance and no other for the purpose of contribution to social security and for calculations of bonus and gratuity and all other payments including other allowances as well as overtime payment together with wages as defined above will be 'remuneration'.

6.43 Term 'retrenchment' should be defined precisely to cover only termination of employment arising out of reduction of surplus workers in an establishment, such surplus having arisen out of one or more of several reasons.

6.48 We, therefore, recommend that in the case of socially essential services like water supply, medical services, sanitation, electricity and transport, when there is a dispute between employers and employees in an enterprise, and when the dispute is not settled through mutual negotiations, there may be a strike ballot as in other enterprises, and if the strike ballot shows that 51% of workers are in favour of a strike, it should be taken that the strike has taken place, and the dispute must forthwith be referred to compulsory arbitration (by arbitrators from the panel of the Labour Relations Commission (LRC), or arbitrators agreed to by both sides).

6.51 A question was raised whether the right to registration as Trade Unions should be confined to organisations of workers only or employer's organisations should also enjoy this right as provided in the existing provisions. We have come to the conclusion that the present system of eligibility for registration may continue. All benefits which accrue to workers as a result of collective bargaining do not distinguish between those who are members of Trade Unions and those who are not. A worker who is not a member of any Trade Union will have to pay an amount equal to the subscription rate of the negotiating agent or the highest rate of subscription of a union out of the negotiating college. The amounts collected on this account may be credited to a statutory welfare fund.

6.66 Negotiating agent should be selected for recognition on the basis of the check-off system, with 66% entitling the union to be accepted as the single negotiating agent, and if no union has 66% support, then unions that have the support of more than 25% should be given proportionate representation on the college.

6.73 Check-off system in an establishment employing 300 or more workers must be made compulsory for members of all registered trade unions.

6.75 The Commission has taken note of the practice of industry level negotiations on interest issues, which obtain in several industries and would like the practice to continue. However, it would also like that as far as possible, negotiations and decision-making on wages, allowances, general conditions including total number of hours of work, leave, holidays, social security, safety and health, productivity negotiations, manpower adjustments, change in shifts, etc. should be concluded at the establishment level so as to maximize the efficient functioning of the individual establishments.

6.76 We would also recommend that recognition once granted, should be valid for a period of four years, to be co-terminus with the period of settlement. No claim by any other trade union/federation/centre for recognition should be entertained till at least 4 years have elapsed from the date of earlier recognition. The individual workers' authorisation for check-off should also be co-terminus with the tenure of recognition of the negotiating agent or college.

6.77 Establishments employing 20 or more workers should have standing orders or regulations. There is no need to delimit the issues on which standing orders can or need be framed. As long as the two parties agree, all manner of things including multi-skilling, production, job enrichment, productivity, and so on can also be added. These standing orders will be prepared by the employer(s) in consultation with the recognised unions/federations/centres depending upon the coverage, and where there is any disagreement between the parties, the disputed matter will be determined by the certifying authority having jurisdiction, to which either of the parties may apply. Any amendment to the Standing Orders can be asked for by either party and agreed to by both parties or referred to the certifying authority or the Labour Court for determination. However, no demand for amendment can be made until at least a year has elapsed. The appropriate Government may prescribe a separate Model Standing Order for units employing less than 50 workers. We append a draft of Model Standing Orders for such small establishments. The employer will have to append a copy of Model Standing Orders or the Standing Orders, mutually agreed upon with the workers, to the appointment letter of every employee.

6.78 The appropriate government may also frame model standing orders, including the classification of acts of misconduct as major and minor, and providing for graded punishments depending on the nature and gravity of the misconduct, and publish them in the official gazette. Where an establishment has no standing orders, or where draft standing orders are still to be finalised, the model standing orders shall apply.

6.79 Any worker who, pending completion of domestic enquiry, is placed under suspension, should be entitled to 50% of his wages as subsistence allowance, and at 75% of wages for the period beyond 90 days if the period of suspension exceeds 90 days, for no fault of the worker, so however the total period of suspension shall not, in any case, exceed one year. If as a result of continued absence of the worker at the domestic enquiry or if the enquiry and disciplinary action cannot be completed in time for reasons attributable wholly to the worker's default or intransigence, the employer will be free to conduct the enquiry *ex-parte* and complete the disciplinary proceedings based on such *ex-parte* enquiry and further, there would be no increase in subsistence allowance beyond 50% for the period exceeding 90 days in such cases.

6.80 Every establishment shall establish a Grievance Redressal Committee consisting of equal number of workers' and employers' representatives. The Grievance Redressal Committee shall be the body to which all grievances of a worker in respect of his employment, including his non-employment will be referred for decision within a given timeframe.

6.87 In the new circumstances of global competition, it may not be possible for some enterprises to continue and meet the economic consequences of competition. In such cases, one cannot compel non-viable undertakings to continue to bear the financial burden that has to be borne to keep the concern going. They should, therefore, have the option to close down. It would be good if there can be a prior scrutiny of the grounds on which the closure is sought. Precisely it is for this reason that the provision for prior permission was incorporated. But experience has shown that governments do not want to give quick decisions, even though they know that delay in taking decisions only adds to the burdens that such enterprises are force to carry. Permission for closure are kept pending for months and years and employers kept waiting. Sometimes managements try to seek some such subterfuges to close the enterprise and disappear from the scene without paying compensation, dues, etc. to workers. In these circumstances the Commission came to the conclusion that the best, and more honest and equitable course will be to allow closure, provide for adequate compensation to workers, and in the event of an appeal, leave it to the Labour Relations Commission to find ways of redressal through arbitration or adjudication.

6.88 Prior permission is not necessary in respect of lay-off and retrenchment in an establishment of any employment size. Workers will, however, be entitled to two month's notice or notice pay in lieu of notice, in case of retrenchment. We also feel that the rate of retrenchment compensation should be higher in a running organisation than in an organisation which is being closed. Again, we are of the view that the scale of compensation may vary for sick units and profit-making units even in cases of retrenchment. It would however, recommend that in the case of establishments employing 300 or more workers where lay-off exceeds a period of one month, such establishments should be required to obtain *post-facto* approval of the appropriate government. We recommend that the provisions of Chapter VB pertaining to permission for closure should be made applicable to all establishments to protect the interests of workers in establishments which are not covered at present by this provision if they are employing 300 or more workers. Necessary changes in Chapter VA in regard to retrenchment and closure will have to be made accordingly. Every employer will have to ensure, before a worker is retrenched or the establishment is closed, irrespective of the employment size of the establishment, that all dues to the workers, be it arrears of wages earned, compensation amount to be paid for retrenchment or closure as indicated in the next paragraph, or any other amount due to the worker, are first settled as a precondition to retrenchment or closure. These provisions will not bar industrial disputes being raised against a lay-off or retrenchment or closure. Having regard to the national debate on this issue and the principle outlined above, the Commission would like to recommend the compensation per completed year of service at the rate of 30 days on account of closure in case of sick industry which has continuously run into losses for the last 3 financial years or has filed an application for bankruptcy or winding up, and other non-profit- making bodies like charitable institutions, etc. and at the rate of 45 days for retrenchment by such sick industry or body where retrenchment is done with a view to becoming viable. It would also recommend higher retrenchment compensation at the rate of 60 days of wages and similarly a higher rate of compensation for closure at the rate of 45 days wages for every completed year of service for profit-making organisations. For establishments employing less than 100 workers half of the compensation mentioned above in terms of number of days wages may be prescribed. However, these establishments will also be required to give similar notice as prescribed for bigger establishments before retrenching the workers or closing down.

6.90 We are recommending the restoration of the original threshold limit for prior permission, increased rates of compensation; consultation with the representatives of the workers without giving workers a right to veto; judicial review by the LRC in case of dispute; and (legal provisions or review by the appropriate Governments) that make it obligatory for employers to purchase insurance cover for employees.

6.91 Arising out of the above, we recommend that while the lay-off compensation could be 50% of the wages as at present, in the case of retrenchment, Chapter VA of the law may be amended to provide for sixty days notice for both retrenchment and closure or pay in lieu thereof. The provision for permission to close down an establishment employing 300 or more workmen should be made a part of Chapter VA, and Chapter VB should be repealed. In case of closure of such establishment which is employing 300 or more workers, the employer will make an application for permission to the appropriate Government 90 days before the intended closure and also serve a copy of the same on the recognised to remain competitive. We would, therefore, recommend that contract labour shall not be engaged for core production/ services activities. However, for sporadic seasonal demand, the employer may engage temporary labour for core production/service activity. We are aware that off-loading perennial non-core services like canteen, watch & ward, cleaning, etc. to other employing agencies has to take care of three aspects—(1) there have to be provisions that ensure that perennial core services are not transferred to other agencies or establishments; (2) where such services are being performed by employees on the payrolls of the enterprises, no transfer to other agencies should be done without consulting, bargaining (negotiating) agents; and (3) where the transfer of such services do not involve any employee who is currently in service of the enterprise, the management will be free to entrust the service to outside agencies. The contract labour will, however, be remunerated at the rate of a regular worker engaged in the same organisation doing work of a comparable nature or if such worker does not exist in the organisation, at the lowest salary of a worker in a comparable grade, i.e. unskilled, semiskilled or skilled. The principal employer will also ensure that the prescribed social security and other benefits are extended to the contract worker. There is a reason that compels us to make this recommendation. At many of the centers we visited, we were told during evidence, that there were cases of contractors making deductions from the wages of contract workers as their contribution towards social security, and then absconding without depositing either the contribution realised from the workers or their own contributions into the appropriate social security fund.

6.110 The Commission would recommend that no worker should be kept continuously as a casual or temporary worker against a permanent job for more than 2 years.

6.112 Minimum wage payable to anyone in employment, in whatever occupation, should be such as would satisfy the needs of the worker and his family (consisting in all of 3 consumption units) arrived at on the Need Based formula of the 15th Indian Labour Conference supplemented by the recommendations made in the Judgment of the Supreme Court in the Raptakos Brett & Co. case. However, before fixing the minimum wage the appropriate Government should keep in mind the capacity of the industry to pay as well as the basic needs of the workers.

6.113 The Commission recommends that every employer must pay each worker his one-month's wage, as bonus before an appropriate festival, be it Diwali or Onam or Puja or Ramzan or Christmas. Any demand for bonus in excess of this upto a maximum of 20% of the wages will be subject to negotiation. We also recommend that the present system of two wage ceilings for reckoning entitlement and for calculation of bonus should be suitably enhanced to Rs. 7500 and Rs. 3500 for entitlement and calculation respectively.

6.114 There should be a national minimum wage that the Central Government may notify. This minimum must be revised from time to time. It should, in addition, have a component of dearness allowance to be declared six monthly linked to the consumer price index and the minimum wage may be revised once in five years. This will be a wage below which no one who is employed anywhere, in whatever occupation, can be paid. Each State/Union Territory should have the authority to fix minimum rates of wages, which shall not be, in any event, less than the national minimum wage when announced; where a state is large, it may, if it chooses, fix different rates of minimum wages for different regions in the state but no such wage can be less than the national minimum wage. The Commission also recommends the abolition of the present system of notifying scheduled employments and of fixing/revising the minimum rates of wages periodically for each scheduled employment, since it feels that all workers in all employments should have the benefit of a minimum wage.

6.115 Where wages are fixed purely on piece rate basis the employer should pay at least 75% of the notified time rate wages to the piece rated worker if the employer is not able to provide him with work.

6.116 We, therefore recommend that fixation of piece rate wages must be so done as to enable a diligent worker to earn after 8 hours work what would be the time rated daily rate.

6.118 There is no need for any wage board, statutory or otherwise, for fixing wage rates for workers in any industry.

6.121 We would recommend enactment of a general law relating to hours of work, leave and working conditions, at the work place. For ensuring safety at the work place and in different activities, one omnibus law may be enacted, providing for different rules and regulations on safety applicable to different activities. (We have appended a draft indicative law on hours of work and other working conditions after this chapter and an omnibus draft indicative law on safety in the chapter on Labour Administration). Such general law on working conditions, etc. may provide for the following:

(a) The law should have a provision for letters of appointment along with a copy of Standing Orders of the establishment (in the local language); and issue of a photo identity card giving details of the name of the worker, name of establishment, designation, and so on.

(b) It should specify the maximum number of working hours in a day/week, and payment of overtime at double the rates of wages. The limitation on employing workers on overtime needs to be relaxed, and we recommend that the present ceilings be increased to double to enable greater flexibility in meeting the challenges of the market. Sub-section (2) of Section 64 of the Factories Act contains a provision that the State Government can give exemptions in certain circumstances. We recommend that the list of such contingencies may be suitably expanded in consultation with the representatives of the industry to include more occupations, processes and contingencies. However, we also recommend that the workers' right to wages for overtime work at the prescribed rate of overtime wages if they are asked to work beyond 9 hours a day and 48 hours a week should be ensured.

(c) There should be reduced working hours for adolescents, prohibition of underground work in mines for women workers, prohibition of work by women workers between certain hours and so on.

(d) On the question of night work for women there need not be any restriction on this if the number of women workers in a shift in an establishment is not less than five, and if the management is able to provide satisfactory arrangements for their transport, safety and rest after or before shift hours.

(e) At the same time, the Commission is not in favour of any exemptions being granted in respect of establishments in export promotion zones or special economic zones from labour laws.

(f) The Commission feels that the appropriate Government may be empowered to grant exemptions from different provisions of law in case of emergent situations that may arise in the workload of an establishment or in cases of extreme hardship.

(j) Creches should not be dependent on the number of women workers or the number of children. Every establishment employing 20 or more workers must run a creche.

(k) There should be provision for holidays, earned leave, sick leave and casual leave at an appropriate scale to the workers, apart from maternity benefits for women workers. We do not approve of the practice of declaring a holiday on the death of a person. Likewise, we do not also see the necessity to declare polling days as holidays. Only half a day's holiday may be permitted on such a day to those who have to go to cast their votes, the timings of which should be decided by mutual consultation amongst employers and workers.

6.147 The labour relations commissions have multiple duties including the important task of identifying collective bargaining/negotiating agents. We have also suggested that all matters in the labour field needing adjudication, be it a labour-management dispute (except collective disputes) or a workman's compensation claim or disputes arising out of and relating to coverage of labour laws or disputes relating to social security and the like, will have to be determined by the labour courts at the lowest level, with appeals to the Labour Relations Commissions. Collective disputes between the negotiating agent and employer, if not resolved bilaterally or in conciliation or arbitration should be dealt with by appropriate Labour Relation Commission. This will need considerable increase in the number of labour courts. The setting up of labour relations commissions also increases the demand for high-level labour adjudicating functionaries. All these compel us to recommend an All India Labour Judicial Service which in the new dispensation will be viable and necessary.

6.148 Equally important in our view is the need for constituting an All India Labour Administrative Service. Labour being in the concurrent list of the Constitution, the advantages of such a service, which will also enable exchange of officers between the Centre and the States, are obvious. It must be recognised that the bulk of the labour administration in the States and union territories relates to implementation and enforcement of labour laws. We are of the view that if all the posts of the labour department of and above the rank of Dy. Labour Commissioners/Regional Labour Commissioners at the State and the Centre are included in the service and also senior level appointments such as Executive Heads of Welfare Funds, Social security administration and so on, there will be an adequate number of posts justifying such a service.

6.150 In spite of the paucity of the time at our disposal, we have attempted to make a draft of what a comprehensive Law on Labour Management Relations, as visualised in this Chapter would look like. It should be taken as our indicative draft, and not the one on groups of industry and occupation. For the purpose of social security measures and cess collection, separate group-based consideration could be necessary.

CHAPTER VIII—SOCIAL SECURITY

8.30 Our Commission accepts the need to consider social security as a fundamental human right.

8.32 We recommend a system in which the State bears the responsibility for providing and ensuring an elementary or basic level of security, and leaves room for partly or wholly contributory schemes. This will mean that the responsibility to provide a floor will be primarily that of the State, and it will be left to individual citizens to acquire higher levels of security through assumption of responsibility and contributory participation. Such a system will temper and minimise the responsibility of the State, and maximise the role and share of individual and group responsibility. Thus, there will be three levels in the system.

8.51 Considering all the conceptual issues as well as the demographic profile of the country we feel that no single approach to provide social security, will be adequate. The problem has to be addressed by a multi-pronged approach that would be relevant in the Indian context.

8.97 The Workmen's Compensation Act should be converted from an employers' liability scheme to a social insurance scheme, its coverage should be progressively extended to more employments and classes of employees, and the restrictive clauses in Schedule II of the Act should be removed.

8.100 So far as the organised sector is concerned, the existing provisions for maternity benefit should be extended so as to be applicable to all women workers.

8.101 There are many classes of establishments where women are being employed increasingly, to which the Maternity Benefit Act is not applicable. We recommend that those classes may be brought within the scope of the Act on priority basis by following the National Industrial Classification.

8.118 Regarding applicability of the P.F. Act, the Task Force on Social Security has recommended that the employment threshold should be brought down to 10 immediately, to 5 during the next 3-5 years, and to one within a short time-frame thereafter. The Commission agrees with these suggestions.

8.129 It is suggested that the Act be amended so as to do away with the distinction between different classes of establishments for purposes of the rate of contribution. This is, however, without prejudice to the suggestions made elsewhere to provide for different packages of contributions and benefits for different classes of employees.

8.136 The Commission is of the opinion that the provision for premature withdrawal of funds should be restricted.

8.138 Proposals to integrate the Payment of Gratuity Act with the Employee Deposit Linked Scheme and also to introduce an Unemployment Insurance Scheme as part of the Scheme should be implemented soon.

8.149 The Payment of Gratuity Act may be integrated with the EPF Act and converted into a social insurance scheme.

8.160 An integrated insurance scheme providing for gratuity, unemployment benefits, lay-off and retrenchment compensation may be evolved, and entrusted to the EPFO for its implementation.

8.175 An unemployment insurance scheme could play a substantial role in coping with unacceptable levels of unemployment resulting from the implementation of the structural adjustment programmes and other economic reforms.

8.177 The unemployment scheme should be financed by a tripartite contribution to be determined actuarially.

8.179 The National Renewal Fund (NRF) was established in February 1992 to provide a form of a wage guarantee which had to be used for re-training, re-deployment, counselling, etc. But in practice, NRF has mostly been utilised for implementing the VRS. There is need to restructure this Fund to serve as a wage guarantee fund.

8.273 The need to provide some form of public assistance to meet the distressing consequences of unemployment has become more urgent after globalisation. The only way to mitigate such stress or insure against such exposures, will be to provide at least a modicum of support that will enable the victim to face the rigours of unemployment during the period of transition.

8.292 Effort to implement a National Employment Assurance Scheme is of considerable importance. Such a Scheme would not be unfeasible and should be given a fair trial.

8.294 We feel that it is the responsibility of the State to provide a basic level of subsistence by an appropriate social security measure to those who have no employment and no source of income. The Central Government should consider introducing a National Scheme of Unemployment Relief to the unemployed persons subject to a means test.

8.347 We reiterate the need for a national policy for older persons. There is no alternative to the Central and State Governments taking the initiative to set-up their own homes in sufficient numbers.

8.351 Appropriate schemes would need to be designed for the health care as well as long-term care of the elderly.

8.365 A National Scheme for Pensions for Physically Handicapped be introduced.

8.393 A permanent commission for disaster management should be set-up on the lines of the Election Commission. It should be responsible for the management of relief and rehabilitation after every drought, loss of crops, floods, cyclones, earthquakes and other disasters. This body could study how disasters are managed in other countries and suggest the equipment to be purchased. It should also be empowered to seek help from the Army, Police and other personnel in times of acute distress due to calamities.

8.415 We strongly recommend the constitution of a high-powered National Social Security Authority, preferably under the chairmanship of the Prime Minister of India. The functions of the Authority will be mainly to formulate the National Policy on Social Security and to co-ordinate the Central and State level programmes.

CHAPTER XI—LABOUR ADMINISTRATION

11.32 The procedure for prosecution for non-payment of wages and payment of less than minimum rates of wages should be simplified.

11.33 To make enforcement effective, there should be commensurately deterrent punishment under all enactments.

11.34 Laws like Payment of Wages Act and Minimum Wages Act should contain a provision for recovery officers to be appointed by the Labour Department, as has been done in Section 8-B of the Employees' Provident Fund & Miscellaneous Provisions Act, 1952.

11.36 Minimum Wages Act should apply to all establishments and not be confined only to certain scheduled employments.

11.40 Industrial disputes not settled in conciliation should go for either voluntary arbitration or by arbitrators maintained by the Labour Relations Commission or adjudication. In the case of essential services the dispute should go for compulsory arbitration. In other cases, it should go for adjudication. Arbitrators should be chosen from eminent persons in industry, conciliators, trade unionists and labour judiciary.

11.61 A Central Labour Relations Commission should be set-up for Central sphere establishments, and State Labour Relations Commission should be set-up for establishments in the State sphere. Above the Central and State Labour Relations Commissions, there will be the National Labour Relation Commission to hear appeals against the decisions of the two other Commissions. The National LRC, Central LRC and the State LRCs will be autonomous and independent. These Commissions will function as appellate tribunals over the Labour Courts. They will be charged with the responsibility of superintendence of the work of labour courts.

11.70 It is also necessary to improve the knowledge, skills and competence of the officers of the CLS to enable them to win the confidence of the employers and workmen. Induction, training and periodical refresher courses are necessary to improve the efficiency and effectiveness of officers of the CLS. To improve the status of these officers, there is need for an All India service, like the Indian Labour Judicial Service. These officers should be given proper staff, infrastructural backup, and support facilities. There should be access to information on all matters concerning industrial relations. A database should be built up on all aspects relating to industrial relations and the officers of the CLS should have access to such database through computer connectivity.

11.79 To make conciliation effective, it is necessary to improve the status and competence and calibre of conciliation officers through proper recruitment, training and placement. A Labour and Judicial Service can be formed.

11.82 Voluntary resolution of disputes should be encouraged over legalistic approach of settlement of disputes through adjudication. Labour Administration should encourage better human resource management practices.

11.83 There should be a legislative framework for voluntary dispute settlement. A basic prerequisite is to place a system of recognition of negotiating agency on the statute. The responsibility of conducting verification of trade union membership for recognition of trade unions should be vested in the Central Labour Relations Commission and the State Labour Relations Commission. The Works Committee required to be constituted under Section 3 of the Industrial Disputes Act should be substituted by an Industrial Relations Committee to promote in-house dispute settlement.

11.84 The National Labour Relations Commission should function as the appellate authority in respect of the decisions of the Central and State LRCs.

11.86 The Indian Labour Conference should be an effective forum for review, consultation and formulation or evolution of perspective and policies.

11.88 We are in general agreement with the proposals in the Draft Indian Labour Code for the strengthening of the Indian Labour Conference. The ILC can be used as a sounding board for proposals of legislations.

11.115 The amendments made in the Factories Act after the Bhopal Tragedy have been salutary and the spirit should be extended to organisations other than factories. The amendments which have been made should be implemented properly and if necessary the responsibilities of the non-technical provisions can be transferred to the Labour Inspectorate so that the Factory Inspectorate can concentrate on aspects of health and safety.

11.129 A competent institution, perhaps on the lines of Occupational Safety and Health Commission of the USA, should be nominated to formulate, implement and periodically review a coherent national policy for the establishment and promotion of OSH Management Systems in organisations.

11.131 Occupational Safety and Health have to be the responsibility and duty of the employer. The employer should make appropriate arrangements for the establishment of OSH Management Systems. The system should contain the main elements of policy, organising, planning implementation, evaluation and means of improvement.

11.144 A disaster management plan must be formulated at every unit and industrial estate, and at the city, district, state and national level. The concept of Mutual Aid Response Group (MARG) provides that workers working in a factory are given information about the hazardous nature of operations in other factories in their vicinity so that workers working in neighbouring factories would be in a position to render assistance during emergency. Similarly, doctors working in major hospitals should be informed of the hazards involved in the factories in their vicinity.

11.154 Arrangements to conduct periodic safety or OSH audits should be established.

11.155 A safety audit policy and programme should be developed.

CHAPTER XII—WORKER PARTICIPATION IN MANAGEMENT

12.54 With globalisation the time has come when we cannot leave the question of participative management to be determined by the management or the trade unions. We believe, therefore, that the time has come for the Government to enact a law to provide for participatory forums at all levels keeping in mind the necessity to ensure that the responsibility and freedom to take managerial decisions are not fragmented to the detriment of the enterprise, the social partners or society at large.

Review of Wages and Wage Policy

12.131 The resources to pay wages have also to be created. They have to come from the economic viability and profit of undertakings.

12.132 Our Constitution accepts the responsibility of the state to create an economic order in which every citizen finds employment and receives a 'fair wage'.

12.178 Till such time as a National Minimum Wage Policy is evolved; the floor level wage may be treated as the current national minimum wage.

12.183 It is difficult to lay down a clear-cut criterion for fixing an appropriate ratio between salaries of the top management and wages paid for the worker at the lowest rung of the ladder.

12.210 The organised sector which accounts for less than 8% of the total labour force of India enjoys privileges and perquisites which are considerably more than that in the rest of the country.

12.247 Our Study Group on Unorganised Labour has recommended that the minimum wage prescribed by the Fifth Pay Commission for the lowest category of Government employees (Rs. 2400 + Rs. 2100 DA = Rs. 45000) should be the minimum wage for a worker in the unorganised sector.

12.303 If a productivity linked wage system is to succeed, it would need the involvement and commitment of all the parties, particularly the employers and the union in coming up with productivity linked wage system acceptable to all.

Labour Statistics and Research

12.338 Statistical information on labour-related matters is basically utilized for framing labour policies, understanding working and living conditions, formulating policies in respect of target groups, monitoring industrial relations, enforcing labour laws and assessing the nature of employment and unemployment, the skills required for different jobs, gaps in the skills development programmes, etc.

12.339 The Government requires a comprehensive, up-to-date, reliable and authentic data base.

12.359 There are many problems in constructing Consumer Price Index Numbers for Industrial Workers. The delay in revising the base year in contravention of ILO Convention No. 160 and Recommendation No. 170 is a serious problem. The ILO Convention requires us to update the base year once in five years and not later than 10 years so that changes in consumption patterns and non-availability of specified items are effectively taken care of. Timely revision of the base year for index numbers has a corrective impact on the weights of various groups of expenditure. The current series is based on the base year 1982. We learn that this abnormal delay is caused by staff shortage and administrative problems, etc., revision of the present poor remuneration to price collectors/price supervisors essential to ensure effective involvement of these field workers and inadequate training of price collectors and supervisors are another shortcomings.

Guarding against Sexual Harassment in the Work Place (SH)

MEANING

Legally, sexual harassment is defined as unwelcome advances, requests for sexual favours and other verbal or physical conduct of a sexual nature.

Most studies confirm that the concept of power is central to sexual harassment. It comes from a superior, a colleague or a subordinate.

In August 1997 judgement of the Supreme Court of India on sexual harassment of working women in the case of *Vishaka* vs. *The State of Rajasthan* has identified sexual harassment as a separate category of legally prohibitive behaviour. The court has laid down guidelines in accordance with international standards to deal with the issue at work place.

In another case the Supreme Court of India has ruled that sexual harassment at the work place is a violation of fundamental rights.

DEFINITION OF SEXUAL HARASSMENT

According to the orders of the Supreme Court of India sexual harassment is any unwelcome:

(i) Physical contact and advances,
(ii) Demand or request for sexual favours,
(iii) Sexually coloured remarks,
(iv) Display coloured remarks,
(v) Showing pornography, and
(vi) Any other unwelcome physical, verbal or non-verbal conduct of a sexual nature.

Supreme Court has further laid down that:

Actual assault or touch is not required. In such cases, the courts are required to examine the broad possibilities of the case and not get swayed by insignificant discrepancies or narrow technicalities or the dictionary meaning of the expression 'molestation'.

RESPONSIBILITIES OF EMPLOYERS TO IMPLEMENT, MONITOR THE GUIDELINES TO TACKLE SEXUAL HARASSMENT

The Supreme Court guidelines lay down certain responsibilities on employers/ management to implement, monitor the procedure in their organisations, public as well as private.

1. Procedure for Complaints by Women

The guidelines direct employer's to set-up procedure through which women can make their complaints heard.

A *complaints committee* headed by a woman, and/or of which half the members are women should be deputed to look into complaints of sexual harassment. To prevent undue pressure from within the organisation, the committee should include a third-party representative from an NGO.

All complaints should be handled in confidential manner within a time-bound framework. Annual report should be submitted to the concerned government department.

2. Preventive Steps to be taken like by Employers

(a) An express prohibition of sexual harassment should be notified, published and circulated.

(b) Amendment of conduct and service rules to include sexual harassment as an offence and provision of appropriate discipline against the offender.

(c) Management also include in S.O. (Standing Orders), personnel manual of their organisation.

(d) Providing such working conditions to ensure there is no hostile environment.

3. Awareness of Guidelines

(i) Employees to be allowed to raise sexual harassment issues at workers' meetings.

(ii) Sexual harassment issue to be discussed in employer-employee meetings.

(iii) Rights of women workers to be notified.

(iv) Where such act is offence under IPC, employer to initiate action and complaint.

(v) Complainants or witnesses not to be victimised while dealing cases.

(vi) Employer to assist the employee if sexual harassment takes place by an outsider.

IMPLEMENTATION PROBLEMS

Several public and private sector organisations have constituted committees and cells to comply with the Supreme Court guidelines. Experience of implementing guidelines has highlighted some issues:

- It is important that the top management takes serious interest on this issue.
- It is noticed that in many cases recommendations of the committee are ignored and thus denial of justice.
- The usual defence that the harasser puts up is of "inefficiency of complainant or it is conspiracy against him."
- In many cases 'caste factor' is brought in.
- Witnesses do not come forward due to job/careers at stake.
- Too much legalities of evidence, proof from witnesses is asked by the committees.
- If harasser holds a very superior position then it becomes difficult for committee members to secure justice to victim.
- The seat of power becomes tool of misuse, and it could be cloaked as a lure for promotion or increment. Most of the times, divorced, separated or submissive women are the victims.

HOW TO MEET HARASSMENT DILEMMA?

It will be relevant to mention views of Nan Demars (You Want To Do What, Which, Where and How To Draw The Line, Simon and Schuster, USA).

"If we remain silent and tolerate harassment, it will continue. I urge you to confront you harassers, document every suspect incident and follow-up conversation. Let it be known that you are taking their inappropriate and unprofessional behaviour seriously. Then, as soon as, you can, try to stop the objectionable behaviour through the use of informal, one to one discussions and incrementally stiffer consequences. When all else fails, resort to formal avenues of protest inside and outside your company."

SEXUAL HARASSMENT AND THE LAWS IN INDIA

(i) There are several provisions in IPC (The Indian Penal Code) and include:
 (a) S. 354—Assault or criminal force against a woman with the intent to outrage her modesty.
 (b) S. 509—Words, gesture or act intended to insult the modesty of a woman.
 (c) S. 209—Deals with obscene acts and songs.

(ii) Case can be filed under Rule 5, Schedule 5 of the Industrial Disputes Act, if an employee suffers unfair dismissal or denial of employment benefits as a consequence of her rejection for sexual harassment.

(iii) A civil suit can also be filed for damages under tort laws. The Indecent Representation of Women (Prohibition) Act, 1987 has also potential to be used for such cases.

(iv) In case of a senior IAS officer Rupan Bajaj and KPS Gill in July 1988. Gill was fined by Supreme Court of Rs. 2.5 lakhs in lieu of 3 months' rigorous imprisonment for offences under S. 294 and S. 509 of IPC.

(v) Sexual harassment has been included as misconduct in:
   (a) CCS (Conduct) Rules, 1964, and
   (b) Industrial Employment (Standing Orders) Act, 1946.

Who can Face Sexual Harassment?

- An individual at the work place.
- A staffer—from a sweeper to a CEO.
- A non-staffer in any capacity—student, housekeeper, volunteer, on honorarium, maid or consultant.
- Dressed in a *sari* or suit.
- Working in public or private sector units or non-government organisations.
- Working in the unorganised sector—large or small.
- A person who believes it only happens to others.
- And it could be either gender, male or female.

The Employer's Responsibilities

- Recognise sexual harassment as a serious offence and include it in the rules and regulations.
- Prevent and punish sexual harassment at the work place.
- Conduct anti-sexual harassment awareness training for regular and contractual employees as well as for new inductees.
- Formulate an anti-sexual harassment policy, which should:
    - o clearly state the employer's commitment to a safe work environment,
    - o define Sexual Harassment with examples and explicitly term it an offence,
    - o constitute a Complaints Committee as per Supreme Court guidelines,
    - o be aware of the fact that the complainant may delay in lodging a complaint,
    - o ensure confidentiality of the complainant and witnesses,
    - o not punish or harass or transfer the complainant and witnesses for complaining, rather should give the complainant the option to seek transfer of the perpetrator or their own,
    - o make the enquiry procedure time bound,
    - o provide for maintenance of accurate records of the enquiry procedure, with a copy of it given to both parties,
    - o ensure that the Complaints Committee makes recommendations in their enquiry report, the duty of the employer being implementation of the recommendations, and
    - o ensure that a copy of the enquiry report along with the recommendations is given to both parties.
- Ensure that the equity be conducted as per the law of natural justice.
- Display/distribute the policy/information about the redressal mechanism.

- Prominently display the addresses/contact number of the Complaints Committee members.
- Ensure that third parties or service users such as hotel guests, airline passengers, are aware of the Policy.
- Take prompt action on the complaint even if the complainant does not have eyewitnesses.

Effects of Sexual Harassment on the Individual

- Physical, emotional and psychological trauma.
- Loss of self-esteem.
- Isolation and ostracism.
- Absenteeism and lowered productivity.
- Loss of job, promotion or job-related activities such as training.
- Suicide and spillover effects into family life.

Now the Effect these will have on the Organisation

- Decreased productivity.
- Lowered profitability.
- Valued employees quitting or losing jobs.
- Poor public image.
- Costly court litigation.
- Expensive compensation payouts.
- Unhealthy work atmosphere.
- Strain and mistrust in interpersonal relations.

Employee's Responsibilities

- Don't blame yourself.
- Don't ignore sexual harassment—it will not go way by itself.
- Recognise the nature of harassment.
- Talk to the perpetrator.
- Talk to others at the work place or in your family about the harassment and talk with the union, if any.
- Maintain a detailed chronological account of sexual harassment.
- Try and have a witness to the incident.
- Write a letter and/or send your organisation's anti-sexual harassment policy to the harasser by registered post.
- Always retain a copy of the documents/letters sent in connection with your complaint.
- Ensure that the employer formulates an anti-sexual harassment policy and has a redressal mechanism.
- Ask for regular awareness programmes and training to be conducted.
- Approach a women's organisation or call the local helpline or both.

- Lodge a formal complaint without delay.
- Seek counselling.

How an act amounts as sexual harassment or not depends between consenting co-worker? In sexual harassment or in ethics, it is the thought that counts. Gifts are given every where.

Box I

Women Safe at Home, Men on Notice

Crackdown against domestic violence begins, law notified, crime punishable with fine or jail or both

by CHETAN CHAUHAN

Finally there is a law to make home safe for women. The much debated law, aimed specifically at protecting women from being abused in any form by their bands or male live-in partners, comes into effect from Thursday Under the Protection of Women m Domestic Violence Act, 2005, Tenders can be jailed for a maximum of one year or fined up to Rs 20,000, or both. They can also be charged under other sections of the Indian Penal Code (IPC), if applicable.

The new law provides an all-encompassing definition of domestic violence including not only physical violence by the husband, such as beating or physically hurting his wife, or sexual violence like forced intercourse, but also verbal or emotional violence such as insulting the wife or preventing her from taking up a job, and even economic violence such as not allowing the wife to use her salary. "The definition includes threats of abuse on dowry demands too," said Renuk Chowdhury, Minister for Women and Child Development.

Chowdhury said around 70 per cent of women in India were victims of domestic violence in some form. "The enactment of the law is a historic step towards ending gender discrimination," she said. The law addresses sexual abuse of children, or forcing girls to marry against their wishes as well.

The Act also gives a married woman the right to remain in her husband's home, or under the same roof in a joint-family household, even if she does not have any rights to the property.

The Act empowers the court to pass protection orders to prevent an abusive husband from aiding or committing acts of domestic violence. The offender, for instance, can be restrained from communicating with the victim and from visiting her workplace or any other place she frequents.

Not everyone is happy with the Act. Pandurangi Reddy Bharati, who runs the Save Indian Family Foundation Aid, "It will lead to the economic blackmail of men."

Chowdhury did not deny that the Act could be misused but said there would "protection officers to ensure it did not happen." "We will sensitise the officers on all aspects of the law," she said.

State governments will have to appoint a woman protection officer in each police station to book and pursue cases. Victims can seek compensation under the law.

Watch your act

- Abusing or even threatening to abuse one's wife is an offence.
- Physical abuse beating, pushing, shoving.
- Sexual abuse: Forcing to have intercourse or look at pornography.
- Verbal abuse: Insulting.
- Economic abuse: Not providing for wife and children.

—*Hindustan Times*

Social Security to Unemployed Workers by ESIC

UNEMPLOYMENT BENEFIT SCHEME

A new scheme called 'Rajiv Gandhi Shramik Kalyan Yojana', the first of its kind, had been launched to provide unemployment allowance to workers during involuntary unemployment. Under the Scheme, effective from April 1, 2005 'workers covered under Employees State Insurance (ESI) Scheme, who lose their jobs due to retrenchment, closure of factories/establishments and permanent invalidity not arising out of employment are to receive a monthly unemployment allowance for a maximum period of six months.

The ESI Scheme has introduced a scheme of unemployment allowance to the IPs who have been rendered unemployed involuntarily due to closure of the factory/establishment, retrenchment or permanent invalidity arising out of non-employment injury.

Affected IPs and their families will also be entitled to medical care from ESI Dispensaries/hospitals during periods of unemployment allowance.

1. Eligibility conditions

The applicant should have been an Insured Person under the ESI Act on the date of loss of insurable employment on account of retrenchment, closure of the factory/establishment or permanent invalidity arising out of non-employment injury. Contribution in respect of him should have been paid/payable for a minimum period of five years prior to the loss of employment.

The period of service of an I.P. need not be continuous with one employer. The I.P. shall be entitled to unemployment allowance.

There shall be waiting period after the retrenchment.

2. Unemployment allowance shall not be admissible in the following circumstances:

- During lockout.
- Layoff/temporary closure of factory/establishment.
- Strike resorted to by the employees.
- Voluntary abandonment of employment/premature retirement.
- Less than five years' contributory service [click here to know the contributory conditions to be satisfied].
- On obtaining the age of superannuation or 60 (sixty) years whichever is earlier.
- Convicted (i.e. punished for false statement) under the provisions of section 84 of the ESI Act read with Rule 62 of the ESI (Central) Rule.
- On being re-employed elsewhere during the period he/she is in receipt of unemployment allowance
- Dismissal/termination under disciplinary action.
- On death of IP.

The claim for unemployment. Allowance shall be submitted by the claimant at any time but not later than three months from the date of retrenchment/unemployment to the appropriate Branch Office with a certificate of unemployment/retrenchment/invalidity.

51

National Rural Employment Guarantee Act, 2005

1. Purpose

The Employment Guarantee Act is a step towards the right to work, as an aspect of the fundamental right to live with dignity

2. The right to work as a "fundamental right"

- The "right to life" is a fundamental right of all citizens under Article 21 of the Indian constitution.
- "Right to life . . . includes the right to live with human dignity, it would include all these aspects which would make life meaningful, complete and living." (Supreme Court)

2.1 The right to work in the"Directive Principles" of the Constitution

- "The State shall direct its policy towards securing that the citizens, men and women equally, have the right to an adequate means of livelihood." (Article 39A)
- "The State shall make effective provision for securing the right to work. (Article 41)

2.2 Provisions in brief

(i) The National Rural Employment Guarantee Act, 2005 is a law whereby: any adult who is willing to do *unskilled manual work* at the minimum wage is entitled to being employed on local public works within 15 days of applying.

(ii) If employment is not provided within 15 days, the applicant is entitled to an *unemployment allowance*:

- At least one-fourth of the minimum wage for the first 30 days.
- At least one-half of the minimum wage thereafter.

(iii) Anyone above the age of 18 who resides in rural areas is eligible for 100 days per household per year in each nuclear family.

(iv) Work be provided within 5 kilometres of the applicant's residence, as far as possible. If work is provided beyond 5 kilometres, a travel allowance has to be paid.

(v) Mandatory worksite facilities:

- Drinking water,
- Shade,
- Medical aid, and
- Creche if more than five children below age 6 are present.

Note: These facilities are to be provided by the implementing agency.

(vi) Priority for women in the allocation of work: at least 33% of labours should be women.

(vii) NREGA: Where and when:

- Act will come into force initially on 200 districts.
- To be extended to the whole of rural India within five years.

3. Employment Guarantee Scheme (EGS)

(a) Each State has to launch an employment guarantee scheme within six months of the Act coming into force.

(b) Implementation

- Block is the basic unit of implementation.
- In each Block, a "Programme Officer" is to coordinate the implementation of EGS.
- Gram Panchayats are the main implementing agencies.
- Accountability to Gram Sabhas.

(c) Permissible works

- Minor irrigation,
- Water conservation, drought proofing, desilting of tanks, flood control, etc.,
- Land development,
- Rural roads, and
- "Any other work which may be notified by the Central Government in consultation with the State Government".

(d) Cost sharing

- Central Government to pay for:
  - wage costs,
  - 75% of material costs, and
  - some administrative costs.
- State governments to pay for:
  - 25% of material costs,
  - other administrative costs, and
  - unemployment allowance.

ANNEXURES

ANNEXURE I

Mahatma Gandhi on Industrial Relations

Mahatma Gandhi emphasised six basic principles in his approach to employer-employee relationship having bearing on ethical functioning of business:

1. Doctrine of trusteeship

Gandhiji believed each capitalist should consider himself to be a trustee of the wealth he possesses. This type of belief would transform the capitalist order of society into an egalitarian one, where the greatest good of all could be achieved. The end of business must be happiness and welfare of the people. This is what corporate social responsibility is all about. In this, he got the support of the Birla's and the Bajaj's to fund the freedom movement. The doctrine of trusteeship has its roots in the Bhagavad Gita in the principles of non-possession and equalism. Management is expected to hold the industry as a trust for the society and avoid unethical practices in business such as providing fake medicines, adulterated food, milk with high pesticide contents, etc.

2. Peaceful co-existence of capital and labour

Gandhiji assigned a paternalistic role to management in their dealings with labour. Capitalist has to treat labour as a family living in unity and harmony helping and serving each other.

3. Mutual trusteeship

Labour and management should both look after the interest of each other. Owners take care of their professionals and they in turn will provide productivity and profits. Thus, both work towards benefit of consumers.

4. Formation of trade unions (TUs)

Being a member of trade unions is workers' right. But he is not to be anti-capitalist. Trade unions to work for material and moral development of workers and give honest attention to business growth. Mahatma Gandhi has played a leading role in trade union movement in western India particularly at Ahmedabad. Workers should seek redressal of demands through collective bargaining.

5. Right to strike

Right to go on strike is an inherent right of workmen for securing justice. According to Gandhiji, strike must be considered as crime once the industrialist accepts the principles of arbitration. Further, trade unions to resort to this practices and remain peaceful and non-violent. Mahatma Gandhi used non-violence and non-cooperation in freedom struggle.

6. Collective bargaining and participation

These concepts are based on his principle of tolerance which mean participation and openness to divergence of ideas. One has to be good listener and hear all that comes your way. He had the courage and persistence to make change happen. He believed in redressal of demands by collective bargaining. He had faith on participation, involvement of people and giving power back to people. He managed all his social reforms on this basis. Thus, Gandhian philosophy plays a pivotal role in shaping modern corporate ethics and industrial relations.

Annexure II

ILO Conventions Ratified by the Government of India

Sl. No.	Number, Title and Year of Adoption by the ILO		Date of Ratification by India
1.	1. Hours of Work (Industry) Convention,	1919	14.07.1921
2.	2. Unemployment Convention,	1919	14.07.1921
3.	4. Night Work (Women) Convention,	1919	14.07.1921
4.	5. Minimum Age (Industry) Convention,	1919	09.09.1955
5.	6. Night Work of Young Persons ((Industry) Convention,	1919	14.07.1921
6.	11. Right of Association (Agriculture) Convention,	1921	11.05.1923
7.	14. Weekly Rest (Industry) Convention,	1921	11.05.1923
8.	15. Minimum Age (Trimmers and Stokers) Convention,	1921	22.11.1922
9.	16. Medical Examination of Young Persons (Sea) Convention,	1921	20.11.1922
10.	18. Workmen's Compensation (Occupational Diseases) Convention,	1925	30.09.1927
11.	19. Equality of Treatment (Accident Compensation) Convention,	1925	30.09.1927
12.	21. Inspection of Emigrants Convention,	1926	14.01.1928
13.	22. Seamen's Articles of Agreement Convention,	1926	31.10.1932
14.	26. Minimum Wage-fixing Machinery Convention,	1928	10.01.1955
15.	27. Marking of Weight (Packages Transported by Vessels) Convention,	1929	07.09.1931
16.	29. Forced Labour Convention,	1930	20.111954
17.	32. Protection Against Accidents (Dockers) Convention (Revised),	1934	13.01.1964
18.[@]	41. Night Work (Women) Convention (Revised),	1934	25.03.1938
19.	42. Workmen's Compensation (Occupational Diseases), Convention (Revised),	1934	13.01.1964
20.	45. Underground Work (Women) Convention,	1935	25.03.1968
21.	80. Final Articles Revision Convention,	1948	17.11.1947
22.[**]	81. Labour Inspection Convention,	1947	07.04.1949
23.	88. Employment Services Convention, 1,	948	24.06.1959
24.	89. Night Work (Women) Convention Revised,	1948	27.02.1950
25.	90. Night Work of Young Persons (Industry) (Revised),	1948	27.02.1950
26.	100. Equal Remuneration Convention,	1951	25.09.1958
27.	107. Indigenous and Tribal Population Convention,	1957	29.09.1958
28.	111. Discrimination (Employment & Occupation) Convention,	1958	03.06.1960
29.[#]	116. Final Articles Revision Convention,	1961	21.06.1962
30.[#]	118. Equality of Treatment (Social Security),		19.08.1964

31.[@@]	123.	Minimum Age (Underground Work) Convention,	1965	20.03.1975
32.	115.	Radiation Protection Convention,	1960	17.11.1975
33.	141.	Rural Workers' Organisation Convention,	1975	18.08.1977
34.	144.	Tripartite Consultation (International Labour Standards) Convention,	1976	27.02.1978
35.	136.	Benzene Convention,	1971	11.06.1991
36[#].	160.	Labour Statistics Convention,	1985	01.04.1992
37.	147.	Merchant Shipping (Minimum Standards) Convention,	1976	26.09.1996
38.	122.	Employment Policy	1999	

* Later denounced. The Convention requires, *inter alia,* furnishing of statistics concerning unemployment every three months, which is considered not practicable.

@ Convention denounced as a result of ratification of Convention No. 89.

** excluding Part II.

@@ Branches (a) to (c), (e) and (g) covered.

Article 8 of Part II.

Source: Government of India (Ministry of Labour) (1998), Annual Report, 1997-98, New Delhi, pp. 179-80.

Annexure III

ILO Guiding Principles on Collective Bargaining

The promotion of collective bargaining occupies an important place in the ILO's mandate. The Declaration of Philadelphia concerning the aims and purposes of the International Labour Organisation recognises "the solemn obligation of the International Labour Organisation to further among the nations of the world programmes which will achieve (*inter alia*) the effective recognition of the right of collective bargaining."

The ILO has been very active in promoting collective bargaining, particularly since the end of the Second World War. Evidence of this is seen in the resolutions and conclusions on the subject adopted by the International Labour Conference. Furthermore, the ILO has published several studies on collective bargaining and has organised a number of meetings on the subject. The most important are Article 4 of the Right to Organise and Collective Bargaining Convention, 1949 (No. 98), and the Collective Agreements Recommendation, 1951 (No. 91).

Article 4 of the Convention No. 98 provides that "Measures appropriate to national conditions shall be taken, where necessary to encourage and promote the full development and utilisation of machinery for voluntary negotiation between employers or employers' organisations and workers' organisations, with a view to the regulation of terms and conditions of employment by means of collective agreements". Recommendation No. 91 is essentially concerned with the legal status of collective agreements and contains provisions on the effects, extension, interpretation and supervision of the application of such agreements. The Collective Agreements Recommendation, 1951 (No. 91) calls for the establishment of machinery appropriate to national conditions "to negotiate, revise and renew collective agreements".

The standards embodied in ILO Conventions are legally binding only on those ILO member-States that have ratified them:

(i) Collective bargaining is seen in the development of various forms of *bipartite* or *tripartite* discussions which are not necessarily intended to result in collective agreements but nevertheless aim at reaching compromises directly or indirectly bearing on matters of wages, conditions of work or industrial relations. Western Europe between the government and organisations of *employers and of workers* with a view to devising policies to combat inflation and unemployment. The same is true of the conversations which take place in the socialist countries between *state and the higher trade union bodies* in connection with the devising and implementation of economic and social plans. Yet a further form of collective bargaining is to be seen in the discussions held in certain countries as part of the system of *works-level consultation or co-decision*: in practice, these discussions often take the form of a genuine dialogue with the aim of reaching solutions to which all the parties concerned can agree. It should also be pointed out that certain forms of collective bargaining are playing an increasing part in the procedures for settling labour disputes. In a number of countries the idea is gaining ground that the main purpose of these procedures should not be to call in an *independent third party to settle the disputes* but, on the contrary to get the talks between the parties going again, with the *help of a conciliator or mediator* so that the solutions eventually reached will as far as possible have been achieved by the parties involved.

(ii) There is yet a further aspect to the development of collective bargaining which concerns the actual bargaining process. Since the end of the Second World War, the law and the negotiating parties have in many countries strengthened the institutional and *procedural framework of bargaining*. Evidence of this trend is seen in the establishment in a number of countries of *procedures for trade union recognition* and the obligation to negotiate in good faith; in the creation of bargaining bodies at various levels; in the banning of certain practices that might impede the bargaining process; and in various other measures whose purpose is to provide the parties with certain information that will enable them to negotiate in full knowledge of the facts.

(iii) Thanks to the development it has undergone in the past five decades, collective bargaining now plays a considerable role in a number of countries from three points of view:

- First of all, it has an important *standard-setting function* in that, together with the law, it constitutes the main source of regulations governing wages, conditions of work and industrial relations.
- Secondly, it represents an important means of rendering the *decision-making process more democratic* since, by definition, it implies that the decisions are reached to agreement between all the parties concerned rather than unilaterally by the employers or the public authorities.
- Thirdly, collective bargaining has in many cases been found to be an effective means of *solving dispute* that may arise between employers and workers and, sometimes, the authorities. In this latter respect there is no doubt that it represents an element of *stability and order* in industrial relations.

(iv) Moreover, bargaining sometimes lands into certain difficulties because the parties have not always received *adequate-training*.

Annexure IV

United Nations Global Compact Principles

PARTICIPATION IN THE GLOBAL COMPACT OF THE UNITED NATIONS

Bharat Heavy Electricals Limited (BHEL), once again expresses its intent to support and advance *United Nation's (UN's) Global Compact (GC) principles* within the company's sphere of influence and commit to make the ten principles—on human rights, labour standards, environment and anti-corruption—as part of its strategy, culture and day-to-day operations.

Significantly, BHEL took a lead role in forming the Global Compact Society (GCS)—an apex level forum of Indian Organizations/Institutions, committed to UN's Global Compact Programme. Through this association, BHEL has got a unique opportunity of networking with other corporate and sharing experiences related to social responsibilities, on a global level. At the National Convention, Delhi and the GC Regional Conclave for South Asia Region, Jamshedpur, BHEL actively participated in the conferences and also highlighted its Corporate Social Responsibility (CSR) activities. BHEL's initiatives were appreciated by Mr. George Kell, Executive Head, UNGO, besides other dignitaries and participants from India and abroad.

Following is a brief report of how the company has addressed each of the ten principles during 2004-05. This Communication of Progress (COP), is also available on BHEL's web site (httpw.bhel.com).

(a) Human Rights

(1) Business should support and respect the protection of internationally proclaimed human rights, and

(2) Make sure they are not complicit in human rights abuses.

BHEL practices the above principles in letter and spirit and has framed its policies in consonance with *upholding the dignity* of its employees.

(b) Labour standards

(3) Businesses should uphold the freedom of association and the effective recognition of the right to collective bargaining

BHEL has an apex level bipartite forum wherein workers are represented by members of recognized unions and the leaders of Central Trade Union Organizations and the Management is represented by Chairman and Managing Director, Functional Directors and the Heads of Units.

This forum is used to settle the problems concerning the workers. In addition, BHEL as a true corporate citizen takes pride in implementing various labour laws protecting the interests of the working class.

(4) The elimination of all forms of forced and compulsory labour, and

(5) The effective abolition of child labour

BHEL neither practices compulsory labour nor has child labour.

(6) Eliminate discrimination in respect of employment and occupation

BHEL does not discriminate its employees on the basis of factors such as sex, caste, religion, race, etc.

(c) Environment

(7) Businesses should support a precautionary approach to environmental challenges,

(8) Undertake initiatives to promote greater environmental responsibility, and

(9) Encourage the development and diffusion of environmentally friendly technologies

All BHEL Units have been certified to ISO-14000 on Environment Management System and OHSAS-18000 on Occupational Health & Safety, after stringent audits by an international certifying agency.

During the year, all major units of BHEL have achieved 'Zero Effluent Discharge' status. Other major achievements included, rain water harvesting systems in all the townships of the Company, mass afforestation involving the employees and surrounding community besides conservation of natural resources, generation of energy from waste and efficient water management. As part of its commitment towards the society and as a responsible corporate citizen, BHEL is involved in a host of community development programmes in various parts of the country.

- The schools set-up for mentally challenged children in various BHEL Units cater to the aspirations and requirements of the under privileged children to help them to become self-dependant citizens.
- As a responsible corporate citizen, BHEL has involved itself in the rural development of the villages in the vicinity of its manufacturing plants. The activities include free medical aid, provision for street lights, drinking water and infrastructure support to schools, etc.
- BHEL family has risen in solidarity with the fellow citizens and victims of natural calamities such as flood, tsunami, etc. in various parts of the country by contributing its mite.

In the area of development and diffusion of environment friendly technology, BHEL is setting up 'Stand Alone' Solar Photovoltaic (SPV) power plants and Solar Power Systems in the rural areas.

(d) Anti-corruption

(10) Business should work against all forms of corruption, including extortion and bribery.

BHEL has initiated a host of 'transparency measures which will help the Company to avoid corruption. The Company focuses more on the preventive and educative aspects, rather than investigative/punitive ones.

Annexure V

Short Answer Type Questions

Define/Explain these terms using not more than 20 words in each.

1. Conflict
2. Trade Union
3. Recognised Union
4. Registered Union
5. Craft Union
6. Lay-off
7. Closure
8. Conciliation
9. Lockout
10. Public Utility Services
11. Settlement
12. Award
13. Wages period
14. Bonus
15. Dismissal
16. Workman
17. Factory
18. Safety
19. Welfare Officer
20. Shift
21. Overtime
22. Minimum Wage
23. Gratuity
24. ILC
25. Unfair Labour Practice
26. Misconduct
27. Standing Orders
28. Suspension
29. Superannuation
30. V.R.S.
31. Tribunal
32. Labour Court
33. Concurrent List

34. Appropriate Government
35. INTUC
36. AITUC
37. CITU
38. BMS
39. HMS
40. Arbitrator
41. Natural Justice
42. Conciliation
43. Disablement
44. Agreement
45. Productivity
46. Incentive
47. Available Surplus
48. Allocable Surplus
49. Occupational Disease
50. Major Punishment
51. Illegal Strike
52. Domestic Inquiry
53. Safety Officer
54. National Commission of Labour
55. Contract Labour
56. Notice of Change
57. Adjudication
58. Works Committee
59. Code of Discipline in Industry
60. Hazardous Process
61. Fines
62. Discipline
63. Charge Sheet
64. Ex-parte Enquiry
65. ILO
66. Re-investment
67. Contractor's Employees
68. Penalties
69. Permanent Total Disablement
70. Equal Remuneration

ANNEXURE VI

Objective Type Questions (Overall)

1. The origin of code of Discipline in Industry is based on an important recommendation made in
   (i) First Five Year Plan
   (ii) Second Five Year Plan
   (iii) Third Five Year Plan
   (iv) None of the above
2. Which one of the following is not one of the cardinal principles of Trade Unions Function?
   (i) Unity is Strength
   (ii) Equal pay for equal work for the same job
   (iii) Security of employment
   (iv) Militance
3. Which one of the following Trade Unions can not trace its origin to AITUC?
   (i) INTUC
   (ii) CITU
   (iii) BMS
   (iv) None of the above
   (v) All of the above
4. Which of the following is not a characteristic feature of collective bargaining?
   (i) A group action
   (ii) A bilateral process
   (iii) A democratic process
   (iv) Legislative, judicial and executive function
   (v) All of the above
   (vi) None of the above
5. Which of the following statement is true?
   (i) A registered union is a recognised union
   (ii) A recognised union is a registered union
   (iii) Political affiliation is a necessary condition for recognition of a Trade Union
   (iv) Political affiliation is a necessary condition for registration of Trade Union
6. Which of the following legislations have provisions regarding recognition of a Trade union?
   (i) ID Act
   (ii) Factories Act

(iii) Trade Union Act
(iv) Bombay Industrial Relations Act
(v) All of the above
(vi) None of the above

7. Match the following:

INTUC INC
AITUC CPI
CITU CPI(M)
BMD Jansangh

8. Which of the following statement is not true about arbitration?
   (i) It is a voluntary method of resolving Industrial Disputes
   (ii) The power to refer an Industrial Dispute to an arbitrator is derived from the written agreement made by the employers and workmen together
   (iii) Number of Arbitrators can be one or more than one
   (iv) Arbitrators are appointed by appropriate Government
9. Under the ID Act, which of the following machinery is relevant to compulsory arbitration/adjudication?
   (a) Conciliation Officer
   (b) Court of enquiry
   (c) Board of Conciliation
   (d) Industrial Tribunal
10. The Conciliation Officer can not do the following?
   (a) Find out the greatest measure of agreement between parties to Industrial Dispute
   (b) Help to arrive at a settlement between parties to Industrial Dispute
   (c) Be a signatory to settlement between two parties
   (d) Can adjudicate over the dispute
11. In conducting a domestic enquiry, following is not an essential principle:
   (i) Consideration of fairplay
   (ii) Consideration of natural justice
   (iii) It must be conducted with open mind and honestly
   (iv) It must adhere to technical requirements of a criminal trial
12. There may be a technical flow in the domestic enquiry if the chargesheeted employee of his representative is not provided an opportunity to cross-examine the management witness:
   (a) True
   (b) False
13. No enquiry can be held if the chargesheeted employee refuses to participate in the enquiry, i.e. addition of Clause 11A to ID Act:
   (a) True
   (b) False
14. Prior to 1971, the Labour Court/Tribunal could not interfere with the quantum of punishment arising out of a domestic enquiry/disciplinary proceeding if a fair and proper enquiry had been held into the case:
   (a) True
   (b) False

15. One of the following statements is not true: Prior to introduction of Section 11A, the Labour Courts/Tribunals had powers to interfere only when
    (i) There was want of good faith
    (ii) There was victimisation or unfair labour practice
    (iii) Management must agree not to increase workload unless agreed otherwise or settled otherwise
    (iv) Management shall not initiate any disciplinary proceeding against any employee without prior consultation with the recognised union.
16. Which of the following is not a function of the Chief Labour Commissioner (Central)?
    (i) Administration of Labour Laws
    (ii) Verification of membership of registered unions for granting recognition under the code to industries which come under the purview of Central Government.
    (iii) Determination of membership of Central federations for representation at national and international fora
    (iv) Adjudication on abolition of contract labour as per Contract Labour (Abolition and Regulation) Act.
17. Code of Discipline in industry has statutory force behind it.
    (a) True
    (b) False
18. One of the following statements are not true about Code of Discipline:
    (i) It is a Government induced, self-imposed and mutually agreed voluntary principles of discipline and relations between management and worker in the industry
    (ii) It aims at preventing disputes
    (iii) It refrains both the parties from unilateral action
    (iv) It was formulated in the year 1949
19. Which one of the following is not one of the cardinal principle of grievance settlement under model grievance procedure?
    (i) Settlement to the satisfaction of the aggrieved
    (ii) Settlement of imaginary as well as real
    (iii) Settlement at the lowest level
    (iv) Settlement as expeditiously as possible.
20. Arrange the following in a proper sequence:
    (i) Industrial Tribunal
    (ii) Conciliation Officer
    (iii) Works Committee
    (iv) Arbitration (Voluntary)
21. The maximum number of members in a Works Committee should not exceed 12:
    (a) True
    (b) False
22. As per Factories Act, there should be a Labour Welfare Officer in a factory employing:
    (i) 50 workers

(ii) 150 workers
(iii) 250 workers
(iv) 500 workers

23. One of the following does not fall within the purview of ID Act, 1947:
(i) Disputes between employees and employers
(ii) Dispute between rival unions
(iii) Payment of bonus/gratuity

24. Labour in matters are the
(a) Central list
(b) State list
(c) Concurrent list
(d) None of the above

25. Which one of the following is not a reason for workers to join a Trade Union?
(i) Economic security
(ii) Irrational, illogical, discriminatory actions prejudicial to the interests of labour
(iii) Communication of views, aims, ideas, feelings frustrations to the management
(iv) An insurance against disciplinary action by the management

26. Point out which of the following is not one of the major functions of a Trade Union:
(i) To promote, defend and protect the interest of their members
(ii) To maintain and improve the living standards of their members
(iii) Providing security of jobs to their members
(iv) Enter into agreements with a view to provide economic benefits to their members
(v) To legislate on matters pertaining to labour welfare

27. A tripartite settlement arrived at under the ID Act is:
(i) Binding on Management
(ii) Binding on the Workmen
(iii) Binding on all the parties concerned
(iv) None of the above

28. Which one of the following is not true to Joint Councils:
(i) It would endeavour to improve the working and living conditions of the employees
(ii) It would be entrusted with the responsibility in respect of administration of welfare measures
(iii) It would be entrusted with the responsibility of supervision of safety measures
(iv) It would be a party in conciliation proceedings

29. Which one of the following statements is not true?
(i) 1918 saw the first organised trade union in India — Madras Labour Union
(ii) AITUC was formed in 1920 under the Chairmanship of Lala Lajpat Rai
(iii) The Railwaymen's Federation, affiliated to INTUC was formed in 1922

30. A Works Committee should not deal with
(i) Wages and allowance
(ii) Bonus and profit sharing
(iii) Matters connected with fixation of work load
(iv) All of the above
(v) None of the above

31. The minimum requirement for applying for registration of a Trade Union is
    (i) 5
    (ii) 9
    (iii) 11
    (iv) None of the above
    (v) Any of the above
32. As per Factories Act, it is a statutory obligation on the part of an employee to recruit a Labour Welfare Officer in factories employing 100 or more workers:
    (a) True
    (b) False
33. One of the functions of Labour Welfare Officer is
    (i) Counselling workers in personal and family matters, helping them to adjust to their work environment
    (ii) Counselling workers regarding ways to organise themselves for bargaining with management
    (iii) Advise workmen regarding workload division
    (iv) Assisting workmen during disciplinary action
    (v) None of the above
    (vi) All the above
34. It is statutory for all employers to formulae standing orders in conformity with the model standing orders:
    (a) True
    (b) False
35. Which one of the following is not one of the aims of Industrial Employment (Standing Orders) Act, 1946?
    (i) To provide for defining with sufficient precision certain conditions of employment in an industrial establishment
    (ii) To regulate standards of conduct of the employers and the employees so that the labour-management relations can be improved
    (iii) To maintain proper discipline, harmonious working conditions and achieve higher productivity by providing satisfactory employment and working conditions
    (iv) All the above
36. Past record of an employee must be taken into account prior to inflicting major punishment:
    (i) True
    (ii) False
37. Following grounds are justified for suspending an employee pending enquiry:
    (i) Where his (employee's) presence might endanger the safety of other workmen
    (ii) Where it is apprehended that the employee may intimidate others or tamper with evidence
    (iii) Both of the above
    (iv) None of the above

38. If all employees refuses to accept the chargesheet, enquiry can not be held:
    (i) True
    (ii) False
39. The chargesheeted employee must lead the case and produce his witnesses first:
    (i) True
    (ii) False
40. Tribunals are
    (i) Advisory Bodies
    (ii) Conciliatory Bodies
    (iii) Adjudicatory Bodies
    iv) None of the above
41. Arrange the steps in grievance handling in a proper sequence:
    (i) Get the facts
    (ii) Acknowledge dissatisfaction
    (iii) Analyse and decide
    (iv) Define the problem
    (v) Follow up
42. Following is not one of the important ways of discovering grievances:
    (i) Direct observation
    (ii) Grievance Procedure
    (iii) Open door policy
    (iv) Exit Interview
    (v) Grapevine
43. Workers' participation in management in real sense was first seen at:
    (i) Indian Railways
    (ii) Indian Iron & Steel Company
    (iii) Ahmedabad Textile Mills
    (iv) TISCO
44. The Indian Labour Conference consists of members from:
    (i) All National Trade Unions only
    (ii) Government and Labour
    (iii) Labour and employer
    (iv) Government Employers and Workers
45. The first recorded instance of collective bargaining in India was at:
    (i) In 1920, at Ahmedabad Textile Industry
    (ii) Tata Iron & Steel Company in 1918
    (iii) Burn Standard and Company in 1926
    (iv) Madras Textile Industry in 1919
46. Joint Management Councils were first set-up in the year 1958:
    (a) True
    (b) False
47. Collective bargaining refers to an institutional arrangement where the representatives of workmen negotiate with management on "interest" related issues like wages, bonus, etc.:

(a) True
(b) False

48. Participate Management refers to a situation where representatives of workmen jointly discuss and decide on "interest" related issues like wages, bonus, etc.:
    (a) True
    (b) False
49. In workers' participation, there is commonality of interests between the participants:
    (a) True
    (b) False
50. The outcome of collective bargaining depends mostly on relative strength of the parties
    (a) True
    (b) False

Source: Distance Learning Programme, IMT, Gaziabad.

ANNEXURE VII(A)

Quiz on Payment of Wages

(Tick Correct Answer)

1. Employer of industrial organisation must pay wage in order to be allowed to continue an industry:
   (a) Fair wage
   (b) Living wage
   (c) Basic minimum wage
2. Wages are a central concern for employers or employees or government for payment:
   (a) For employer
   (b) For employees
   (c) Government
3. Wages in industrial establishments shall be paid (less than 1000 persons) after last day of the wage period:
   (a) By 2nd day
   (b) By 7th day
   (c) by 10th day
4. When wages of an employee, whose service is terminated, shall be paid?:
   (a) After one month
   (b) Before 2nd day
5. Can an employee ask for advance from wages?:
   (a) No
   (b) Yes
6. Average monthly wage is determined by dividing by number of days:
   (a) 30 days
   (b) 26 days
7. Is an employer obliged to pay wages to a worker who has been suspended?:
   (a) No
   (b) Yes
8. What action can be taken by an employer if 40 workers acting in concert, absent themselves without due notice?:
   (a) No
   (b) Deduct wages upto 8 days
9. Can an employee relinquish his right to minimum rate of wages?:
   (a) Yes
   (b) No

10. Can employees insist for a claim of housing or house allowance?:
    (a) Yes
    (b) No
11. Is it obligatory on an employer to pay stiffen allowance to workers?:
    (a) Yes
    (b) No
12. Can minimum wage be linked with performance or output?:
    (a) Yes
    (b) No

Annexure VII(b)

Quiz on Payment of Gratuity Act, 1972

Answer Yes or No or as required *Answer*

1. Is permanent employee entitled to payment of gratuity for the years he remained absent without leave and has actually, worked for less than 240 days?
2. Can a gratuity payable under a scheme, be attached?
3. An employee was paid gratuity under a particular scheme, whether he will be estopped from making a claim for additional sum of gratuity under the act.
4. Can gratuity be forfeited, if services of such employee were terminated for an act involving moral turpitude?
5. An employee was retrenched and was not paid gratuity. Correct or wrong?
6. Whether an employee re-employed after superannuation be eligible to payment of gratuity?
7. Is an employee entitled to gratuity for those years when he has not rendered service for 240 days?
8. Is there any punishment prescribed for non-payment of gratuity?
9. Can an employer withhold the payment of gratuity when the employee failed to vacate the accommodation allotted by the employer?
10. Whether the payment of gratuity act will be applicable to the establishment of lawyers?
11. Can an employer plead lack of financial capacity to pay gratuity?
12. Can gratuity be withheld after affording opportunity to employee?

Annexure VII(c)

Quiz on Payment of Bonus

Answer Yes or No or as required *Answer*

1. Will bonus be payable to an employee on the commission received by him?
2. Whether a probationer or trainee will be eligible for bonus?
3. Can bonus be claimed by employees in excess of allocable surplus?
4. Will over-time payment form part of wages for calculating of bonus?
5. Whether bonus will be payable to employees working on part-time basis?
6. Whether an employee be entitled to bonus on the payment received due to encashment of E.L.?
7. Can the employee of one unit of the company claim bonus that employees of other units have been paid bonus?
8. Can bonus be denied to an employee on the condition that on the day of the declaration of bonus he was not in employment?
9. Can an employer recover excess bonus if paid by him to the employee?
10. What is the time-limit for payment of bonus?
11. Is payment of bonus statutory obligation or voluntary payment as share in profits?
12. Whom employees have to approach for non-payment of bonus by the employer under the act?
13. Can employer deny bonus to employee dismissed from service?
14. Can employer deduct from the bonus payable to an employee for the loss caused?
15. Can employer enter into agreement for payment of bonus linked to productivity instead of profits under the Bonus Act?

Annexure VII (d)

Quiz on Validity of Settlements with Union

(Answer Yes or No)

1. A settlement was reached with the recognised union, which is expected to protect the interest of labour. Will this agreement be binding upon the minority union ?
2. A settlement was made by the Management with the recognised union when there were allegations of mala-fide coercion and false promises, will this agreement be binding upon on all workmen?
3. Whether an existing settlement between an employer and his employees, will be binding upon a new employee as he was not a party to the said dispute?
4. The Management and the majority union arrived at a settlement, in all respects to be applicable to all employees, when dispute is already referred to Conciliation Officer, will this be binding?
5. A settlement was arrived at between employer and two office-bearers of the recognised union. The constitution of the union is silent whether authorisation by the executive committee of the union or by the workmen is to be obtained for this. Will it be binding?
6. An employer enters an agreement with one of the labour unions which represents only crane operators.
   (a) Can another union representing slingers claim its applicability to their members?
   (b) Will this agreement be binding only to crane operators who are members of that union which is party to that agreement?
7. A settlement was arrived at otherwise than in the course of conciliation proceedings, and was signed by the parties, thereto in the manner prescribed by rule and copy was not sent to the appropriate Government. Later on the union backed out. Can the employer claim it is binding on the parties to the agreement?
8. A settlement was made with the union which represented a large majority of the workmen of the company. Out of the 1928 workmen, who were in service of the company on July 1993, only 995 workmen signed the settlement and also accepted their dues thereunder and 242 workmen accepted their dues under the settlement by actually signing the receipt though they had not signed the settlement. Further 910 workmen who left the company between January 1, 1988 and July 31, 1993 had also accepted their dues under the settlement. A section of employees approached the tribunal that settlement was not just and fair. Do you agree?

Annexure VIII

The Workmen's Compensation Act, 1923: Practical Problems

Attempt the following problems, giving reasons:

1. Is the employer liable to pay compensation in the following cases?

(a) A railway company provided a hostel for its workmen in a certain place where the engine-drivers who lived somewhere else could take rest a while off duty on payment of small charge. They could utilise their time in any way they liked. An engine-driver while on the premises was injured in an accident.

(b) A workman goes to attended to his work riding on a bicycle and is involved in an accident in the course of the journey.

(c) A watchman whose duty was to guard the property of the premises of a rest house, had his quarters within the premises of the rest house. His duty ended at 11 P.M. At 2.30 A.M. (i.e., within 3-1/2 hours of the said 11 P.M.) he was found murdered near his quarters.

(d) A worker lost his mental balance as a result of an injury by accident while working in the factory and committed suicide.

(e) A workman suffered an injury by an accident arising out of and in the course of employment and was permanently disabled. But the accident had been caused by his wilful disobedience to an order issued for the purpose of securing the safety of workmen.

(f) A firm of engineers contracted with the owners of a cotton spinning factory to put a new driving wheel into the steam engine belonging to the factory. While engaged in the work of fixing the new wheel, a workman employed by the engineers met with an accident which caused his death. The dependents of the deceased workman demanded compensation from the owners of the factory.

(g) A worker working in a shed was injured by the fall of a wall which was not the property of or under the control of the employer.

(h) A boy employed in a shoe-factory took home a pair of boots for repairing them in order to improve his skill. This he did contrary to the order of authorities. While repairing the boots at home he injured an eye with an awl, and it had to be removed.

(i) A worker leaves his workplace after his duty hours. He returns after one hour to pick up his articles. He receives injury in an accident at the time of taking his articles.

(j) A driver was employed by a truck owner to carry petrol in a tank. The driver found the tank to be leaking at some point. He entered the tank with the permission of the owner with a view to detect the point of leakage and lighted a match stick. The tank caught fire and the driver received some burn injuries, and died afterwards.

(k) A driver of a concrete mixer, while working thereon, found some part of the machine loose which required immediate tightening. In the process of rectifying the defect, his thumb and index fingers were cut-off.

(l) A workman, on completion of his day's work, was going home. On way he was injured by an accident without any fault or negligence on his part.

(m) A workman, who was a heart patient, complained of chest pain during the duty hours on a ship. He was treated in the ship's dispensary before leaving the ship but he died on way back home of coronary thrombosis.

(n) A workman was serving in a railway as an assistant driver of the goods train. While he was on his duty with the goods train, he received heart attack. He first complained of chest pain near a station and after leaving that station and while performing his normal duties with normal strain, he again complained of chest pain. He was admitted to a hospital at the next station where he died.

(o) A worker suffering from heart disease worked for 4 hours in the factory premises. While he was coming out of the factory, he profusely sweated and died of heart failure which resulted on account of severe stress and strain inside the factory premises.

Annexure IX

Case Studies

Case Study-I: Introduction of a Computer

Mr. Rajender Kumar is the head of the accounting section in a fast growing manufacturing company. In the section, he has 30 employees under his control. The company has three hundred employees, mostly drawn from nearby areas. The recent changes in science and technology have prompted management to introduce mechanization in the accounting section. Mr. Kumar is asked to explain the importance of having a computer in the accounts department to his employees. The introduction of computer, undoubtedly, affects the lives of all those who are working in the section. Some fifteen employees will have to restructure their job responsibilities; ten employees require training in the use of computer and the remaining five employees may have to knock the doors of other companies for jobs. Of course, all these changes, through painful, will take a place gradually.

This situation is quite similar to another situation witnessed by Mr. Kumar some time back. Eight months ago, the company had hired a computer on lease basis to handle the production inventory. The management is highly pleased with the arrangement, for the inventory processing has improved tremendously afterwards. But unfortunately, the production people have resisted the move strongly. Now, Mr. Kumar is in a tight corner. Strangely, he is entrusted with the responsibility of introducing the computer in his own section.

Questions

1. Examine whether notice of change is required in this case?
2. If notice of change is required then under which act/provision you would give notice of change?

Case Study-2: It's the Same Story Everywhere

Prakash hails from a hard-working, immigrant family. Right from his childhood he wanted to achieve something and acquire power for himself. Unfortunately, he could secure only a low paid job in the assembly line in a large manufacturing firm. It was a charmless job having no promotional opportunities. Since he has to support a large family, he needed a well-paid job and all his efforts in this direction had gone waste. To blow off his steam and to relieve himself from wordly woes, he started living in a "fool's paradise" and spent most of his days in day dreaming. Not surprisingly, he fell a prey to drinking and other vices. After exhausting his meagre financial resources, he would get depressed and start worrying about his family.

It has been a vicious circle and he wants to come out of it. Unable to bear with this miserable situation, one fine morning, he wanted to seek advice and counsel from his supervisor. But since his relationship with his supervisor was not-too intimate, he sought help from his union leader. The union leader has listened to Prakash's woes patiently. He told Prakash in a sympathetic one: 'There is no use working in this company, we have innumerable problems and not a single problem has been solved by the management so far. The working conditions are pathetic. Our salary is too low. And let's not talk about our benefit plans. After our contract finishes let's unite together and fight with management for better salary and working and working conditions".

Questions

1. Analyse the nature of role conflict experienced by Prakash in this case.
2. What type of conflict resolution strategy is the union leader suggesting in this case?
3. What would you advise Mr. Prakash?

Case Study-3

The chairman of a small unorganised company believed in unions and was pleased when told that his employees were forming a union. Their negotiating committee submitted a list of demands in advance. The chairman studied them carefully and found them reasonable, so he decided to surprise his workers and grant all demands in full at the first meeting of the negotiating committee. This magnanimous attitude would, he thought, set a firm basis for good union relations. At the first meeting, he granted all demands as he had planned, but much to his own surprise, the union representatives were not all pleased. The contract was duly signed, but relations deteriorated instead of improving.

What happened in this case?

Case Study-4: Grass-cutter v. Gas cutter

In the public sector undertaking with a chequered past, a line manager was appointed as the Chief of personnel. Within a year after taking up the assignment, he had to sign a wage agreement with the worker's union. The union at that time was dominated by non-technical staff. The union's charter of demands favoured the interests of its dominant member groups. It asked for a significant revision in gardener's pay, but was not equally vocal in pressing for the increase in the pay scales of workers in certain technical grades. The management conceded these demands, because the union cooperated with them in keeping the burden of the pay revision well within the guidelines of the bureau of public enterprises (BPE).

Once the agreement was signed and communicated to employees/members by the management and the union respectively, there was commotion among the technical staff. They walked out of the union, formed a separate technical staff union and marched round the company premises holding placards which read, "Here grass cutters get more than the gas cutters." In the engineering assembly unit, till the pay revision occurred welding was a highly-rated job. But not any longer. Now gardeners get more than welders.

Questions

1. What happens if grass-cutters get more than gas-cutters?
2. Evaluate pros and cons of the approach of the management and union in this incident?

3. List the lessens learnt.
4. Suggest a way out of the problem on hand.

Case Study-5: Bharat Petroleum Corporation Ltd.

Read the Case Study of Bharat Petroleum Corporation Ltd. and answer the questions given at the end.

In the instant case, under the shadow of Trade Union agitations, both the parties the employer, Corporation and the employees' union were continuing mutual discussions and negotiations. Management was desirous of and willing to have a long-term settlement on a condition that the employees' union should withdraw the pending cases filed by them.

A general meeting of the workmen, members of the union were convened to take secret ballot to find out the willingness or otherwise the workmen to go on an indefinite strike. On 13th January 1982, the workmen informed the management that 92% of the workmen had voted for going on indefinite strike. No formal notice for strike was given and no date for commencing of said strike was fixed and communicated by the Union to the Management. The Management started shutting down the refinery plant from midnight of 13th January 1982 and early morning of 14th January 1982. As a result of the shutting down of back process the workmen were without work on 14th and 15th January 1982, till midnight. The management continued to display notices requesting the workmen to join back on duty. Both the parties however, continued to negotiate and finally reached a settlement on 17th June 1982. Dispute of wages during strike period from 14th January 1982 to 16th June 1982 was not amicably settled. The workmen therefore raised an industrial dispute to get wages of the said period of illegal lockout. Industrial dispute was referred for adjudication to the Tribunal. By the Award of Tribunal dated 13th May 1995, the learned members of Industrial Tribunal put the blame on both the parties. Held workmen were not entitled to full back wages for the period hence awarded 50% of the back wages. Both the parties filed a writ petition before the High Court challenging the same.

Questions

1. Explain in detail with examples the essential elements for a strike? How many kinds of strikes are there?
2. Do you consider it an illegal lockout? When can the employer do lockout?
3. What you will decide in this above scenario as High Court Judge? Explain Why?

Case Study-6: Grievance Procedure vs. Collective Bargaining

The Andhra Pradesh State Road Transport Corporation has been providing passenger transports facility since 1956. It has been extending its operation from one region to another by nationalizing the private passenger transport companies on a phased manner. Presently it is operating its services in 80% of the routes in the State. It nationalized two routes in East Godavari District in the State in October 1988. Normally it absorbs all the employees working in passenger transport companies before nationalization and fix their wages at par with the scales of similar categories of jobs.

The pay scale in the corporation are determined on the basis of mutual agreement between the management and the recognized trade union. The scales are revised once in three years. The recent agreement came into force with effect from September 1988. There are two classes in the drivers' category, i.e. class I (drivers working on long distances buses) and class II (drivers working on short distance routes). The pay scale of class II drivers is enhanced from

Rs. 600-1200 to Rs. 900-1600 (with effect from September 1988) in consequence to the latest agreement. The agreement further says that the pay scales of the drivers drawing the scales of Rs. 600-1200 will be fixed in the scale of Rs. 900-1600.

The corporation absorbed 10 drivers who were with the private passenger transport companies consequence upon the recent nationalization of two routes. The personnel department fixed the scale of these 10 drivers in the scale of Rs. 600-1200 and it rejected their plea of fixing their pay in the scale of Rs. 900-1600 saying that only drivers drawing the scale of Rs. 600-1200 are now eligible to draw the new scale of Rs. 900-1600. The company has set-up both the grievance machinery and the collective bargaining machinery to resolve employees problems. Then these drivers submitted this issue to the foreman who is their immediate superior. The foreman told them to raise this issue in collective bargaining with the help of trade union leaders as it is a policy issue. These drivers approached the trade union leaders and persuaded them to solve the issue. The trade union leaders included this item in the draft agenda to the collective bargaining committee to be held in January 1989. But the collective bargaining committee deleted this item from the draft agenda saying that this issue can be settled through grievance machinery as only 10 drivers out of 3,000 of the corporation are concerned with this issue.

Questions

1. Who is correct? The personnel department or the foreman or the collective bargaining committee?
2. Where do you place this issue for redressal?
3. How do you redress this grievance?

Annexure X

Amendment to Labour Laws

(i) A Bill to amend the Payment of Wages Act, 1936 for enhancement of existing ceiling of Rs. 1600 to Rs. 6500 per month has been introduced in Parliament. This has been done to enlarge the scope as well as prescribe more stringent grievance redressal machinery. The Rajya Sabha has passed the Bill while it awaits consideration in the Lok Sabha.

(ii) To provide flexibility in the employment of women, the Cabinet has approved to amend Sec. 66 of the Factories Act, 1948 to allow women to work in factories during night shifts with adequate safeguards.

(iii) Enforcement of Minimum Wages Act

In order to monitor the Minimum Wages Act, 1948 more effectively, the Central Government directed States/UTs to develop and introduce a new system of external monitoring through civil society. Accordingly, State Governments are now including more persons from the civil society to the Advisory Boards constituted to oversee the implementation of the Act.

(iv) Skill Upgradation

Skill upgradation and imparting of modern skills to workers is another priority as only 5 per cent of the total labour force are skilled. The Labour Ministry has formulated a scheme for upgradation of 500 existing Industrial Training Institutes (ITIs) into Centres of Excellence for meeting international standards. The upgradation process is estimated to cost Rs. 160 crore. To begin with 100 ITIs were taken up for upgradation during the year, meeting the cost through internal resources. The World Bank has been approached for financial assistance for upgrading the remaining ITIs. The measure has been taken to improve/employability of workers in global and domestic markets.

(v) Elimination of Child Labour

Efforts to elimination of child labour particularly in hazardous occupations and processes in a sequential manner received further impetus. The Government decided to extend the National Child Labour Projects (NCLPs) Scheme from 150 districts to 250 districts during Xth Plan to rehabilitate children withdrawn from work. Implementation of 100 additional NCLPs has started with increased inputs for nutrition, health, vocational training, etc.

(vi) Welfare of Unorganised Sector Workers

For the welfare of workers in the unorganised sector, who constitute 93 per cent of the total workforce, the Ministry is redrafting the Unorganised Sector Workers' Bill, 2004. The objective of this legislation is to regulate employment and conditions of service of workers in the unorganised sector and to provide for their social security, safety and health.

(vii) Extension of ESIC Scheme

The Employees State Insurance Corporation (ESIC), has increased wage ceiling limit from Rs. 6,500 to net in more workers into ESI Scheme. It has also extended its coverage to new geographical areas bringing within its ambit 1.5 lakh more workers. Adding more sectors to coverage, ESIC decided to extend the scheme to educational institutions and to all municipal corporations, municipalities, cantonment board areas and other notified town areas in a phased manner.

Index